INTEGRAL MUSIC

MODERN AND CONTEMPORARY POETICS

# INTEGRAL MUSIC

## Languages of African American Innovation

Aldon Lynn Nielsen

THE UNIVERSITY OF ALABAMA PRESS
*Tuscaloosa*

Typeface: New Baskerville

∞

The paper on which this book is printed meets the minimum requirements of American National Standard for Information Science—Permanence of Paper for Printed Library Materials, ANSI Z39.48-1984.

Library of Congress Cataloging-in-Publication Data

Nielsen, Aldon Lynn.

Integral music : languages of African American innovation / Aldon Lynn Nielsen.

p. cm. — (Modern and contemporary poetics)

Includes bibliographical references and index.

ISBN 0-8173-1433-4 (cloth : alk. paper) — ISBN 0-8173-5139-6 (pbk. : alk. paper)

1. American literature—African American authors—History and criticism. 2. American literature—20th century—History and criticism. 3. African Americans—Intellectual life. 4. African Americans in literature. I. Title. II. Series.

PS153.N5N535 2004
810.9′896073′0904—dc22

2004008878

*For Jerry Ward and Marjorie Perloff*

# *Contents*

# *Acknowledgments*

Anna Everett has brought me from those austere and lonely offices to love. An increasingly eminent scholar and writer in her own right, she has taken time to take notice of my own efforts, and her offerings to my thought are too numerous ever to be properly tabulated. By her good graces I may occasionally achieve grace.

A portion of the research and writing of this manuscript was completed during the period of a generous fellowship from the National Endowment for the Humanities. Further research trips were supported in part by grants from Loyola Marymount University, where Dean Kenyon Chan and Chair Linda Bannister were unfailingly in my corner.

I am particularly grateful to poets Jayne Cortez and Russell Atkins for granting permission to quote far beyond fair use from their works. Additionally, I would like to thank Gerrit Lansing, literary executor for Stephen Jonas, for permitting extended quotations from the late poet's writings. Amiri Baraka, in scattered conversations (and, in the early years, some strategically placed red marks on my papers) scattered across more than two decades, has given me good information and, perhaps more important, strong debates. I am forever in his debt. Short selections from this book appeared previously, often in different form, in *African American Review, Diacritics, Callaloo,* and in the *Impercipient Lecture Series,* and I want to thank the editors of those publications for their encouragement and kindness. Similar kindness has been shown me by colleagues and students who have allowed me to road test these ideas and readings at various conferences and lectures around the country and around the world. Having helped me kick the tires, they were good enough to offer me a place to park as well. As always, the staff at several research collections have been especially helpful to me. The Baraka collections at UCLA and at the Moorland-Spingarn in Howard University's Founders Library have been a treasure trove of insights and leads, as have been the materials at the Poetry and Rare Book Collection at the State University of New York at Buffalo.

The sort of scholarship I attempt here would simply be impossible were it not for those who have given themselves so wholly to the preservation and care of these valuable, albeit neglected, documents of our culture and history. Hank Lazer, Charles Bernstein, Daniel Waterman, Joe Abbott, and the staff of The University of Alabama Press have been both farsighted and forbearing, an increasingly rare combination in these days of downsized (austere) offices and cut budgets. Readers of my previous works will have as much reason as I have to thank Paula C. Durbin-Westby, who is responsible for the marked improvement in indexing. My anonymous readers are as important to me as those whose names I know, and I thank them both, with an extra note of gratitude to the reader who reminded me of the Jackson Pollack painting on the cover of an Ornette Coleman LP, my copy of which languished forgotten in a closet after I had digitally removed its music to my portable player. And a thank-you to the anonymous graduate student at the University of Iowa who reminded me of Maya Deren's *Meshes* after I'd screened a clip from Sun Ra's *Space Is the Place* and just as I was thinking about Bob Kaufman. It was the same weekend that I met Funkadelic's lead guitarist in an elevator. Iowa is that kind of place, as Kaufman would have comprehended.

And none of this would have made it to the page had it not been for the permanent traveling colloquium afforded me by my colleagues and students at Loyola Marymount University and Pennsylvania State University. I not only would like to but will offer a special note of appreciation to Robert Caserio, who, in the short time that I have known him, has been an unparalleled, serial inciter of good scholarship and considered writing.

For sub-sub-librarians, factors and extractors everywhere, an unending note of gratitude.

## *Extracts*

(Supplied by a Sub-Sub-Librarian)

The other answered that I talked too good English. I replied I believed I did.

—Olaudah Equiano

An old man in the South one time had said to me, "Some folks speak too clear," talking about my clipped northern speech. But, hey, that never registered.

—Amiri Baraka

A Negro has been instructed since stepping foot on the land to choose his words, watch his diction, precheck his grammatical construction.

—Carlene Hatcher Polite

The Negro will learn to read and write before the white will.

—Ralph Waldo Emerson

Bad English. Broken English. Dialect. None of these was a safe house.

—M. Nourbese Philip

I have come to chew up yr language.

—Steve Jonas

There are always language*s* in language.

—Jacques Derrida

# *Introduction*

"Can we take it to the bridge?"
—James Brown

"And these are the breaks;
Break it up, break it up, break it up!"
—Kurtis Blow

" . . . chain-dancing to freedom . . . "
—Alan Rice

With Middle Passage as the "X" that marks the spot of both origin and sea burial, vanishing point of horizons both coming and going, small wonder that there should be some ambivalence, some shifty perspectival multivalence, as African American artists take to the bridge, only to break it down. Some bridges break open for the passing of a ship. Some ships have bridges affording a commanding view, where even a sailor might take a break. Africans in transport to slavery in America sometimes made a break to take the bridge.

One break in American history was marked within the writing of our Constitution, a date with destiny, a date after which it *might* be legal to make the Middle Passage illegal. Efforts to interdict that passage were too often halfhearted, marked ambiguously by *Amistad*. Subsequent history, through the Civil War, Reconstruction, Black Codes, the seeming impossibility of multiple nadirs, Renaissance, Depression, affirmation and contraction, Black Power and backlash, has been continuously and irrevocably marked by such ambiguity. We may be forgiven for thinking we deserve a break, an interdiction.

*Interdiction* has much to recommend it as a critical term. While the word intends a prohibition, it seems to seek an opening, an in-between space in which folk etymology might read a felt history of differing dictions brought into frictive contact. To interdict racism would appear to require a polyglot tongue-lashing, an interruption and eruption, a critical insertion of oneself in a dangerous space between people speaking in tongues. It has often seemed to me in my reading that this is just what many of the most interesting African American poets have accomplished. If there is such a thing as Du Boisian double-consciousness, it must take place in a single and singular soul, it must constitute both a differing and a deferral, and it must prohibit the very racist imaginings that called it into being. It must, therefore, make a break for the territories, as Ellison and Twain would differently have it, and it is only in the making of that break that the territories can begin to be delineated.

The space of race has demarcated the range of both popular and academic reading throughout our troubled history, though that space has itself been only infrequently and inadequately charted. If it is true that poets, always playing, like jazz musicians, out at the edges of possibility, test the limits of language (and what else can it mean to acknowledge them as legislators), then it is also true that American poets write beyond reach of our belated dictionaries of race. This is not to say that they are raceless or that they in any way transcend race; rather, it is to remark the moving targets that they make of race.

Which invites hard listening out there at what Jayne Cortez has recently called the *Borders of Disorderly Time*. On the recording of that title, where Cortez joins together with that floating band of signifiers she calls the Firespitters, it is ultimately impossible to declare secure boundaries between poetry and jazz, bridge and break, chorus and canto, solo and background, digital dance and analogue type. That we can think these terms while listening legitimates them as still useful devices; that we can discern no firm dividing lines between them demonstrates that Cortez has construed our languages and musics in the very place of their possibility, that she has escaped any prison house of language and is, in Alan Rice's words, chain-dancing to freedom. If there is a signifying chain to break, the possibility of breaking is built into every link. The possibility of breakdown is built into the building as an opening for dance. Fred Moten has analyzed the break as *The Aesthetics of the Black Radical Tradition,* finding in his listening to jazz that "the break animates the entirety of the solo rather than simply functioning as the 'home' of something that approaches the solo, some local and locatable habitation (of the name)" (268). When Bob Kaufman breaks down the names of his subjects, when Amiri Baraka breaks open the syllables of Kaufman's name (as when he breaks apart and then breaks with his own names), they are practicing within the letter, to the letter, what Moten calls "the dissemination of the break" (268), even as they write a bridge work conjoining their poems to poems past and future.

Poet Ed Roberson writes of a *Lucid Interval as Integral Music*. Writing to the letter of his invitation, I borrow my title from his works, as I did before with *Black Chant*. *Integral Music* stands as a break between two other books, as a bridge passage between beginning and end. As the title implies, *Integral Music* has its own structural and thematic integrity and can be read on its own, with no knowledge of its fellows. Still, disseminating the break and following the structural logic of the bridge, the present book is of a piece with the other volumes of a trilogy in progress. There are practical as well as philosophical reasons for this. On the one hand, I have known—ever since the day that an earlier editor made it plain to me that my reputation had not yet reached a stage, might never reach a stage, where a six-hundred-page volume of criticism might be a safe undertaking for an academic press—that my ongoing research and reading of African American postmodernisms would, as it turns out, fortuitously, of necessity be a multivolume work. Still, this seemed at the outset and now indicative of something more important, sign of the disseminative nature of bridge and break, of solo and reprise, of the very future anterior that is so often found in those African American writers here and there addressed.

While the ordering of chapters in *Integral Music* is roughly chronological, there are other footings to be found. The primary link backward to *Black Chant* and forward to the next volume is the continued exploration through a wide variety of writings of blackness and the postmodern. The root argument in the most rudimentary sense is that African American creators of what we might call innovative works or, better yet, "experimental" arts (in the now less familiar sense of experiential, as when Puritans spoke of an experimental knowledge of God) engage in a perpetual reopening of the question of modernity; reopening the modernism that, through its obsessive primitivism and its racial politics, tended to posit black people anywhere in the world as atavistic or as simply being outside of modernity (as Hegelian thought had placed them outside history). Black poets of the experimental, though, find again and again that black arts are at the very heart of the modern. In order for them to produce this rereading of the blackness of modernity, a modernity that is, as both C. L. R. James and W. E. B. Du Bois argued more than six decades ago, the absolute condition of possibility of the modern West, modernity had to be already there before them for critique. Thus, and here is where the echoes of Lyotard become strongest (the same Lyotard who had been a colleague, after all, of C. L. R. James), the black artists who rediscover a blackness within modernity must simultaneously posit a priority and a culmination. This explains the continual reappearance of the future anterior in their works and in this book.

There are other themes woven throughout. Beginning with the first chapter, on Russell Atkins, the issue of black thought, of the philosophical contributions of black thinkers, is at the forefront. In league with that set of discussions is a reiterated concern with issues of black creativity and technology, both the adoption and anticipation of technologies and the critique of current technology in the racial state. And any book that presents itself as break and bridge passage, of course, will address music as well. As the first chapter will take up Atkins's "deconstruction," the second will recover Stephen Jonas's "reconstructed disconnection," which should be seen as related to, while departing from, the critical categories of Baraka then and Nathaniel Mackey's "discrepant engagement" now. Similarly, passages in the Jonas chapter that discuss the "bridge" themselves serve as a bridge to the music/poetry of Jayne Cortez and to "The Bridge" by Baraka. The commentary at the close critiquing Sartre's inability to anticipate black thought, black readers as knowing and critical subjects, brings together again, just before we take a leap of faith into the empty space surrounding the third volume, this book's considerations of the evolution of black thought and languages.

There are, also, recurring characters in this repeating verse drama. Amiri Baraka was a presence throughout *Black Chant;* he appears on the first page of this book, is the subject of a chapter, and wends his way through the rest of the pages. In the later portions of *Black Chant* I turned to the performances of poetry and jazz created by Jayne Cortez; *Integral Music* concludes with a chapter sketching the diasporic reach of her work, and she is not finished with us yet, will be back in volume three. Russell Atkins appeared in *Black Chant* in the context of Cleveland's Free Lance group, of which he was a mainstay. In *Integral Music* I have the opportunity to take a much broader perspective on this crucial, though often overlooked, figure.

As the chapters appear in rough chronological order, it falls out that we move from readings of barely discussed poets to discussions of widely read poets. I adopt a strategy of writing much more about the less well known poets, hoping that those few readers so fortunate as to already have read deeply in their works will be forgiving. At the same time, there may be those who wish I had written much more about the poets here who are more widely recognized. All I can say in response is that I have written more about them and will again.

If the past is prologue, then this preface should be seen as a forward-looking description of a past that looks different, that will look different yet again, that will ever after make for a difference that makes a break for the future; a past that may well serve as bridge, as lucid interval.

# INTEGRAL MUSIC

# 1

# *Carrying Deconstruction to Cleveland: Russell Atkins*

. . . for some time now his books
had no dishevelled about them, no open;
all shut with rare and seldom.
—Russell Atkins, *Here in The*

"What does *that* signify?"
"It don't signify nothin' Mr. Warner."
—Russell Atkins, *Maleficium*

## I. HERETOFORE

I did not want to be "well-rounded."
—Russell Atkins, "Russell Atkins"

At a time when the dating of even so broadly studied a phenomenon as the Harlem Renaissance remains a subject of torrid debate, few would care to supply a date for the heretofore little noted emergence of an identifiable avant-garde among African American poets. Still, the breaking of some rigidities is worthy of rereading. Even before the first poems bearing the signature of LeRoi Jones began to appear in small-press magazines around the country, Russell Atkins had established himself as a prominent advocate of avant-garde poetics in America. Atkins published his first poems when he was only eighteen years old, and, according to Casper LeRoy Jordan's afterword to Atkins's 1961 collection, *Phenomena,* Atkins's characteristic devices and ideas "were in effect" as early as 1946 to 1950 in poems that circulated in magazines such as *Experiment, View, Beloit Poetry Journal,* and others. Jordan remarks, "A perusal of poetry publications in which Mr. Atkins' poetry appeared reveals that he remained one of the very few consistently experimental poets" (76). In the author's biography that accompanies Atkins's fullest collection of his life's work in verse, *Here in The,* the poet is quoted as stating, "I was *avant garde* before I knew there was an *avant garde*" (52). Although too many current-day critics still evidence no awareness that there has been an African American avant-garde in America, Atkins was an active and recognized force for experimental poetics across a span of four decades. Early champions of his work included Carl Van Vechten, Langston Hughes, Parker Tyler, Charles Henri Ford, and Marianne Moore; and he has been one of the most prolific black experimentalists in American literature, publishing more than ten books along with numerous articles, notes, and dramatic pieces contributed to little magazines here and abroad. (An even earlier supporter was Atkins's Latin teacher at Cleveland's Central Junior High, Helen Chesnutt, daughter of Charles Waddell Chesnutt.) Atkins was a mainstay of the *Free Lance* journal, which Conrad Kent Rivers once called "[t]he oldest black-bossed magazine around" (qtd. in Redmond 328) and which the editors of *Black American Literature Forum* described as "the longest continuously published black journal" (Atkins, "Henry Dumas" 159). Atkins did receive a degree of recognition for his tireless and highly individual efforts. He was a frequent reader on the poetry circuit, reading at universities, galleries, and coffeehouses around the country, and he was invited to both the Bread Loaf and Iowa writers' workshops. Atkins was awarded an honorary doctorate from Cleveland State University and was for a time the writer in residence at Cuyahoga Community College. Karamu House, where Atkins taught creative writing for more than a decade, produced a "Tribute to Russell Atkins" in 1971, featuring performances and critical discussions of his works in music and literature. Dudley Randall, of Broadside Press fame, journeyed from Detroit to join in that retrospective evening, presenting a reading from Atkins's correspondence. At other times, members of the Cleveland Orchestra performed his "Objects" for cello, violin, and piano. Composer Hale Smith wrote his "In Memoriam" based on a poem by Atkins, and Stefan Wolpe introduced Atkins's "Psychovisual Perspective for 'Musical' Composition" at the Darnstadt Festival of Contemporary Music in 1956. Atkins's work in music theory is cited by H. H. Stückenschmidt in his 1969 study, *Twentieth Century Music.* Marianne Moore was sufficiently taken with Atkins's poem "Trainyard at Night" that she read it as part of a WEVD radio broadcast in New York as early as 1951. In July of that year Moore wrote to Atkins, saying that she had mutilated and mangled the reading of his poem, despite an earlier, successful rehearsal. She reported to Atkins that despite her reading she had heard quite good reactions to the poem from her listeners, concluding that it had been the distinctive element of the broadcast (Moore).

When *Free Lance* published a special issue in tribute to Atkins's career in 1970, the issue's editorial commentaries, written by Casper Jordan and J. Stefanski, placed Atkins's experimental works against a background in which "Conservatism dominated contemporary American poetry through the early fifties." They proceeded to argue, "In spite of a highly visible attempt to deny the fact, Atkins has been among the most subtle influences of the last two decades" (1). Elsewhere in the issue they term Atkins's poem "Night and a Distant Church" "the masterpiece of 'concretism'" (9) and "the most exquisitely suggestive 'concrete' piece of the last twenty years" (8). They credited Atkins with having published some of the first examples of concrete verse in the United States, and they argued that "the bridge between typographical and 'concrete' is difficult to define until one knows of Atkins's ingenious combination of elevated tone and meticulous application of device to thought and subject" (8). Given the occasion of a tribute, some overstatement (perhaps even a misplaced modifier or two) can be forgiven. It would probably be difficult, though, for literary historians to prove the "high visibility" of attempts (by critics or by Atkins himself) to deny Atkins's importance and influence, but he has indeed been omitted from almost all histories of American literature in general and American poetic experimentalism in particular. It is somewhat easier to point to published attempts to deny the importance of African American literature in toto, stretching from Thomas Jefferson through Allen Tate, and the general ignorance about Atkins's extensive contributions on the part of literary scholars is no doubt attributable in part to the legacy of that history of racism. Despite Atkins's valuable exchanges of correspondence with Charles Henri Ford, Parker Tyler, Marianne Moore, Carl Van Vechten, and Edith Sitwell, the published histories of the movements from modernism to postmodernism have not yet found reason to mention Atkins, and despite his early associations with Langston Hughes, the critical efforts to recover important black writers who have been overlooked have yet to renew the reputation of Russell Atkins. (A herald can be seen, though, in the special section devoted to Atkins in a recent issue of the small-press magazine *Crayon*.)

In part, this critical invisibility can be blamed on a tendency, too widespread among academic critics, to ignore small-press publications until such time as an author has achieved a modicum of public critical interest. With the exception of his 1976 collected poems, *Here in The,* which was published by Cleveland State University's Poetry Center, and his chapbook in Paul Bremen's Heritage series, published in London, Atkins's books were all limited editions from small avant-garde presses. Roughly half of his books were printed by Free Lance Press, and others were brought out by Cleveland's Renegade Press and California's Hearse Press. As a result the volumes *Here in The* and *Heretofore* are the only collections among Atkins's works that are likely to be found in many research libraries, and they were also the only books of his readily obtainable in literary book stores, so long as they remained in print. But far more than this, Atkins's critical invisibility is likely the result of the combination of the nature of his writing and his identity as a black experimentalist. It has often proved difficult for white authors of avant-garde texts to get published, enormously difficult in fact, and although it has taken a very long time indeed for critics to come around to the reading of such works, we do now have a body of critical studies available to students of such modernists as Mina Loy, Gertrude Stein, and Louis Zukofsky; and the critical bibliographies surrounding the texts of such contemporary poets as Clark Coolidge, Susan Howe, and Charles Bernstein are thickening appreciably. Still, even though collections of Atkins's papers have been on deposit for some time at Atlanta University and at the Chicago Public Library, Atkins remains, as Ronald Henry High notes in his article on the poet in the *Dictionary of Literary Biography,* "[b]etter known abroad than in America" (24). High concludes his entry by predicting that "as more people get familiar with Atkins, his approach to literary expression will be better appreciated and more fully understood. As his work is more performed and more read, as it garners more critical attention and documentation, his genius will come to be recognized in the United States as it is in Europe" (32). (A mark of Atkins's renown overseas is that the scholar of neo-African culture Jahnheinz Jahn made a point of stopping to visit with Atkins during one of his trips from Germany [Simon 8].) High made his predictions more than ten years ago. A check of the most recent Modern Language Association bibliographies yields few citations of critical work devoted to the study of Atkins's poetry.

As early as 1950 Russell Atkins, who by that time had been publishing poems in magazines for six years, was already known as a significant new talent among African American poets. When Langston Hughes guest-edited a special "Negro Poets Issue" of the magazine *Voices* in 1950, he included Atkins along with Waring Cuney, Owen Dodson, Robert Hayden, Melvin B. Tolson, and Gwendolyn Brooks. By the next year Marianne Moore was introducing some of his most experimental work to New York radio audiences, and Atkins's commitment to his avant-garde stance seems never to have wavered since. Abby Arthur Johnson and Ronald Maberry Johnson, in their history of African American magazines, identify Atkins as "the most technically experimental" writer included in *Free Lance*. They go on to complain that "[h]e was so experimental in both essays and poems that it was often difficult to trace his ideas" (157). They are not alone in their complaint. In his reply to Adelaide Simon's praises of Atkins's work in the special Cleveland issue of *Input* magazine in 1964, Kirby Congdon claims that Atkins has done all in his power to deserve his public obscurity. Simon, who had worked as Atkins's coeditor at *Free Lance*, had written that "there is a great deal of sadness in the lack of critical acclaim for Russell Atkins's work in the very avant garde itself" (8). Congdon concedes that Atkins's ideas, the matter of his work, are original and provocative. It is the work's form and language that Congdon finds objectionable. Congdon claims that if Atkins has been neglected, "it is only because he chooses to write in a lush, archaic take-off of Shakespearean lingo that sounds great at first but does the author a disservice, since it comes off as pretentious and unnatural" (9). In the end, though, Congdon is not so much concerned about the disservice Atkins may be inflicting on himself as he is about what he thinks Atkins is doing to his readers. As is all too often the case when a critic wishes to dismiss experimental poetics, Congdon accuses Atkins of writing this way in order to curry favor with critics (apparently without success). Congdon advises Atkins, "I am still hoping he will write for *us* readers & . . . forget the students, explicators, and scholars, whose interest he apparently wishes to capture." It would seem that no "lack of acclaim" from students and critics will ever be enough to protect a writer from this charge. As Congdon concludes, he states, suddenly adopting the royal first-person plural: "We don't think, though, that the sadness lies in our neglect of [Atkins]; but rather in his neglect of us," and the critic offers the poet, as a model to follow, the translations of Robert Graves (9). Atkins, in his own critical comments scattered through successive issues of *Free Lance,* has often attacked this sort of legislating of the allowable in language and in form. "The 'authority,'" he writes, is in the "teaching values racket" ("Of" 1963, 22). The authority has at his disposal an effective disciplinary apparatus. "Conferences, classrooms and magazines are his to cultivate the merely presentable poem for which he knows what 'techniques' are 'proper' and who is proper for them" (21–22). In that same collection of notes in 1963, Atkins, speaking of Robert Hayden, indicates his own acute awareness of the critical facts of life facing black poets in America. "It is not surprising in America," Atkins observes, "that we would hear *less* of an accomplished non-white poet, for it is bound up with ethnic obstacles in connection with the mainstream of literature in America" (23).

Eugene Redmond's assessment at the end of his summary of Atkins's career in *Drumvoices* is both more measured and more fair than either Congdon's or that of the Johnsons and is more temperate in its appreciations of Atkins than Simon could be about her coeditor. In Redmond's reading, "Once Atkins's technique is understood, . . . his poetry can be enjoyed for its witty, wacky, yet serious philosophical musings" (329). There is a central wackiness, it must be conceded, to Atkins's writing that we should not lose sight of even as we read his more convoluted critical essays, but it is a motivated wackiness. Sterling Brown frequently quipped to those of us who knew him in Washington, DC, that "any black man who isn't paranoid is crazy." As Russell Atkins worked his way through the madness of America's racialized languages, trying to make art out of discourses designed to deny his entry, he developed a characteristic mode of writing that, although it resembles some aspects of the works of his contemporaries in local instances, is finally unlike that of any other black writer of his time, perhaps unlike any writer of his time. Always, though, he evidenced an ironic sensibility about his projects and about his reception. He knew that some of his methods brought resistance from those committed to more traditional reading strategies, and he sometimes used more traditional writing strategies to comment on that fact. Perhaps Kirby Congdon had never read Atkins's "Notes on Negro Poets," a 1954 poem composed after Atkins had read Hughes and Bontemps's *Poetry of the Negro*. The poem is anything but an example of "lush, archaic lingo," and few readers would have any difficulty making their way through its stanzas. One must, however, have read some of Atkins's more experimental forms in order to appreciate just how far into his cheek he has worked his tongue when he offers the following self-assessment:

I cannot make heads or tails
of the new poets among Negroes.
But then why bother?
Could anything be made of them
would it matter?
But some say that they
cannot make heads or tails
of ME! How can that be?
I am so clear! not like
Gwendolyn Brooks—
all blear. (16)

This from a poet who more frequently wrote lines like the following:

Clad of shrub shreds to rush
and for the exodus'd
difficult will snow. (*Podium* n.p.)

Juxtaposing such lines as these to Atkins's humorous claims to clarity is not the revelation of a grand contradiction. We should, instead, understand that Atkins, like the early Objectivist poets, conceived of a clarity that differed substantively from the model offered by mainstream poetry at midcentury. None of the words Atkins uses in the second example of his verse sends readers scurrying for their dictionaries, and the only unusual word formation is his transformation of *exodus* into a past-tense verb through the use of an apostrophe (a technique used perhaps too frequently by Atkins—but in this instance I can't help hearing an intertextual echo of the "exodusters" in his line). Neither does Atkins's poem "Demolition," with its "clad of shrub," burden readers with extensive and opaque allusions (though both Euclid and Medusa get mentioned). What readers face here is a kind of formal opacity. Most readers are not used to encountering phrases like "Clad of shrub shreds to rush" in their daily experiences of language, even in verse, and so may tend to resist reading such phrases despite the fact that one can, and fairly quickly, begin to make a series of sensible readings out of the phrases of the poem. What Atkins jokingly suggests is that his poems are at least as "clear" as those of his more celebrated contemporaries. It is true that if we compare an Atkins line like "Clad of shrub shreds to rush" to some of the denser of Brooks's lines, their poetics might appear somewhat less disjunct. In "The Second Sermon on the Warpland" Brooks writes:

> Salve salvage in the spin.
> Endorse the splendor splashes;
> Stylize the flawed utility; (*Blacks* 454)

In the face of such a passage (and it is important to recall that these lines occur in one of the poems Brooks wrote after she had begun communing with Don Lee and Sonia Sanchez), it may be harder to argue with Atkins's ironic assertions that his own poems are actually less "blear" than those of Brooks. His concluding stanza to "Eloge" might well pass as a fair imitation of the Brooks of the 1950s:

> Such seer ones who had
> no repose and to whom
> nothing trophied came,
> who strove to save the world
> I threnody them all
> remorse, for it is drear to tell
> how lacked is of them
> sculpture (27)

Only in the last two lines do we find the characteristic twist of those syntactic displacements that mark a poem as quintessentially Atkins. It is not that Atkins inhabited an entirely disparate poetic universe from Brooks and others of the time; the differences are matters of degree. (And Atkins is more likely to be up to mischief when he violates modernist admonitions against poetic inversions of phrase grammar than is Brooks in her earlier works.) One effect of the sequestering of experimentalists like Atkins from the more recent genealogies of black verse has been that we are no longer able to see the continuum that stretches from the avant-garde of the 1950s and early 1960s to the more widely read and discussed later poems of a figure like Brooks.

Atkins wrote his "Notes on Negro Poets" several years before the younger Amiri Baraka published his controversial essay "The Myth of a Negro Literature." In that 1962 essay Baraka claimed that "Negro" literature had in the past been "a method or means of displaying . . . participation in the 'serious' aspects of American culture" (*Home* 108); he then went on to complain of some contemporary African American poets that they would "reject the gaudy excellence of 20th century American poetry in favor of disembowelled Academic models of second-rate English poetry, with the notion that somehow it is the only way poetry should be written" (113). Baraka would subsequently revise his reading of some earlier black authors, but his complaint was shared by Atkins. The older poet's 1954 poem reaches a hilarious peak of racial punning when Atkins sighs, "Ah Negro poetry where perfect sham / is passing!" ("Notes" 16). The pun itself is one instance of Atkins's own gaudy excellence. This doubled figure, which also echoes a Melvillean "Ah, humanity," conjoins a complaint about the sham of passing mediocre and imitative verse as thought and the high art of poetry, and the sham of passing for white. To underscore his estimation of the banality of what he later was to call "the remaining Kipling zealots and the Paul Laurence Dunbars [and] the Tennysonians . . . " (*Free Lance* 13, 22), all those African American poets who rejected the new poetics of the postwar era, and even those of the modernists, in preference for continued mining in the played-out vein of archaic verse forms, Atkins resorts to doggerel to record his ironic critiques. "I'll tell you when I'm crushed / by books—when I read / Gwendolyn Brooks!" Atkins exclaims in "Notes on Negro Poets" (17). Of a prominent voice from the Harlem Renaissance Atkins says: "When I think of Countee Cullen / I grow sullen" (17). As far as Atkins is concerned, Cullen should not have marveled that God would make a poet black and bid him sing. For Atkins the really curious thing was that no one bade Cullen cease (a criticism that, as we have seen, is ironically returned to Atkins by Congdon's later ripostes). Though Atkins would subsequently describe Robert Hayden's imagination as "freely decorative" and speak of his poetry as a "relief from an exaggerated preoccupation with 'content'" ("Of" 1963, 23), here he writes: "'How like the consummation of' too much / Are the poems of Robert Hayden / With too many big words laden" (17).

It was what he saw as an "exaggerated preoccupation with content" on the part of critics as well as poets that most exercised Atkins in these "Notes." It was not that Atkins denied the political implications of literary art nor that he refused politically oriented readings of poetry and poetics. To the contrary, he exhibited a sophisticated understanding of the culturally constructed nature of race and prejudice and of the role literature and literary education played in both the construction and defense of racial hegemony in the realm of culture. In 1964, ten years after he wrote his "Notes," he recorded in the *Free Lance* editors' column "Some Thoughts Defining 'Mainstream' in Relation to 'Education' and Destructive Power." These later ruminations indicate Atkins's estimation of the role played by institutions of state power, such as education, in the naturalizing of hegemonic discourse, as well as his comprehension of the essentially arbitrary nature of signification: "Educated prejudice—the most difficult of prejudices—is not based on ignorance, but upon 'knowledge' that has been *created* and culturally adjusted under Military control. It is in command of enough information that it can usually refute arguments employed to convince it of something with arguments equally valid. Even should this fail it is aware of this: *that in the realm of semantics, abstraction, types of creativity, and on the plane of values, little can be proved to be other than arbitrary*" (26).

Some thirty years later, what the American media came to call the culture wars in education continued to rage over just these grounds. As poststructuralist theories, feminism, cultural studies, ethnic studies, new historicism, and even new poetries increasingly challenged mainstream education from within the institutions of education themselves, frequently issuing their challenges in terms much like those used in the *Free Lance* of 1964, the mainstream's cultural authorities and politicians like George H. W. Bush and William Bennett attempted, often with considerable militance, to reassert control. As far as Russell Atkins and his *Free Lance* colleagues could see, canon construction and publication are an integral force in the "military control" of cultural values. "Often enough," we read in *Free Lance,* "anthologies reveal or confirm or even determine a group's relationship to the 'mainstream' as defined above" (27). On this view the critical preoccupation with the content of African American poetry is a means of determining, adjusting, perhaps even policing group identity and group subject positions. A mirroring preoccupation on the part of writers effectively sustains the assumptions and agendas of critical hegemony. As Atkins puts it in his "Notes," again turning the humor against himself:

> Negroes, Freedom, etc., in poetry!
> (a word dear reader;
> they weary). Many frowns and all
> pass over them mysterious,
> and some die over them,
> and I—I've been so heroic—
> I've sighed over them. (16)

Atkins also recognized the intimate critical association in American thought between the preoccupation with the content of African American verse and the continuing demand for a "realism" of linguistic surface in the literary forms of black writing. As we've seen in Congdon's attacks on Atkins's style, as we can see in Sarah Webster Fabio's attacks on Melvin B. Tolson's language, and as we can see in Professor Joyce Ann Joyce's attacks on black critics who make use of the language of poststructuralist theories, American criticisms of African American writing continue to posit an audience (always vaguely out there, somewhere, congregating in virtual ghettoes as "the people") befuddled by forms of English that purportedly could never be their own. (Interestingly, critics making this type of charge seldom present themselves as unable to comprehend the language under attack, although they do present themselves as "among the people"; it's always "the people" who will not be able to understand.) Such attitudes tried and tired Atkins, as did those "tea party" poets who thought of the poem as a therapeutic baring of the emotions. At the close of his "Notes on Negro Poets" Atkins condemns that conservative adherence to literary realism (not to be confused with "the real") that would again be condemned in the next decade by Amiri Baraka and Clarence Major:

> You know how sensitive I am and all
> and cannot bear writers ungeneral—
> Realists and so on? How they do bore!
> because there are not a few of them
> but a few *more*! (18)

Precious little of Atkins's poetry is written in this mode, though he is sometimes this precious. Atkins was having a good deal of fun matching the banality of form in his "Notes" to the mediocrity of technical accomplishment that passed among so many poets wedded to traditional forms. Always, Atkins wanted forms that suited his subjects. In his memorial poem to Langston Hughes, which is for the most part written in Atkins's more familiar syntactically disruptive style, the poet suddenly inserts a traditionally rhymed couplet in the manner of Hughes's best known poems. "May Twenty-Second, Nineteen Sixty Seven," included by Atkins in the 1967 Hughes memorial issue of *Free Lance,* is an elegy honoring that older poet who encouraged (and published) the wilder and younger experimentalist. "Few fugitives had been sheltered by him / as had I" (23), Atkins remembers of the poet whose prefatory note had introduced the very first issue of *Free Lance.* Atkins rails against "eternal syndicates" that "won't dare countenance things free" (22), and he contrasts them to Hughes, who, whatever doubts he may have harbored about the more extreme formal revolutions of the next generation, was willing to lend his name and prominence to the idea of free-verse experiment. In what has to be one of his most eloquent couplets, Atkins follows a citation from Hughes with lines in which his apostrophied verb forms seem more than usually "natural" and sound as if they were drawn from Hughes himself:

> "Ain't no sense in my being dead."
>
> They cannot prey on him: he left instead,
> jazz'd in fire, funeral'd in red. (21)

Atkins obviously remembers Hughes's written reminiscence of the lyric, "Fire gonna burn my soul." Historically minded readers of this elegy will also remember, whether intended to or not, that decades earlier the magazine of experimental literature by young black writers that Hughes had helped to found, a forerunner of *Free Lance,* was titled *Fire.* Hughes recalled in later years that *Fire* represented a desire to "*épater le bourgeois,* to burn up a lot of the old stereotyped Uncle Tom ideas of the past" (18–19). That magazine was itself "funeral'd in red" when the bulk of the press run was immolated in a building fire (Johnson and Johnson 79). Having briefly adopted a Hughes-like diction and form, Atkins then immediately reverts to a language more his own, to those yet odder verb and noun forms that gave Kirby Congdon so much consternation. The metrics of Atkins's lines here remain traditional, but, like John Ashbery, Atkins floats "normal" sounding sentences atop that measure that seem to float loose from normal modes of predication and subordination: "Which facts are worst to their abhor / of the valuables, his, that I possess" (21).

Atkins often employs forms that hover close to the traditional, only to twist the direction of readerly expectations aroused by the generic cues offered by those forms. His particular mode of experiment took the history of genres (including the genre of the concrete poem) as the givens on which he worked his improvisations. In the course of a *Free Lance* review in 1966 Atkins declared his belief that

> *[a] poet cannot change, for whatever purpose, the fundamental units of perception in terms of accents, trochees, etc., can only be permutated.* American poets hint of a complete liberation from a tradition. However, they must employ that tradition's own devices, viz., syntactical logic, morphology, etc., compounded of words of "the latine & mo from the French and mo from the Italian—" according to one Renaissance purist. Regardless of the pros and cons of the dispute, any originality toward figurative effect through the *English* language may inescapably *resemble* that language's traditions at, say, the drop of a hat?" (Rev. of *Musophilus* 13)

One of the disarming things about Atkins's nonconcrete works is just their resemblance to traditional forms. Atkins's way of contesting the mainstream was often to contest it within its own structures so that his originality frequently resembles, in shape at least, the poetry that he attacks as insipid repetition of the past.

This is certainly true of a late poem that pays a peculiar tribute to one of Atkins's early correspondents, Marianne Moore. The 1978 collection *Whichever,* published as a Free Lance Press chapbook, includes a poem whose title will be immediately recognized as a wry appropriation from the modernist canon. Where Moore offers as a trope for that touch of the genuine that may sometimes be found in modern poetry her imaginary gardens with real toads in them (how unlike an admiring bog), Atkins writes of "Imaginary Crimes in a Real Garden." The poem follows a portrait of an "Old Man Carrying a Bible in a

High Crime Area" and continues a decidedly off-center argument about the changing neighborhoods of late twentieth-century America. Atkins's poem precedes by many years the concerted attacks on public funding of controversial art works that gathered impetus during the presidencies of Ronald Reagan and George H. W. Bush; but even the Ohio Arts Council of 1978, which helped to fund publication of *Whichever,* might have been disconcerted by the nature of the crimes imagined in Atkins's real garden.

The poem begins in traditionally stressed syllabic lines. With its opening conceit, the poem appears to be headed in a predictable direction, only the odd modifier *asthma'd* sticking out as something out of the ordinary: "a spring already short of breath / on its way to asthma'd summer" (7). The very regularity of these four-stress, octosyllabic lines implies the ordered artifice of the real garden. Significantly, this regularity is disrupted by the entrance of the first-person pronoun, the graphic representative of the imagining criminal. The third line reads in its entirety, "I gather," and from then on the poem is composed of variant lines, sometimes echoing the opening's regularity, always marking with their deviation from that opening "chord" their disruptions of pastoral traditions. Atkins's poem is not a replication of the literary archetype of spring's cyclical fertility. Here the grass itself is allergic, the roots of shrubs sterile and useless. Then, with a terrifying sexual pun, Atkins begins the catalogue of his metaphorical carnage:

> faggots in a bunch, their necks
> snap of twig's necks            crunched!
>                         thick earth—
> between the hands, against knuckles            (7)

In Atkins's gathering of dried twigs and flowers (this is too like your usual domestic outing to be anybody's Waste Land) he imagines a rampage against a fat man, a fetus, "a shape of a female twig." Each is violently rent, violated and collected. In the end:

>                         I shove
> them down               bind the bag
> with a short wire
>
>                         this is the kill

It is somewhat as if the poet, having come across Moore's real toads, crushed them against the rocks. This is no doubt the mode Adelaide Simon had in mind when, in her "Salvos for Atkins," published in *Input,* she spoke of his "[i]nexorably Gothic lyrics" (8). In Simon's summation, "[t]he poetry of Russell Atkins is one long strong elegant preoccupation with horror. DEATH DECAY LUST MURDER ABORTION ADDICTION NECROPHILIA," and she goes on to make the at first odd-seeming remark that Atkins's poems produce "a new shudder that outpaces Williams and Baudelaire" (8). The connections to the Baudelaire of *Spleen and Ideal* are probably made readily enough; and given the context, it may be Tennessee, rather than William Carlos, Williams that Simon has in mind. Still, the kind of shudder Simon has invoked here is the feeling that awaits readers of Williams's short stories like "The Use of Force" or of passages like the one in *Paterson* that describes a womb held up by a door knob. Like that Williams, too, is the frequent note of bizarre humor accompanying Atkins's horrific imagery. A 1955 poem titled "How Would I Come upon a Corpse (on recent occurrences in Cleveland)" derives its hilarity from a perfectly commonsense response to an imagined question:

How would I come upon a corpse?
With a Look what's here for God's sake!
Or would I profoundly
mystery hollows who?
Hushed as if "Sorry, am I intruding?" (26)

That same sort of humor attends Atkins's poetic responses to those who might condemn the sense of the "fantastic" in his work on the grounds that it constitutes an apolitical escape from reality. In one of the poems in his 1960 volume, *A Podium Presentation,* the poet is briefly confronted by the surreal image of "Mrs. Rhone" appearing in the doorway as a shrouded figure from her crypt:

Furious'd garb.
Listen: More spoken of "reality"
and face to face with it as the at desk
at ink at phone at typewriter
and business'd in coat and tie, et al., sons & co. (n.p.)

Surely one of the things that sets Atkins's verse apart from that of so many others is that he seems to have scripted a postmodern role for the largely abandoned poetics of Poe. Atkins's Poe is not exactly the Poe who haunts the stanzas of Hart Crane's poetry, nor does he seem to be the revisionist Poe rediscovered by William Carlos Williams at the end of *In the American Grain*. He does seem to be a close American cousin to Baudelaire's Poe. Like Williams and Crane, Atkins appears to want a reclaimed and remade Poe, one saved from his dusty corner of *The Best Loved Poems of the American People* in order to redirect contemporary poetics. In Poe's morbidity and emphasis on technique Atkins locates a counterargument to the mimetic aesthetic that continues to call for a realism of language even as it accepts, sometimes, a critical conception of the poem as self-contained, iconic, even as a machine made of words. For Atkins, as he argues in a note appended to his collection *Phenomena* in 1961, an "uncreative *realism*" was to be shunned. "Realism in the sense of a 'disposition to think (perceive) or act in the light of things as they are' is unprogressive, dull. No definable contribution is effected. The intention in the created DESIGNED IMAGINATION is obstructed" (79). Atkins's distance in his aesthetics from such slightly later postmodernists as Baraka, Major, and Spellman is locatable in part here in his emphasis on the work of the DESIGNED IMAGINATION and in his exhumation of a premodernist Poe in a postmodernist poetics. Atkins does not share with Baraka and the others the powerful influence of Williams's insistence on an art constructed out of the idioms of daily speech. Atkins would argue for a more expansive notion of speech, one that would make room for the artifice of the speaking subject of the fantastic. While Atkins may thus seem yet more distant from the Objectivists' program of thinking *with* the things of the world (and perhaps closer to a novelist like James Purdy), his refusal to accept any reification of that thinking places him as an early figure in one strand of the postmodern that will include such later writers as Will Alexander.

Atkins rejects aesthetics based on a transcendent appeal to realism, though he will contend that a poet following his strictures is every bit as capable of contributing social value as one following a more traditional poetics. Atkins asserts that the poet of "DESIGNED IMAGINATION," following a type of nonrepresentational aesthetic, "*creates* an experience evolved independently of the stimuli that [emanate] from 'real' as experienced by himself" (*Phenomena* 79). A poetics of radical artifice and "CONSPICUOUS TECHNIQUE," then, is just as likely as "an artist preoccupied with 'other people' or social problems" (79) to make what Atkins saw as the vital contributions. Such an aesthetic clearly presents problems for any who come to black poetry as to a "native informant," looking to pry out of the work relatively direct reports of the "minority sensibility." Atkins, for all his education as much an antiacademic poet as the often Ivy League trained Beats, would respond in 1963 to an earlier generation of traditional readers:

> Is this the teaching-values racket? What critic-teachers of values and "techniques" teach is what poets are told is best to have in their poems (for sundry unpoetic reasons such as a position on some faculty, editor in some publishing house, promising lecture tour, etc.) then everybody is told how to find it there. There are poets, no doubt, who put accepted "enrichments" in their works. Thus dupes are disposed to find these while critic-teachers "discover" them to review the book and so demonstrate such *sensitivity* to what has been standardized! After all, how would the critic-teacher "authority" of no literary ability keep his job? ("Of" 1963, 22)

One present-day version of the "teaching-values racket" that so exercised Atkins is a classroom version of the corporate sensitivity sessions organized within the framework of "managing diversity." In the classroom, poems are managed as students, sensitized by their teachers, pluck out evidence of the sensitive ethnic subject responding to the world, all the while leaving the rest of the poem behind. The remainder that is left behind is largely that very "conspicuous technique" that Atkins employs to disrupt such reductive reading strategies. Reading for "difference" should not mean simply charting and freezing in place an array of ethnic elements that mark a poet's difference from or identification with the reader. It should be an ever unfinished reading of differentiation on a constantly shifting territory of meaning-in-progress. As Derrida was to write many years later: "The identity of a language can only affirm itself as identity to itself by opening itself to the hospitality of a difference from itself or a difference with itself. Condition of the self, such a difference *from* and *with* itself would then be the very thing, the *pragma* of its pragmatics: the stranger at home, the invited or the one who is called" (*Aporias* 10).

Derrida has explicitly defined deconstruction as "a certain aporetic experience of the impossible" (*Aporias* 15). Atkins, who described his own forms of deconstruction in a series of essays in the 1950s, presents the imaginary crime in the real garden as the aporetic experience of the impossible, and for Atkins this mode of being the stranger in the garden of one's own language (How would I come upon a canon?) is the real "realism" of poetry and the daily experience of black native speakers in American English. Atkins's postmodern reclamation of Poe through Baudelaire is a way of making Poe differ from himself. Within the texts of that quintessentially racist southerner, whose only novel is wrapped around the mysterious polar inscriptions of ancient Ethiopic script, Atkins rewrites a counterracist gothic, once again demonstrating that originality "toward figurative effect" that inescapably resembles the traditions of the language in which he works.

Thus Atkins also counters arguments that a poetry of political use must necessarily employ prescribed language registers. In his 1966 review of an edition of Samuel Daniel's *Musophilus* Atkins offers his contemporary version of an Elizabethan controversy over the justification of a life of the intellect and study. "Similarly today it is: If one is not on picket lines (civil rights, Viet Nam) or in 'community action' (poverty politics) one is 'a fool wasting time writing poetry.' Or else, the insinuation goes, if one *does* 'waste one's time' doing so, he must write in 'the language of ordinary men' (W. Wordsworth & W. C. Williams) artless, in a sense, and straightforward" (12). (One can't help hearing a pun on literary traditions of vaunted American innocence inside Atkins's complaint about poetic strictures prescribing verse that is "artless, in a sense.") As he has done in "Imaginary Crimes in a Real Garden," Atkins writes in "Narrative" a poem that begins by sounding its resemblance to traditional narrative verse before turning the language strange. It is an overtly political poem but one that uses "natural" language as a material out of which to construct a work rather than as a prescribed and transparent medium of instruction. Atkins's "Narrative" uses the first person to place us among John Brown's men as they assault Harper's Ferry. "I sat with John Brown," the poet begins. "That night moonlight framed . . . " (*Heretofore* 28). The third line of this 1956 poem is equally congruent with traditional narrative practice. In fact, it sounds a good deal like Stephen Vincent Benét in *John Brown's Body:* "He came and said 'It's Harper's, men!'"

But what interposes itself between the first and third lines is distinctly unlike Benét. What the moonlight framed, it transpires, was "the blown of his beard like a portent's undivulged." The first phrase of this line is not at all difficult for readers weaned on e. e. cummings or Kenneth Patchen to accommodate. "The blown of his beard" summons a familiar image, no matter its grammatical oddity, but the second phrase of the line entangles tenor and vehicle in such a way that the simile itself, rather than its possible referents, becomes the driving force of the poem's signifying. Again, if we only listen to the poem without looking at it, we might seem to be on more conventional ground. We would seem to be pointed in the direction of a similarity between Brown's blown beard and an undivulged portent, though even then the apparent disagreement between the indefinite article and the audibly plural noun we might think we heard would tell us that something is out of kilter. The visible presence of the apostrophe on the page, however, twists that simpler simile out of focus. Is it the beard of an undivulged portent that resembles Brown's, the "blown" of that beard, or is it that Atkins has chosen to omit whatever it is that belongs undivulged to a portent that resembles Brown's blown of beard? Or, are we to read the line as "the blown of his beard like a portent that is undivulged"?

The rest of the poem continues this alternation of quite accessible, even sometimes maudlin, constructions with other, counternormative artifices. Even when Atkins's phrases are strikingly out of the ordinary, they are often easily glossed and sound quite natural given their context. As Atkins imagines himself among Brown's band preparing its raid, for example, he sees the horses as "exhumed" terrors. Then, simply, he writes: "We dared off." No one in contemporary conversation would be likely to use such an expression, but neither would most have any difficulty comprehending it. Further, it has a somewhat archaic air about it; it sounds like something that could have been colloquial in Brown's time. What cannot be read aloud, though, is the exclamatory punctuation that interrupts our reading of the line in which Brown approaches Harper's Ferry. Lloyd Addison, a poet who, despite the publication of his magazine *Beau-Cocoa* and his inclusion in the same Heritage chapbook series that included Russell Atkins, remains even less known than Atkins, practiced a mode of typographical disruption in some of his most memorable poems. As Lloyd Addison would do, Atkins here interrupts the flow of letters in a word form with final punctuation, allowing, not the town itself but the appearance of the town to be discerned in the dust of print: "Harper's a!p!p!e!a!r!e!d! /—into it we went in a dust!" The poem ends by reprising its concrete representation of the unrepresentable, the dreadful rush of men and horses storming Harper's Ferry on their ultimately failing mission:

> "ft passed'ierced
> "if's,in,ss'd
> shsh"erced
> "ft
> "isk

It is possible to sound this out, but it is doubtful that any two successive soundings might coincide. It can be read as mimetic representation of the sound men make chasing their fate or as miming the barely comprehensible rush of rumor that spread out from Harper's Ferry and aroused a nation on the brink of war over the issues of slavery and secession. It could even be read as the dust into which the men rode. At some level, still, it has to be read as alphabetic letters inscribed on a page, summoning sounds but remaining ultimately uncertain, undetermined. This is perhaps not the "language of ordinary men," but it participates in a tradition of such soundings. Stephen Henderson has argued that African American music "is not afraid of new philosophies or new technologies; for the music deals with time filtered through the pulses of African sensibility. So no ideological hangup should prevent Black poets from writing 'sound poems,' especially with the model of Bob Kaufman, and Ella Fitzgerald, Louis Armstrong, and the moaning of the Baptist preacher" ("Modernity" 143).

It may also be, as Atkins's notes on "Egocentrical Projection as Object" have it at the end of *Phenomena,* that these techniques are the mark of "[a]n artist preoccupied with a neuro-psychophenomena of ego" (79), the poet designing a sound artifice to stand in relationship to a narrative history rather than simply pass us into that history as if "we were there." "We" are in the poem, however, thinking about the politics of race and history and rebellions.

Atkins's mode of relating his works to lyric tradition follows his mode of relation to history. Though he rejects Wordsworth's admonitions about poetic language in the "Preface" to *Lyrical Ballads,* Atkins does write "The Prelude," a lyric and philosophical autobiographical poem. The later poet's "Prelude" both parodies the theses of Wordsworth and demonstrates Atkins's mode of radical artifice (at the same time it also parodies *Hamlet*):

Being is appalling. Not as appalling
    However, as Not-To-Have-Been. Inertia
    'Death,' Night, Space, Time greatly Gravity
    Aspects of a mysterious realming
Substance? Thus in Not-Having-To-Be-More
The Thousand-length's luminous hideoum,
    From whose head of bloom,
The striking of flames conspicuously
    Adder'd in a gloom. (*Phenomena* 2)

This may be the sort of thing Redmond has in mind when he speaks of Atkins's "witty, wacky, yet serious philosophical musings" (329). New York School poets like Frank O'Hara, Kenneth Koch, and John Ashbery were evolving parallel mixtures of campy parody with serious meditation at about the same time. In the same year that Atkins published his "Prelude" in *Phenomena,* Frank O'Hara and Bill Berkson coauthored a poem that strikes much the same mood as Atkins's but without his signature deformations of words:

heaven is where you hang yourself
so dress up        the French will have ideas about it
                if you don't (104)

Though Atkins's poem resembles this piece by O'Hara and Berkson in subject matter and tone, Atkins goes much further in the direction of what he came to term "conspicuous technique." Atkins believed that "just as contemporary composers had challenged Western diatonicism with chromatic dissonance, [he] could distort grammar to a similar purpose by shifting parts of speech and exaggerating the distortion" ("Russell Atkins" 12). O'Hara and Berkson's poem appeared in the 1962 issue of John Ashbery's journal *Locus Solus,* and they, as well as their editor, have been the subjects of considerable critical and literary historical attentions. Atkins's *Phenomena* was, like so many of his works, published as a *Free Lance* book and is seldom mentioned by any critics at all.

A later Atkins chapbook, published by Cleveland's 7 Flowers Press, finds the poet celebrating another lyric tradition. Here Atkins follows his predecessor Langston Hughes in revisiting the traditions of black sacred song. Where Hughes (or any of a number of other African American moderns, including Sterling Brown and Owen Dodson) carried out their revisionist aesthetic by a recontextualizing or relining of the hymns, Atkins engages in the reformation of forms by articulating the poetics of the African American spiritual within the aesthetics of the concrete poem. He signals this remastering of the spiritual text by a respelling of it. The single poem contained in this chapbook is titled *Spyrytual,* and in it Atkins makes the quotation mark a concrete sign of citation visually glossing the spiritual's lyric:

Oh didn't it      “““      “““      ”””<br>
“““      ”””<br>
“““      ”””<br>
“““      ”””<br>
“““      ”””<br>
”<br>
““      ”<br>
““<br>
““<br>
““      ””<br>
rain (n.p.)

The words of the spiritual are here to be repeated, but the additional spirit writing of Atkins's cloudburst of quotation marks can only be transcribed and read, it cannot be recited at all. The poet has opened out the oral text and affirmed it in writing, offering the poem's material embodiment of the song as an affirmation of his experiment's rootedness in tradition. As a popular radio minister of my youth used to say, he takes his text and he takes his time. Once more Atkins is seeking to reassert what he saw as a neglected third stream (following the Emersonian tradition and the Eliot-Pound stream of influence) of America's poetic lineage represented by Hughes's modernist, urban recitation of blues and spirituals in the experimental typography and juxtapositions of innovative lyric forms.

Even in the writing of dialogue Atkins eschews the demands for natural language. Atkins's plays were experiments in sound text to be set to music and not naturalist drama. Of his nine plays, *The Exoneration* was produced as part of the 1971 Karamu House tribute, *The Corpse* was revised for presentation as part of a 1969 workshop performance in Cleveland's inner city, and *The Abortionist* was given a partial public reading; but, as Atkins explains in a recent letter, his aim in drama was "to make the play completely dependent on the poetry doing the *acting,* so to speak,—*not* having the poetry dependent on the plays" (letter of July 28, 2003). In his endnote to *2 by Russell Atkins* the poet writes, "The foregoing drama-poems have not sought to effect 'strong characterization' or the usual 'insights' into 'human behavior,' since these were incompatible with the experimentation" (32). These verse dramas should not be regarded simply as closet plays; some were given public production. Atkins's aesthetic in these pieces is not antihumanist so much as it is posthumanist in the sense that we have come to understand in those critiques of Western humanist philosophy launched by Foucault and Derrida. Atkins did not choose to write verse as a means of peering into the recesses of the human spirit, although he did hope to have an effect on humans through his writing. Likewise, although Atkins took some pride in having been the first playwright to address abortion on a Cleveland stage (*The Abortionist* was first published in 1954), he did not write either of the plays in *2 by Russell Atkins* as a means of conveying his positions on subjects such as abortion. *The Abortionist* appears in this book alongside *The Corpse,* which had first been published in *Western Review* in 1954. Atkins's Free Lance Workshop colleague Casper LeRoy Jordan wrote in an endnote of his own that "*The Abortionist* was *not* designed as a comment, pro or con, relating to abortion, but it is, as is its relative *The Corpse,* an object poem in play form to be set to music" (*2 by Russell Atkins* 32). Nonetheless, Atkins does communicate poetically in these dialogues, but their political import is not the transcendent limit of their interpretation. No one speaks or sings as do the characters in Atkins's musical drama, but the dialogues do appear to take colloquial speech as a point of departure. In *The Exoneration* a series of exchanges between two police officers is a riotous reformation of spoken language whose humor is as effective a protest against racist police brutality as composer Steve Reich's far better known 1966 piece "Come Out." The more meditative officer identified as "Cop of

Desk" observes: "We have Quaker'd jails: / Franklin'd penalties: / Emerson'd justice" (67). The character identified as "Cop 1" has apparently had about all of such reform that he can stand:

Ask me. I say that those old
Had what it takes. Ask!
GIVE'M THE WHACK I'D
SET TEN ON AND WHAM
BLUNT BELOWA BACK
SWEAT SOPS BLOOD EKES
FLESH OFF! (67)

Three decades later the Rodney King beating case and the murder in New York of Amadou Diallo demonstrated the staying power of such attitudes as Cop 1's. The response this draws from "Cop of Desk" is the same response many might want to offer to former Los Angeles police chief Daryl Gates and his disciples: "You're sick" (67).

In the play that is joined with *The Exoneration* in *Phenomena, The Drop of Blood,* we can see how, in the midst of the fantastic, Atkins is wont to create verse dialogue that comments on its own author's favored techniques. The situation of the play is sufficiently unreal to lift it out of the genre of naturalist drama even before we begin to listen to the lines themselves. Among the speaking characters in the drama is the titular Drop of Blood (possibly an allusion to the infamous "one drop" rule of America's racial definitions?), though how this would be managed in stage productions I have not yet ascertained. The "Blood" speaks lines that are characteristically in the mode of Atkins, lines like "Things with extremely like a head of tree— / Innumerable impenetrable intricacies," a line that appears to describe its own convolutions. But more interesting in this regard is a line spoken by the Blood's interlocutor, "The Wife." One of Atkins's most reiterated and conspicuous techniques is his use of the apostrophe to create new word forms, a device that Casper LeRoy Jordan calls particular attention to in his notes on Atkins. But what Jordan has not noted is an instance in *Phenomena* when Atkins redoubles his reliance on apostrophe. In *The Drop of Blood* Atkins makes dramatic use of a literary device that has fallen somewhat out of favor among lyricists of the postmodern era (except, perhaps, in the field of country music, where song choruses such as "Oh, Whiskey, if you were a woman . . . " occur with some frequency). The direct address to the personified object or the absent person is a mainstay of literary practice, as when Ben Jonson addresses himself to Shakespeare, "Soul of the age"; when Shakespeare's Cassius, while conversing with Brutus, calls out "Age, thou art sham'd"; when Wordsworth speaks to the deceased Milton; or, indeed, when the country-&-western singer desperately pleads with her rival, Whiskey, to release its hold on her straying spouse. What is unusual about Atkins's use of this traditional device of apostrophe is not just that the personified drop of Blood answers The Wife but that The Wife, in the act of speaking an apostrophe, also uses the signal apostrophe of Atkins's poetics:

> I am those years of up come down—
> Shut through which direction's ceased:
> The yearn'd, blood, of which he wished blown,
> Exhalations as when all is done and gone! (30)

The Wife's apostrophe to the Drop of Blood, underlining itself and punctuating itself with its namesake, is a textbook example of mise-en-abyme that has as yet entered no textbooks.

Despite Abby and Ronald Johnson's complaints about the "impenetrable titles" (157) of much of Atkins's work and the correlative difficulty of his style, and despite the complaints of such writers as Kirby Congdon regarding the supposed pretense of Atkins's unnatural language (of which the dialogue from *The Drop of Blood* might be another textbook example), passages such as the exchange between the police officers in *The Exoneration* provide a hint that there is yet another political effect registered in Atkins's verse. It would be the gravest of errors to claim, as some have tried to argue about the late style of Melvin B. Tolson, that the mode Atkins develops is a massive put-on. Still, the parodic mode of *The Exoneration*, and perhaps of the apostrophes in *The Drop of Blood,* enact overtly what Atkins's other poems enact somewhat more covertly: a direct challenge to the authority of racialized language in America. As unlikely as it is that any police officer ever uttered a phrase much like "BLOOD EKES / FLESH OFF," certainly no officer ever uttered such a phrase in verse; yet many white police officers over the decades have spoken similar intent toward black Americans subject to their authority. Atkins's parody of police speech voids white authoritarian language of much of its power to police speech. In Atkins's hands the language becomes a tool of counterterror, writing back to the military powers of hegemonic language. That effect is continued in the nonparodic poems of Atkins's unusual body of work. His language is not a lush aping of Shakespearean style, an archaic reach for "poetic"-sounding effects. Rather, it is a challenge issued to tradition from within the language of poetic tradition itself. Nobody, black or white, is likely to speak as do the voices of Atkins's poems, except for those who speak them aloud, but this is no reason to decline the reading of his poems. Their language is a contesting of the very authority of the concept of the "natural" in language.

Although T. S. Eliot's contemporaries complained that he did not write using the natural language of man speaking to man, as Michael Bérubé points out, few "would pause to ask whether *The Waste Land* is truly the spontaneous speech of 'the people' of Eliot" (177). Eliot's departures from "standard" English form are recognized as departures, but they are not seen as departures from a normative whiteness. What radical transformations in critical discourse would have to transpire before any critic would think to take Eliot to task for not sounding white? (In fact, Eliot's occasional use of "black" minstrel dialect would appear to have the effect, more than anything else, of operating as a continual guarantee of his whiteness.) The syntactic disruptions committed by Russell Atkins bear a relationship to the similar aesthetic revolutions of white poets, but they bear an added ethnic ambiguity within the racialized reading spaces of American literature. The avant-garde techniques of Atkins are not a white imposition on an essentially black language. They are a black American's remastery of the signifying materials of American English. They are a form of loud talk, wolfing, audacious reformation, deliberate deformation of hegemonic forms, and a reinscription of modernism as black writing. As such, Atkins's poems are the earliest sign of what Eugene Redmond has termed the "'signifying' poets of the 1960s and '70s (such as Baraka, Crouch, Touré, Eckels)" (96), in the same way that Redmond's critical deployment of the term *signifying* serves as a precursor to the later and fuller elaborations found in Henry Louis Gates's *The Signifying Monkey*. Atkins's innovative forms are graphic devices by means of which he explores networks of language for the purpose of deconstructing their unacknowledged dependencies and oppressions and of setting the stranger in motion within the home of his own tongue. As he writes in "At Night Keep Still":

There are, everywhere unheard
(as one might see deep in an electron microscope)
rigidities
        violently breaking (*Whichever* 4)

## II. HERE IN THE

With the prominent exceptions of poets like Amiri Baraka, June Jordan, Larry Neal, and Haki Madhabuti, the critical writings of recent African American poets have not been collected and circulated as assiduously as those of their Caucasian colleagues. Characteristically, Larry Neal's essays were gathered into a book posthumously, and Madhabuti's have been published and distributed primarily through his own publishing house. Even Baraka's collections have been allowed to pass out of print in most instances, only the books on music remaining readily available throughout his career. This may change for black poets who write in more mainstream modes in the near future. Now that Rita Dove has served a term as poet laureate of the United States and Derek Walcott has won the Nobel Prize, we might expect a modest increase in interest by publishers and readers in critical works by poets whose forms are less troubling than their content. And black poets who attain academic credentials and write scholarly/critical essays, such as Nathaniel Mackey and Harryette Mullen, may succeed in getting their works published by university presses. However, surveys of shelves in bookstores and libraries will confirm that there has been little concern among even university and small presses to collect and preserve the critical legacy of black experimentalists in the way that the essays of Charles Olson, Ed Dorn, or Robert Creeley (or even more recent poets, such as Charles Bernstein and Lyn Hejinian) have been maintained before a public. Russell Atkins has been one of the most prolific and demanding of black poets writing criticism and theory in the last four decades, but like Percy Johnston he has had to publish most of this work through his own magazine and workshop press, and there has never been a published collection of his critical work. The special Russell Atkins number of *Free Lance* included a section surveying his work in critical prose, but little of that work has found its way into the broader critical discourse of literary scholars (it has fared a little better with musicologists), and Atkins's prose is infrequently cited (save perhaps to denounce its style). As eccentric as Atkins's prose can sometimes be, these works are important early signs of a break with the "rigidities" of traditional humanist discourse among African American writers. Atkins's statements on music, literature, politics, and education parallel the works by Baraka leading into and out of the Black Arts Movement, but Atkins, as he does in his verse, travels an independent and often disturbing path.

Speaking of Anthony Braxton's experimentalism, Ronald Radano observes that it "emerged from the changing landscape of urban American life, from a new order that encouraged new ways of thinking about black art and the black artist" (28). One of the earliest and most persistent theorizers of, and creators of, these new orders was Russell Atkins. Much as "[m]usical modernism became, in the form of free jazz, the new tool of resistance in black performative expression" (Radano 21), Atkins viewed musical composition and poetry as areas in which new forms of conspicuous technique and black artifice could become tools of resistance. Atkins saw the postwar period as a creative moment when previously enforced codes of composition and reception had been shattered. In the realm of music, which for Atkins closely parallels the situation of the poet, this created both an enormous opportunity and a potential impasse: "the value-context base between audience and composer has finally vanished altogether. What is a value-context base? A context within which the composer can establish his composing aims knowing that it is also the context within which the audience can listen for purpose, meaning and discrimination, viz., approvals, disapprovals, good, bad, shocking or pacifying, interesting, surprising or dull" ("Of" 1980, 1). Atkins understood that there had been a violence implicit in the assertion of the previously existing value-contexts, just as there had been a violence associated with the sundering of that controlling set of discourse agreements. This accounts for Atkins's earlier references in the editorial columns of the 1964 *Free Lance* to the "military" control involved in the creation and cultural adjustment of knowledge ("Some Thoughts" 26), notes that so closely parallel Foucault's analyses of the disciplinary effects of discourses. The modernist era had been one violent series of ruptures in the skein of official culture in America, and Atkins saw the period following the Second World War as another. Conservative critics have also tended to view the period in this way, and that accounts for a good deal of the vituperation expressed against cultural shifts of the 1960s in the course of the recent culture wars conducted in the writings of Allan Bloom, Dinesh D'Souza, William Bennett, Shelby Steele, Carol Iannone, and others.

As far as Atkins was concerned, though, too many postwar artists were taking what amounted to a conservative turn of their own by "emulating past poses" ("Of" 1980, 4). Even though Atkins believes that creative ruptures must be made within the existing texts of the tradition's own devices, he never believed that the fresh and the daring could be accomplished by reasserting a previous value-context, by emulating "the old semantics of the 'new' which may have been a misinterpretation in the first place" (4). The contemporary artist, according to Atkins, was between horrific alternatives. In music, on the one hand, was the "popular" insistence on the familiar, the electronic media's "still powerful supports for the 'old' diatonic sounds (the darlings of rock, country, soul and disco)" (4), to which we might add the success of minimalism as an avant-garde that enjoyed wide popularity among the educated upper classes. On the other hand, the "'serious' avant-garde contemporary composer has finally been divested of anything to work with except fragmented discord—discontinuousness, if you prefer" (5). This led to an "ultimate dead-end" in the opposition between what Atkins terms "continuousness of motion in a piece versus discontinuousness." Representative of the latter end of that scale would be aleatory techniques, described by Atkins as "a near hopeless meandering succeeding only in extending the Webernian sparseness, plus a few mathematical addenda, which, when heard, are indistinguishable from all the rest" (5). An analogous dichotomy in poetics might be seen in an opposition between the much heralded New Formalism (and the popular success of writers such as Vikram Seth and Dana Gioaia) and the aleatory verse of a Jackson Mac Low. Neither possibility is attractive to Atkins, and he sees them as more dependent on a shared value-context than proponents of either might be willing to concede. It would not be enough simply to avoid sounds and forms one disapproved of (either the conservative aversion to syntactic innovation or the avant-garde allergies to sentiment, for example), and Atkins steadfastly rejects such avoidance therapy, which is one reason that his poems sound so little like those of most other postmodernist writers, particularly those following in the Pound-Williams-Objectivism lineage. What would be required would be a spiritually violent conflictual split that might provide an opening for new regimes of truth.

While there was a split in the available value-contexts for artists in the wake of the social turmoil of the Second World War, Atkins perceived clearly the intention expressed in "Dominant Group" forms to reassert control over the future availability of such contexts. Russell Atkins did not have to read Louis Althusser on the subject of ideological state apparatuses and their domination of the subject to reach an understanding of the disciplining effects of education. "Some Thoughts Defining 'Mainstream' in Relation to 'Education' and Destructive Power," in the 1964 *Free Lance,* proposed a sharp response to traditional humanist assertions that education would, of itself, destroy racial prejudices rooted in ignorance. The counterargument in *Free Lance* was that education produced rather than ameliorated these prejudices: "These arbitrary prejudices dominate the 'mainstream' and derive largely from 'education' CONTRARY TO THE FALLACY THAT 'EDUCATION' IS THE PREVENTIVE OF THEM and can be summed up thus: '*Liberal' and technological education, especially today, additively, produce destructive might that maintains and increases power that imposes and controls values*" (27). This analysis will seem almost overly familiar today, as will the directions toward an alternative laid out by Atkins in *Free Lance*. The need for community-based production of knowledge and alternative institutions of cultural production would, in the years following publication of Atkins's notes, become a foundational assumption of Black Power ideology. Atkins is not the originating author of such ideas, but he published his analysis at a time when such statements were not ordinarily found in literary journals and before they had become the common ideology of many black-oriented magazines. In the previous year's volume the *Free Lance* editor had devoted his "Of" column to an essay titled "The Invalidity of Dominant-Group 'Education' Forms for 'Progress' for Non-Dominant Ethnic Groups as Americans." Fleshing out his theories of "egocentrical phenomenalism," Atkins had introduced there the concept of the nationalistic phenomenalist as one who does not entirely reject the concept of "education" but who sees that the forms of education constructed by the dominant group are forms for the militant imposition of the dominant group's will. Atkins recommended a "perspectival objectivity" that requires "appreciating that 'education' is often the mere objectification of another group's thinking processes; that words such as 'mind,' 'intelligence' etc., do not represent incontestable properties of anything and need not be taken as seriously as they are taken in the dominant group's definition's context except as concepts involving the DEFINING OF 'KNOWLEDGE' " (32). In part as a result of the naturalizing effects of hegemonic discourse, as Atkins sees things, some individuals within nondominant ethnic groups are guided into a series of epistemological errors. They become unable to distinguish between that which is knowable by any consciousness, what we might think of as a sharable, transcendent real, and that which the mentality of the dominant group, in Atkins's terminology, "creates-into-knowledge." It is not entirely clear what provides the phenomenological ground for this act of distinguishing in Atkins's thought, but it is clear that he feels many minorities have been led to confuse sources of knowledge *as* education with education as a source of knowledge (19). Some members of nondominant groups, having seen that the dominant group has constructed institutional education as its own vehicle of social control, may then reject both forms of education: the institution of education falsely portrayed as source of knowledge, and material sources of knowledge by which the mind educates itself. A freedom to make use of or not make use of available stimuli is, according to Atkins, a requirement for good relationships between ethnic groups. In the absence of that freedom "[t]he misfortune of *some* non-dominant ethnic groups is that they cannot extricate themselves from dominant-group created-into-knowledge and 'education' in such a way as to *select* and *re-constitute* it by employing or *not* employing elements of it in a 'mind's' margin independent of it" (24). Atkins burdens his essay with a series of algebraic equations as a means of establishing through a sort of formalist logic some points that really are practically unarguable. It is not possible to learn that which has not been created, he establishes, using the word *created* in a relatively loose sense, but it is always possible to create the not-yet-learned (22). While it would be senseless to contest these propositions, what is more important here is Atkins's point that dominant modes of education have the effect of leading students away from analysis of how something has been created-into-knowledge and of convincing many of them that all that can be created has been created already, perhaps even "always already." One thing that nondominant minorities "learn" through this process is that education and intelligence are associated with progress and that the most progress has been made by the dominant group. Meanwhile, the "original and assertive heritage" of mind is oppressed and devalued (30). The object of the minority student is to learn that which has already been created as knowledge by the dominant group. If something more is needed, the dominant group will create that something more into knowledge for the nondominant to learn. This form of mastery still presents itself as the educational ideal in its more recent forms under labels such as "outcomes assessment." Almost three decades after Atkins's essay, the avant-garde poet Erica Hunt, in her "Notes for an Oppositional Poetics," is compelled to make many of the same points, so little having truly altered in the interim: "Dominant modes of discourse, the language of ordinary life or of rationality, of moral management, of the science of the state, the hectoring threats of the press and media, use convention and label to bind and organize us" (199).

As an integral part of this process of binding and organizing, dominant modes adapt to the increasing heterogeneity of subjectivities in society and in the schools by reorganizing them within a homogeneous form of discourse. In this way cultural dominance may continue even as it speaks a language of diversity and identity politics. Through enforced modes of cultural pluralism and managing diversity, education can contain heterogeneous creation in the very guise of encouraging students to esteem their "self" identity. It is recognition of this process that leads Cornel West to declare that he doesn't "consider identity politics ipso facto left at all; those politics amount primarily to a mode of middle class entrée" (*Beyond II* 122). Atkins's "nationalist phenomenology" was not the identitarian form of multiculturalism that now dominates American education without actually reforming the institutions of education themselves. As West details current educational practices in his speech "Beyond Multiculturalism and Eurocentrism," it is a practice that survives reconstruction of its canon of master texts by constraining modes of reading and responding to those master texts: "Students read Toni Morrison and simply look in her text and see themselves rather than the challenge of a great artist who is dealing with collective memory and community breakdown in *Beloved,* for example. Challenge. If you look in a text and see yourself, that is market education, done in the name of education. But education must not be about a cathartic quest for identity. It must foster credible sensibilities for an active critical citizenry" (*Beyond I* 19). Russell Atkins in 1963, like Erica Hunt in 1993, calls for an oppositional poetics, new forms of heterodox creating-into-knowledge. Atkins never believed, nor does Cornel West, that hegemonic discourse is an impermeable seal on our consciousness or a monolithic power against which we are helpless dupes. For Atkins the creative use of language and art affords opportunities for the production of contestation, regimes of knowledge and heterogeneous sites of resistance beyond the predictive powers of state educational institutions. According to Atkins, education can only predict or control potential sources of creating-into-knowledge "ARBITRARILY OR DICTATORIALLY THROUGH ITSELF AS CULTURAL BUREAUCRACY" ("Invalidity" 31).

Atkins predicted the growth of these cultural bureaucracies with the merging of education and technology. Those of us who conduct our cultural work within the academies are now implicated daily with the demands of educational technology (hardware, firmware, software, shareware, courseware, learnware; the rubrics are unending). Atkins also predicted that as a society attempts to tighten its educational bureaucracies it will occasionally err, act against its own best interests, and subsequently be forced to enact corrective measures. In a further prediction, one that will strike many instructors of college and university writing courses as eerily accurate, Atkins argues that following such an error, educational bureaucracy "will seek to compensate by group-work. Examined, the ration between group-work and the complexity of its achievement's attendant problems, might reveal that the achievement in toto is decrescent, really" ("Invalidity" 31–32).

Atkins perceived the dangers that awaited segments of nondominant ethnic groups who sought to gain entry to dominant society by merging their interests with those of the educational apparatus. This move, in the end, would prove equally catastrophic as the error of reactive rejection of sources of knowledge *as* education. A sort of cultural suicide awaits those classes who are willing to accept the masquerade of diversity management as the mode of middle-class entrée. "A non-dominant ethnic group," Atkins holds, "(especially one whose tradition of creating-into-knowledge was cut off) that seeks to accept or join this expanding bureaucratic rigidity without future plans, may kill its powers of 'mind'" (32). The only real alternative is the production of heterogeneous ruptures, the production of countermemories, anticanons, new historicisms; but that is also one of the most daunting of possible projects: "To begin a new history is a prodigious undertaking. A non-dominant group might have to assume the DEFINING OF KNOWLEDGE (what can or cannot or should or need be 'known,' and how much treated as such). It may have to create what it knows and know what it creates: and create what it learns and learn what it has created" (32). Although Atkins labels his educational phenomenology "Nationalistic," his is not an essentialist cultural nationalism. He does not believe that nondominant ethnic groups can simply turn from the nationalist education of the commanding culture to an already-in-place-and-waiting stable tradition of alternative knowledges. In order to transform the legacy of past traditions into usable counterknowledges, the group must create what it learns, must transform the traditions daily into an always self-differing knowledge in motion. Freedom of judgment must continue to distinguish mind from learning. Indoctrination cannot simply be replaced by training. "A member of a tradition can depend upon (C) ['learning-into-known'] of its own culture while remaining 'intelligent' 'mindlessly' and be secure about doing it" (23), according to Atkins, but true creating-into-knowledge moves from tradition into the newly creative; it never just applies tradition to the new circumstance.

In 1967 Russell Atkins returned to these issues in his "Of" column for *Free Lance*'s eleventh volume, this time taking a yet more provocative position that, while never abandoning a commitment to the use values of knowledge, struck a blow at links traditionally made in African American writing between education and amelioration. His point in this column is really quite simple, but it is not one that the United Negro College Fund would be likely to use in its fund-raising literature. A popular slogan among civil rights speakers in the 1960s made a plea for learning as a substitute for burning. My own most vivid recollection of this slogan is of the day that James Brown appeared on our television sets in the nation's capital during the rebellions that followed the assassination of Martin Luther King Jr. practically singing the slogan: "Don't burn. Give the kids a chance to learn." Atkins has a rather obvious question regarding this linkage. It is not, after all, that the rebels in the streets were burning school buildings or books. And they certainly were not, as their white countrymen were shortly to do in Boston, attacking school buses full of black children on their way to getting an education. The rebels' attention was much more directed by capitalist consumer ideology than that. And as Atkins innocently argues, "conceivably, you could 'learn' prior to or during the burning of something" ("Of" 1967, 49). What Atkins then undertakes is an audacious deconstruction of the binary opposition asserted by advocates of moderation and nonviolence between burning and learning, two terms whose economy of exchange strikes Atkins as a classic case of mystification. Whatever we might finally make of the poet's political positions, his irreverent common sense in this instance is a refreshing counterpoint to the hypocritical pronouncements of the Lyndon Johnsons and Nelson Rockefellers of the day. Atkins establishes quite easily the undeniable fact that it would be impossible "to *prove* that 'learning' and 'burning' mutually exclude each other as acts" (49).

Like a good student of logic, Atkins uncovers the unspoken presuppositions of leadership statements that ask the populace to behave *as if* burning and learning were mutually exclusive: "(1) If one 'learns' more, he will not employ violence ('burning,' riot, etc.); (2) Persons who are 'educated' do not use violence; (3) 'Education' is opposed to violence; (4) 'Education' prevents violence" (50). Of course, none of these propositions will bear close scrutiny, particularly the scrutiny of those who have been educated in the history of the United States. Atkins asks, "Would it not be devastating to this claim to really detail the history of 'learning' in regard to uprisings, violence, etc.?" (51). Not only do we have to contend with the record of violence among even our "best" educated citizens and political leaders (Atkins cites the campus riots at southern universities following the Supreme Court's desegregation decision of 1954), but we must also account for the role of education, even literary education, in perpetuating the violence of racism. In the course of his discussion titled "Racial Knowledge" in his study *Racist Culture: Philosophy and the Politics of Meaning,* David Theo Goldberg argues effectively that "[t]hrough various primary ordering concepts and root metaphors, contemporary knowledge production reinvigorates racialized categories or launches new ones and so subtly orders anew the exclusiveness and exclusions of racist expression. . . . In the seeming informalities of its modes, literary and cultural production is particularly well-placed to mold, circumscribe, and stamp racialized identity, since racial significations are deeply implicit in the signs employed and employable. Racialized connotations are embedded in the locus of ordinary social meanings that cultural expression reflects in the various space-time contexts of modernity" (149). Again, Russell Atkins neither believes that racist discourse is monolithic, eternal, and natural nor that education itself is to be abandoned as a useful concept. Even within the presently constituted educational apparatus it is possible to learn differently. I am sitting in a university office writing these words (though not in my own office, I must admit), and Atkins proposes that one might learn things in educational institutions that would then lead to revolutionary violence.

Similarly, Atkins's logic rejects parallel suggestions that education, in addition to producing a morality that would rule out violence, will produce economic effects that would in turn remove all material impetus for rebellion: "Some Civil Rights Speakers infer that: *If one 'learns,' he will have no use for violence because he will have a job, and that only the 'unlearned,' 'uneducated' or 'unschooled' people have ever resisted oppression by the use of violence— 'the language of the ghetto,' etc.* The former statement presumes too much; the latter is in defiance of much of recorded history" (51). In the end Atkins returns to a point made powerfully in his earlier reflections on knowledge and education, that whatever their many claims to effectiveness, educational institutions cannot accurately predict the improvements or changes of mind and character produced by their disciplines: "In fact, there's every eventuality that the ghetto riotous, attending schools, might 'learn' how to riot" (52). There is little to marvel at in the continued omission of Atkins from university surveys of education theory.

Though occasionally unwieldy, Atkins's writing in these statements concerning the politics of education offers little that would produce any difficulties of comprehension among an audience of nonspecialists, or even among "the people." On the other hand, a survey of Atkins's fuller statements of his aesthetic theories will turn up much material for citation by those who fulminate against the jargon-filled obtuseness of writing by scholars in the humanities. Of course, Atkins was not, at the time he produced his most developed theories, a professor of anything. Despite his many friendships with college staff, he was about as far outside the mainstream of academia as a writer could get in the 1950s and 1960s. The life of bohemian poets in Cleveland was not a ticket to New Critical embrace in those days, and indeed much of Atkins's writing on aesthetics was directed against the critical establishment then dominating the larger journals and departments of English in the United States. It was obviously not in hopes that he was speaking the acceptable critical jargon of the academy that Atkins provided his essays with titles like "Pseudo-Problematical Critical Values for 'More' in Poetry as Opposed to Technique" or "A Phenomenalist Perspective for Poetics Based on C (Negative) and B (Positive) Probabilities for Maxima and Minima," nor were all his titles meant to be ironic (though many of them are as mischievous as those of Wallace Stevens). In 1964 he titled an essay in *Free Lance* "The Hypothetical Arbitrary Constant of Inhibition's Continuumization." The entirety of the essay couldn't fit in one issue, so he followed this installment in 1967 with an additional "Abstract of the Hypothetical Constant of Inhibition's Continuumization Becoming 'Consciousness' (Nervous System, Etc.)," an abstract accompanied by enough charts and formulae—explaining such fine points as "The Phenomena of Summation between (2)b and (4)d as the Threshold"—to choke a structuralist.

As someone who hopes that more readers will pick up Atkins's texts, I hesitate to highlight such titles. But, then, the daily sports pages of my local newspaper are replete with equally arcane jargon and formulae, none of which seems to give its readers much trouble. (One such reader has generously devoted considerable time to making me understand that sports writers are not merely attempting a poetic "making strange" of the language in saying of a baseball player that he "flied out.") Admittedly, Atkins's chart explaining his theory of the "Positive Neural Sub-Continuum" may not prove attractive to critics of American poetry, but it bears a strong and curious resemblance to certain pages of composition instruction manuals in wide circulation today, with their use of brain charts and chaos theory to explain principles of expository writing and to encourage freshmen and sophomores to write, to free write, or even to prewrite. At moments Atkins's prose nearly collapses into self-parody, as in his statement that "When maximum excruciation of the sub-atomic, and chemico-statical into observable mass as organic continuum function is anesthetized by increasing frequency-velocity mass tendency acting as a resistance to 'motion,' brain becomes an approximation center acting as a *gauge*" ("Hypothetical" 50). Even in this extreme example, however, there is something of value, easily grasped, and that is Atkins's marvelous (and astute) description of the human brain as "an approximation center."

When Atkins addresses himself to subjects about which he is most assured, such as the aesthetics of poetry and music, his essays are both more interesting and more interesting as reading experiences than most others appearing in literary journals of the period. His many diagrams are certainly no more distracting than those of Charles Olson, and Atkins has as much of value to offer readers in his theoretical statements as can be found in far more influential and critically examined essays such as Olson's "Projective Verse" or Adrienne Rich's "Compulsory Heterosexuality." The key to Russell Atkins's aesthetic philosophy is in his theoretical treatise on music, "A Psychovisual Perspective for 'Musical' Composition," published for the first time in successive issues of *Free Lance* from 1955 through 1958. His subsequent essays "Egocentric Phenomenalism" and "Phenomenalist Perspectives" are a further working out of those early theories in the domain of composition and critique of poetry. A major component of Atkins's aesthetic is the concept of deconstruction, which he defines in 1958 as "the taking apart of objects as Ideas" ("Psychovisual Perspective" 37). Just a few years later, writing in France, Jacques Derrida was to make a strategic decision to deploy an already existing word as a descriptor for the mode of critique he was then conducting rather than to coin a new term. One advantage of the word *deconstruction* was that it clearly differed from, while being articulated with, the Heideggerian destructive poetics that was one subject of Derrida's deconstructions. *Deconstruction* also already existed as an English word when Russell Atkins chose to apply it in an aesthetic and philosophical context in his own writing. The first meaning of the word *deconstruction* offered by the second edition of the *Oxford English Dictionary* is "the action of undoing the construction of a thing"; to deconstruct is, then, "to undo the construction of—to take to pieces." In this sense the term dates back to the late nineteenth century. The earliest print source given by the *OED* is, significantly enough, in a political context, referring to "[a] reform, the beginnings of which must be a work of deconstruction." The only appearance of *deconstruction* in a philosophical and literary sense recorded by the *OED* is associated with Derrida's usage, and the earliest English occurrence in print noted is D. B. Allison's 1973 translation, *Derrida's Speech & Phenomena,* fifteen years after the publication of Atkins's essay. Atkins's usage is patently not identical with the *OED*'s initial definition. For Atkins deconstruction is not only the undoing of a construction. "The taking apart of objects as Ideas" is a veritable transformation. Neither is Atkins's usage coextensive with Derridean deconstruction. In one of his frequent usages that will strike many readers as counterintuitive, Atkins describes deconstruction as an act of composition. In his "Psychovisual Perspective" Atkins explains that "[d]econstructing to communicate through sounds, the 'composer' need not *organize* by calculation and control, rather he should maintain control as he *disorganizes* into discursion" (28). The compilers of the *Oxford English Dictionary* have not yet come to Cleveland or to Russell Atkins.

The point here is not to argue that Atkins is an unacknowledged influence on Derrida. In 1958 neither writer knew of the other's existence. Nor is the point to find an African or African American origin for each and every putatively white development in philosophy (especially since Derrida is himself from North Africa). Rather, the point is to conduct an interdiction in American philosophy's conduct of business as usual, a conduct in which white historians simply are unlikely to go looking for black thinkers when they seek early citations of philosophical terms and concepts. There is absolutely nothing new in the revelation that African American writers have always conducted philosophical investigations. But something new must occur in American philosophy when the thoughts of black people are included in the discussions or when they are finally allowed to set investigative agendas. Lucius Outlaw, writing in *The Philosophical Forum*'s special triple issue devoted to "African-American Perspectives and Philosophical Traditions," says this:

> When considered against the context of the history of western philosophy as narrated and practiced by some of the dominant figures, and against the explicit derogations of African peoples by a number of these figures, the advent of discussions about African and *African-American* philosophy is necessarily "deconstructive." Thus, for example, each instance of an attempt to identify and/or articulate a philosophizing effort as distinctively African or African American is, at the outset at least, an important challenge that decenters the very idea, as well as the discursive practises, of "philosophy" into the history of their construction and maintenance, into the historicity of philosophical anthropology, that informs them via the valorized and racialized notion of "rational man." (76)

Russell Atkins does not deploy "deconstruction" as a distinctively African American philosophizing effort, but the fact that a distinctively African American poet, working out of Cleveland in the 1950s, provides one of the earliest intertexts for our readings of the subsequent texts of a Francophone North African Jewish thinker certainly should cause some interesting disturbances in what we thought we knew about American and "Continental" philosophies and what we thought we knew about black American poets and their relationships to "theory."

It is as a source of some disturbance that Russell Atkins wished to enter the critical debates in poetics of his time. His "Pseudo-Problematical Critical Values" opens with a seemingly innocuous thesis statement that turns out to be deeply problematical, not just "pseudo-problematical," again gesturing in the direction of the counterintuitive logic of the supplement in writing and language: "'More,' per se, is sufficient enough often by implication alone" (45). Poetry is generally thought to have "more" of something than prose, and good poetry is supposed to have "more" of whatever that is than bad poetry. Nearly all of us fall into this sort of statement whenever we are in casual conversation about aesthetics. We tell each other that we prefer works that give us "more" to experience and think about over those that have "less" to offer—unless, of course, we are a certain breed of postmodernist who believes that less is more. "Critics," Atkins tells us, "set themselves the task of divulging or discussing what that 'more' is to be thought to be" (46), and Atkins sets himself the task of identifying "segments" of critical modes of divulging that "more," most of which he disapproves of. Atkins's "Segment I" critic is a somewhat old-fashioned sort who believes that poetry conveys more meaning as knowledge. Atkins will not wait further in his cataloguing process to reveal his own sense of "more." The great sin of the Segment I critic is that this critic refuses to "admit" that the meaning, the value, of a poem is the quantifiable effect of its techniques, "to which everything else is, or may be intentionally, subservient" (49). The Segment I critic, in Atkins's estimation, is locked into the view of poetry as primarily a conveyor of knowledge and therefore values those poems that reveal new information to the critic. Atkins is able to identify any number of reputedly "great" poems that only meet this test in the broadest of interpretations.

"Segment II" critics Atkins describes as the "add to experience" critics, who, however, always want more than "mere technique" (50). These critics Atkins portrays as sufficiently cautious as to avoid careful cataloguing of the nature of these additional experiences that are brought to us by poems but are supposed quickly to transcend the materials of the poem "itself." What Atkins then calls the "Segment III" critic is a vague amalgam of the first two types, constantly discerning between the "significant" and the "insignificant" in poetry. Typically, these critics appeal to traditions and values as measures of significance in an idealist manner, seldom describing the social and historical contexts for the production of these measures or touchstones. The significance of the poem under consideration is, then, a measure of the "quality" of the verse. Prefiguring later works such as Barbara Herrnstein Smith's *Contingencies of Value,* Atkins notes that "[c]ommonly enough, this 'quality' turns out to be the pseudo-problem maxima of 'truth,' 'knowledge,' 'add to experience,' etc., and all the rest" (51). The search for significance proves to be motivated by unexamined presuppositions that elevate arbitrary designations to an ideal realm of eternal verities; in other words, it is axiological logic at its worst. The critics that Atkins assigns to this segment are the type who argue that poems are significant to the extent that they embody values that have stood the test of time and that those values wouldn't have stood the test of time had they not been significant.

Atkins's "Segment IV" critic sounds more like the author of innumerable blurbs and reviews that fill most current poetry journals than like the ascendant New Critics of Atkins's early years. These are the "insight" critics, who Atkins believes are the dominant group of his period. These are the critics, as the name implies, who look to poetry for "deep" perceptions; and "[i]n some ways," Atkins thinks, "Segment IV has been the most destructive of all in transforming poetry into a standardized discussion of minutia, intricate details, specifics" (51). Here, the charged detail of the imagists has devolved (beyond even "Amygism") into the standardized epiphany of the poetry workshops. This segment has also encouraged poetry to adopt the wisdom voice, the shamanic function, the stance of the sensitive poetic soul who can "see" things, usually things about "life," that the unassisted reader would be too dim to perceive, not being a poet or, the poet's first cousin, the critic. "Under a pose of unpretentiousness, quiet wit, wisdom—surpassed only by the ancients—Segment IV would have us believe that they proffer the true 'knowledge,' 'revelation,' 'content,' 'meaning' for poetry" (52). In the years since Atkins's essay appeared, poets of this type have come to draw the largest audiences on the official poetry reading circuits, audiences that often sigh audibly as they greet each poem's delivery of the expected and satisfying epiphany. "Segment V" critics, in Atkins's description, are the inseparable companions to Segment IV, but, as Atkins details their characteristics, they sound more akin to a sort of undergraduate classroom model of the New Criticism. These are the "fusion" critics, and what they value in a poem is the "'fusion' of 'content' and 'emotion' or 'thought and emotion,' or 'stimuli and perception'" (53).

Last, Atkins takes to task the "idea" poets, or "Segment VI" in his schema. Atkins's primary objection as a phenomenalist to this mode of public criticism, most characteristically identifiable by its oft-repeated complaint that bad poems have no ideas in them, is that these critics are unfamiliar with "the long philosophical history of the word 'idea'" (53) and hence are constantly committing forms of categorical error. Atkins runs through a brief list of propositions, images, technical ideas, inferences, and so on, noting that "there are philosophical ideas, many of which automatically carry with them the poetically destructive burden of logistics" (54). In the end Atkins effectively establishes the fact that it would be impossible to write a poem that was truly devoid of ideas, just as it is impossible, despite the nostrums some of our students and colleagues have learned to repeat, to write a poem that doesn't "make meaning." "Perhaps," Atkins concludes, "the idea critic is better off misusing the word 'idea'—better off than he would be attempting to wrestle with the semantics of 'originality.' But too often the idea critic confuses idea with 'new' or with 'originality.' He errs in saying that a poem without 'originality' has no ideas" (54). The idea critic resembles the New Critics in emphasizing condensation. "For some reason," Atkins suggests, "he's obsessed with a 'few' words (which might well be a suppressed hatred of poetry)—and he proceeds to demand that poets pack and pack while the 'meaning' gets bigger and bigger and out of proportion philosophically while the 'few' words have long since given up the ghost plus their 'economy' and the poor reader is left with loads of 'meaning' in some tight little word body that if not already dead will be in a matter of minutes" (56). This would seem a surprising turn, and it marks a separation point of one form of postmodernity from its modernist precursors. The "high" modernism the academy came to identify as modernism as such was characterized by an emphasis on exactitude and *condensare*. Mortal sins for this critical modernism include "over"-writing, sentiment, and strained "poetic" effects. Atkins, in open revolt against the institutionalized forms of these once revolutionary principles, suspects that this masks a hatred of the very materials of verse (a suspicion suspiciously close to those voiced by recent New Formalists), rather as if a composer worked by erasing, as some composers in fact do, more and more notes from a score, hoping to arrive at some irreducible minimum.

It may well strike a reader today that Atkins has stuffed a bit too much straw into the man that he is knocking down in this essay, but extensive reading in the larger circulation poetry journals of the post-war era will show that the abuses he charged were in full effect in poetry reviews. The essay never really comes to grips with either the strengths or the weaknesses of the New Criticism, but then Atkins's target wasn't really the ivory tower theorists of his day but the mixture of affective response with a smattering of New Critical vocabulary that filled the review columns of most literary magazines. Neither does this essay chart a better course for criticism, save by negative example. Where one might ordinarily expect some such suggestions to appear in the conclusion to an essay of this type, Atkins simply signs off, saying: "Well, so much for critics, segments I, II, III, IV, V, VI etc." (57). His footnote on "exactness," on the other hand, extends for another two pages past the end of the essay.

Having in the late 1950s elaborated his psychovisual perspective for music, and having in the 1960s extended his philosophy to an examination of mass and matter, Atkins in 1977 began to extend a theory of poetics. This, unfortunately, turns out to be the shortest and least developed segment of his theories. Many will wish that he had spent less time contemplating "The Arbitrary Constant of Inhibition's Continuumization" and more time discussing his poetics. But there is the poetry, forty to fifty years of published works, much of it much clearer on the subject of its own operations than "A Phenomenalist Perspective for Poetics Based on C (Negative) and B (Positive) Probabilities for Maxima and Minima." Atkins's psychovisualism adopts the concept of inertia from physics, describing relationships of energy and mass, and posits it "as the basis for *all* coherent human thought" ("Phenomenalist Perspective" 17). He then posits any departure from the inertial lineage of the human species as "positive" and the inertial lineage itself as "negative," taking care to insist that no moral meaning attach to these heavily connotative terms. "Life," in his calculations, derives from the positive, whereas "human consciousness" derives from the negative. What he means by this is that consciousness is "rest energy" or "nonmoving," whereas life is in a "lineage towards energy" (18). Analogously, at least in Atkins's cosmology, "non-phenomenalist" poetry is negative, still in a nonmoralistic sense, despite the fact that he clearly dislikes such verse because of its emphasis on compression, "rest energy," and what Atkins terms "negative significance transitivity" (18). The symbols and equations accompanying this portion of the theory amount really to a graphic display of the critical "segments" he had outlined more discursively four years earlier in "Pseudo-Problematical Critical Values." The negative axial direction of nonphenomenalist verse is a representation of an effort in much poetry to inhibit "discussion in terms of stimuli functioning against restrictions of length or poems set to mean 'more' in 'less' time, or attempts at density increase" (20). The "B" positive, or phenomenalist poetry of Atkins's theory reduces "rest energy," increases motion, tends toward energy and the decrease of inertia. The real thesis of this exercise is actually quite simply stated by Atkins and flagged as an "EXTENSION INTO POETICS": "phenomenalist poetry . . . has its end-result in focusing the reader's attention on the poem as mood, or effects, or something *done* in terms of device or events in a poem, or the employment of words to approximate or embody that which is visual (image recalled)" (20). In this relatively straightforward expression it is easier to see the relationship between Atkins's phenomenalism and more familiar forms of phenomenology. The focus is on the poem as it appears in the consciousness, bracketing metaphysical appeals to a transcendent ideal to which the poem might give access (even though there is a transcendental form to some of Atkins's arguments).

Atkins's predilection for accompanying his theories with explanatory formulae will try the patience of many readers. It is not immediately evident that we need to contrast this phenomenalist definition to the formula "$\Sigma$ (Aa < C)," an expression describing the critical segments that seek "fusion," "more," and so forth (22). But it is also the case that many of these formulae are in fact readily grasped. The symbol "Wv," for example, simply stands for "Written volume, that is, the amount of apparent writing on the page" (23); not much to argue with there. What all this comes back to in the end is the position Atkins has been staking out in his notes, reviews, poems, and music theory all along, an emphasis on conspicuous technique and "designed" imagination. As we read on the positive, phenomenalist side of Atkins's equations in his "Phenomenalist Perspective for Poetics," his poetics emphasizes "technique as the thing experienced in the service of *imagination*" (21). Since Atkins's perspective does not value significance over temporality, technique can permit "a poem to 'mean' 'less' in 'more' time by increasing discursion on behalf of action, narrative, since B (positive) does not value meaning as C (negative) over expended time" (21), just the opposite of the emphasis presently privileged in many writing workshops in America. In Atkins's phenomenalist charting, the positive directs us toward "Stimuli: (1) sound; (2) syllabic effects as discursion (or 'motion') eye movements; (3) other sensory effects (smell, taste, touch) for themselves autonomously; (4) that which is imagined only" (22). As clotted as this set of expressions may be, it can serve useful purposes even now by reminding readers that the visual and the image are not confined to the photographic. Atkins would have very little patience with attempts to assert a binary opposition between the written and the visual, between graphic verbal learning and "visual" learning. This is one reason that, in Atkins's calculations, the increased degree of "departure from conventional syntax" (24) can increase "Metaphorical paradoxa" (23) wherein even the most "visual" image can be a verbal abstraction. In fact, Atkins's theories may provide a useful vocabulary for the discussion of such nonphotographic images as Emily Dickinson's "Zero at the bone," or Atkins's own line in the poem "After": "There is Spain in it of amber'd wander" (*Objects* n.p.). This last example is unarguably a visual image, but it is not a still-life, not a picture. Further, Atkins's emphasis on the connections between discursivity and eye movements is a healthy corrective, reminding us of the materiality of reading and writing practices and countering casual presuppositions that have the effect of rendering reading as "passive" in binary opposition to a presumably more active "visual" that does not involve looking at alphabetic characters in a text.

Sounding once more like a strong precursor to Jacques Derrida, Atkins opens his 1955 essay "A Psychovisual Perspective for 'Musical' Composition" with the statement, "Psychovisualism does not try to frame new concepts" (2). Atkins then moves rapidly to what can only be described as a destructive reading of the very terms of music, concluding that "The term 'music' persists . . . as a definition of things it does not define creating a figurative error that has guided the 'music' world for centuries" (4). While Atkins is not out to frame new concepts, he obviously intends to place some old concepts under erasure. He declares the death of music as tone system and as a language and proposes "a day of absolute Composition." Then, and here may be the most direct link to his theories of poetics, Atkins proposes that musical composition is primarily a visual art. It is in this sense that we must understand Atkins's description of composition as the creation of "Object-Forms" and his subsequent definitions of compositional deconstruction as the "taking apart of objects as ideas" ("Psychovisual Perspective" 1958, 37). As in his "Phenomenalist Perspective" on poetics, Atkins's emphasis here is on conspicuous technique, designed imagination, and motion. In Atkins's view the mind's "inertial system *deconstructs* into comprehension-motions of eye-movement," and the composition and reception of music is analogous to the writing and reading of verse because "[a]t this point a poem and 'music' meet for a poem, too, is such a distribution of 'motion' achieving a maximum" ("Psychovisual Perspective" 1958, 9).

Again, the poem or musical composition is never simply a mode of communicating a stable and preexisting meaning from the mind of the author into the mind of the audience. The artificer of a poem provides "the experiential for the imagined (*imagined,* not 'experienced' by author or 'believed' nor out to *convince* the reader)" (*Phenomena* 79), as Atkins explains in his 1961 notes on "Egocentrical Projection." Atkins does not deny that poems can and do convey ideas (their purpose *is* one form of communication), but he believes that this is not their larger purpose. "Small meanings," he believes, can be created with tone relationships in music, but these are derived from and less significant than (Atkins appears unable finally to evade the claims of significance) the larger phenomenal world of "Composition as Object-Form" ("Psychovisual Perspective" 1955, 3). Musical notes in themselves are simply vibrations in the air, neither "high" nor "low," and this is why Atkins argues that "[t]he ear is not a conceiving organ" (5). What the ear senses is imagined into relationships of high and low by the mind, and "[c]onsciousness of a spatial relationship of form-significance derives from or IS visual perception" (7). We might well argue against Atkins's view that the eye is also only a sensing, not a conceiving, organ, but he is speaking of the "mind's eye" here, not of the organ of sight, although that distinction does not entirely save his position. The object-form of music is a "COMPOUND MOTIVIC ORGANIZATION," which Atkins explains by means of an analogy: "The word 'house' carries with it its spelling and its reference and regardless to what use it is put it maintains its identity as representative of a specific thing. A compound motivic organization acts similarly throughout a psychovisual composition in a presentational way" (9). In this analogy we can see Atkins's most marked difference from later poststructuralists. Derrida would no doubt agree that the word *house* carries all these things along with it, but he would probably have questions about the specificity of its representations. Atkins observes that much of the vocabulary of music discussions, terms such as "chord coloration," "architecture," etc., rely on visual phenomena, and he proceeds to argue that music must present its object-forms in the visual fields of the mind. At this point, bringing the first installment of his theory to a conclusion, Atkins tells his readers that space does not permit reproduction of the "mind-form graph" that was to have demonstrated the mind's progression toward an ever greater complexity of relationships, far beyond anything easily representable by means of traditional counterpoint. In 1958 he was able to devote a portion of *Free Lance* to "A Psychovisual Manual for Compositional Deconstruction and Sound Applied," the concluding and "practical" section of his theory, and here he offers a number of graphs and formulae to assist our understanding of "a 'composing' process through which stimuli, irrelevant to the retina, [depend] upon the visual *mechanism* as a total process to achieve comprehensive shape as organization. It is necessary to point out that the 'eye' or retina does not 'see' objects directly. Vision is a paradoxical mechanism" (25). Figure 8 among Atkins's illustrations is again eerily reminiscent of parallel developments in poststructuralist thought.

This small figure, directing readers in the requirements for determining the number of measures occupied by a musical figure, affords a powerful intertextual mirror of a phenomenon of which it is completely independent, Jacques Lacan's explications of the *objet petit a* (Lacan 240, 144), while also prefiguring the diagrammatic titles of Anthony Braxton's compositions:

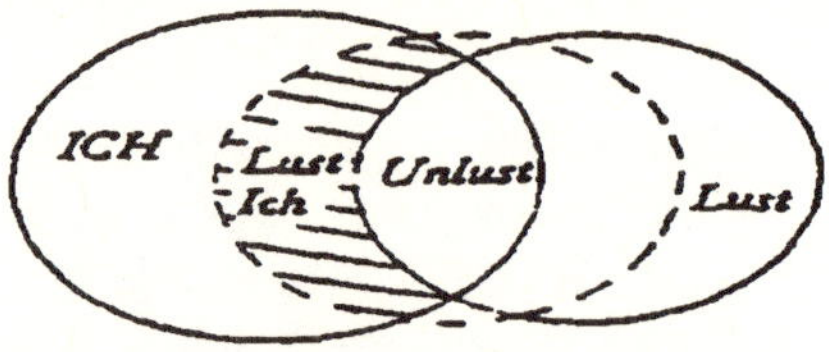


The proof by the object a

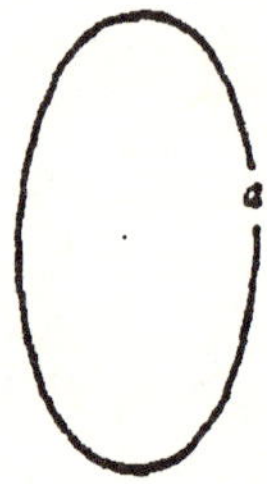


Schema of the hoop net

(Lacan 240, 144)

It may prove helpful, too, to remember that "[m]etaphor and metonymy as Lacan thinks of them are 'objects'" (Metz 169). Atkins's diagram is not intended to mime the entrance of light into the eye and its subsequent translation into neural impulses. To the contrary, Atkins is describing "visual" phenomena that exist independently of light. His diagram is meant as a heuristic device to aid our comprehension of the mind's inertial system and its deconstruction into comprehension-motions (9); further, his diagram is itself a form of spirit writing. Composition, in this schema, is "the art of beautiful 'motion'" (11). A musical work is "a congealing continuum" of forward motions with simultaneous "*contractions* into images" (37). This allows the situating of the object-forms in a fashion determined by the composer. "A psychovisualist manipulating tones is involved in an act of meticulous deconstruction for discursive presentation" (28).

In summary, we can see in this theoretical work the paradigmatic, counterintuitive direction of Atkins's writings. In the poet's theories music is discursive, but discursivity is visual. The visual, however, is not dependent on light and the retina but is a set of processes in mind fields independent of the eye itself. Obviously the "visual" exists because we have eyes to receive light, but Atkins's deconstructive composition relies on the presentation of nonpictorial images in the form of compositional objects. The reader or listener does not reproduce the encoded "message" of the artist, made out of materials previously experienced by the artist. The "meanings" in art are just one of the techniques presented by the artist as experiential stimuli. The editors of *Free Lance,* in their introduction to the theory section of their Russell Atkins special issue, call this a music space theory of eye and brain. They go on to remark that "[t]he entire rigamarole of 'multi-media' in its *recent* outlines dates back to and fades at Atkins's theory of psychovisualism. From this work flowed a strange uncanny set of concepts that influenced the avant-garde ideas of European music, resurrected a number of faded 'experimentalists' from decline and instituted a score of imitators" (19). It may prove difficult to enumerate a full score of Atkins's imitators today, and he is himself now an experimentalist whose works are in need of resurrection. There is much, though, to be gleaned from the experience of grappling with Russell Atkins's work in theory. In the first place it is crucial if we are to have anything approaching an adequate understanding of the history of African American philosophy that we include in our tracings such marginalized thinkers as Atkins. His "Psychovisual Perspective" may well be the single most eccentric theoretical statement on music to come from a black writer prior to Anthony Braxton's *Tri-Axium Writings,* but in its very eccentricity it marks a much expanded border of black music theory. Further, as multimedia once again become a topic of theoretical work and hypermedia are placed ever more prominently on our critical agenda, the theories of Russell Atkins will help us to remember that these modes do not supplant text and discursion; rather they participate in the supplementary logics of text and discursivity.

## III. PHENOMENA

Ronald Henry High has said of Russell Atkins's 1961 collection *Phenomena* that "[t]he entire book has an unsettling mood which overtakes the reader, even when the meaning escapes one" (29). Later in his essay High remarks that Atkins's works "are disparate and perhaps need to be collected in order for readers to recognize him as one of the most innovative forces in poetry of the past thirty years" (31). When we do collect Atkins's works and read them in association with his theory, we see that one reason some readers have found his poetry so unassimilable to their existing understanding of what it is that poems do is that in Atkins's work meaning is subsidiary. This does not mean, I hasten to add, that Atkins finds meaning inconsequential. Indeed, he takes considerable pride in having been among the first to have treated certain subjects and meanings. But for Atkins meaning serves technique, and meaning *is* one technique. Perhaps not since Edgar Allan Poe has American poetry seen a writer so strongly committed to the production of effect. And while this places Atkins in a stylistic relationship to a strand of postmodern verse that includes John Ashbery and Clark Coolidge, it has also served to place him well outside the dominant modes even of the outsiders and innovators of American postmodernity. As a black man working independently to create a postmodernity that contested the directions of William Carlos Williams, the Objectivists, and much of the Black Mountain School, Atkins has been multiply obscured by the workings of recent literary history.

By age fourteen Atkins had determined himself on a course "out of the traditional milieu and into the 'modern' in art, which," he remarks, headed him "toward the avant-garde" ("Russell Atkins" 7). As early as the period 1947 through 1950 he had developed an identifiable style that has obvious surface affinities with works soon to appear from poets such as Frank O'Hara and Kenneth Koch. Atkins's "Lines in Recollection," already making use of the poet's signature deformative apostrophe, would have sat comfortably alongside O'Hara's poems in *The New American Poetry*. They are among the funniest opening lines of the postmodern era:

> I had just arrived on the advanced slope and I
> did think of Grant Wood and some others:
> no trouble at all
> to see the around'd spanned circular far
> moving hills . . . (*Podium* n.p.)

Arrived at the "advanced" slope, the poet, represented by those upright ski poles of the first-person pronouns that bracket the poem's first line, finds his experience of nature mediated by his experience of art. In much the same way that Wallace Stevens's jar set in the slovenly wilderness takes dominion, Atkins discovers that his prior viewing of Grant Wood's art—Grant Wood, whose very name is seemingly redolent of the outdoors—organizes his circumferential scene, as some proprietor has organized the sides of hills into slopes for the beginners and for the advanced. These lines are further ordered by another prospect. In *Podium Presentation* this advanced slope is met on its facing page by the advancing and sloping graphic lines of Atkins's concrete composition. The humor implicit in this situation is characteristic of Atkins's poetry throughout his career, as is this linking of the world of the "natural" to the mediations of the "cultural." His later poem "Probability and Birds" is a mathematical and philosophical meditation on the food chain as it operates in the poet's yard. The rodent resident in the yard becomes the proximate cause of the cat's continued attention to a particular space. The presence of water in the yard would be the chief attraction to a bird, who must balance thirst and quickness against the danger represented by the cat. At the poem's conclusion, the variability of measure is marked by variable line lengths, which in turn parallel the variables in this equation of chance and hunger. New variables, human emotions, and dogs also suddenly appear at poem's end:

> The cat is variable
> The rodent becomes the death of the bird
> Which we love
>           dogs are random (*Here* 5)

Finally, as if to underscore the variability of each component in the scene, Atkins concocts a concluding uncertainty. In the complete absence of punctuation from this last stanza (the first stanza is punctuated), we cannot tell for sure if it is the bird or the death of the bird that the poet loves.

As early as the period of 1947 through 1954, Atkins was including typographical manipulation and concrete verse among the more conspicuous of his techniques. The editors of the special Atkins issue of *Free Lance* in 1970 selected a number of representative pieces from this transitional period to track the development of Atkins's use of these procedures, a use that he increasingly came to link to his emphasis on visual motion and narrative. Atkins evolved a "double image" technique, as he termed it, a technique first developed in response to "Dali's double-image device" ("Russell Atkins" 12), that often involved the unfolding of words inside of other words in a continuously readable line. Many of his concrete poems can thus be recited, but they contain among their more conspicuous elements visual effects that cannot be read aloud. Some of these techniques look back in one direction to the typography of e. e. cummings, while others prefigure the interdictive punctuation of Lloyd Addison and Norman H. Pritchard and the "scored" pages of Amiri Baraka. One untitled poem provides a visual enactment that operates in opposition to the commandment it seems to record:

```
            Firmly repulsed/    ///    ///    /br/
ea/    k/  not the solem      l    mMMM
M  m  NM    NM       l        l
                  l      l  ll
                  Ll
more   so             emnly thought on
seems   more    resigned
when like the long-awaited  (swift)
a w- i - nn  nn  -  d oo
      ___________
" ! b r / e aks th" g l        m    (13)
```

The eye scanning across this text can reach above the dividing line and recapture the floating "oo," drawing it down into the waiting "gloom"; indeed, it would be difficult for the eye trained in the reading of English not to do so. Few readers could force themselves to regard these isolated letters simply as isolated letters. In the same way, despite the spelling problem that it creates, we cannot help reading in the sixth line both the phrase "more so" and "more solemnly." We cannot, though, repeat verbally those repeating slash marks that break up the commandment to "break not the solemn." The tongue is firmly repulsed by this interdiction. Similarly, we cannot read aloud the long line of division between the word and the gloom it breaks, nor can we pronounce the quotation marks around the break (and who is being quoted?). The poem is not at all difficult to read and to make sense of, but it can be reduced neither to an oral presentation nor to a single sense. It remains in mind as a visual object-form that self-deconstructs, literally in this case, *avant la lettre*.

Likewise, when reading the next poem in the sequence presented in the Atkins special issue, we can easily produce a straightforward paraphrase, but the poetry that gets lost in the translation into orality here is precisely the sloping and breaking of the word forms and the momentary uncertainty about where to begin our reading when we first see the piece:

t
h
g
i r x
a e r x
r n e T
t i w T
s n oTT
th' gTTTT
are in the bre-a-t-h
h hhhhhhhh hhhing gn ng ngn
just as "C" !D"AWN! now com
mmMMMMMMMMMMMMM a long-

W ————
——dAwn————
Y
" (14)

It takes some time before a reader spots the word *snott* hidden in this breathy poem, and another microsecond to reread it as the contraction "it's not," because we have by that point begun reading up and down precipitous slopes rather than straight across the line. It is easier to see the word *way* slowly rising across a typographic horizon, but how is one to read that horizon itself or, again, the "quoted" letter "C"? The matter of these poems is often relatively simple, even commonplace, but the matter is only one element of the poetry, not its telos. The poem does not exist so that we may recollect the break of dawn in tranquility. It exists as a series of deconstructive compositions to provide experiential readings. The experience of moving about inside the poem *is* the poem far more so than is the poem's meaning.

Such verse serves as a forceful reminder of the role played by the actively reading eye in the constitution of the poem, and as sentimental as some sections of Atkins's concrete poems may seem, their violently disruptive syntax and shape afford little space for the sympathetic reader looking for what Atkins in another poem calls "typographical composition" (*Here* 15). Often, the motion of the eye is itself thematized in the poems. In "While Waiting for a Friend to Come to Visit a Friend in a Mental Hospital," Atkins aligns the appropriative gaze of power and authority with the presuming eye of reading:

> eyes thieve with prickled stir:
> the attendant has ideas about me
>
> the attendant keeps watch, watching
> that abrupt wild uranium grow a bat's ears,
> sardine flowers, moons' eggs,
> stomach guitars,
> a double-bass rump—but he's err:
> one shrewds to his inferences (*Here* 14)

Atkins hangs a title on this poem that he knows will direct the reader's anticipations in a very deliberate way. Like the mental hospital attendant, the reader will begin with certain presuppositions about what kind of poem this is to be and about what kind of poet lurks behind the poem's "I." Still, the trick of the poem is telegraphed by its opening conceit. The surreal thoughts that the attendant is supposed to suspect fill the mind of the person he is gazing on are, obviously, attributed to him by a poet gazing at the attendant. Later in the poem, Atkins writes that "the eyes direct / devilishly in this 'catch me' business," and this turn at the poem's beginning is exactly the most devilish catch of all. Those surreal images *are* in the mind of the poet (and the reader) as he eyes suspiciously the suspicious attendant. At the end we learn from this narrative that the poet, who has "about the least to do / with white coated attendants," is merely standing and waiting for a friend who has gone banking. The infectious duplicity of the poem, however, mirrors the duplicity of the poet's language and the cultural instability of perspective. As we, in our reading, watch the poet watching the attendant watching him, we read the uncertainty of subject positions. The figure-background shift enacted in Atkins's poem replicates the constant shifting about in language of self and other. Stuart Hall, in arguing against essentialist views of race and culture, argues for a conception of black popular culture forms as "the product of partial synchronization, of engagement across cultural boundaries, of the confluence of more than one cultural tradition, of the negotiations of dominant and subordinate positions, of the subterranean strategies of recoding and transcoding, of critical signification, of signifying" (28). Atkins's poems are such moments of critical signification. As the white-coated attendant watches the waiting black poet, the poet imagines the thoughts that the other must imagine are his. The double-consciousness of the veil is at once rent and redoubled upon itself. The poem catches itself and the reader in a moment of mirrored presuppositions and then smashes the mirrors. It is a movement beyond essentialism, one that answers before the fact Stuart Hall's call for "a new kind of positionality, a different logic of difference" (29).

And it may well be the case that Atkins still awaits rediscovery by critical readers because the form of his critical signifying is not the stable form of difference currently expected of African American poetry. The critical attendants of institutionalized poetry, like the white-coated attendant of Atkins's poem, "err" when they fail to read that which he supposes they suppose of him, and thus they fail to read his different logic of difference. Rey Chow has commented that "it is ironic that in much of the work we do in cultural studies today, we resort to cultural/ethnic/local 'difference' not as an open-ended process but as a preordained fact" (47). The type of reading for difference Chow describes as the dominant approach in contemporary academia reinstitutes an instrumental view of language in which the reading of texts by minority authors produces information about minority consciousness. It does. How could it not do so? Yet, as Atkins would rush to point out, that particular experience of the "more" to be gotten from the reading of poetry is not the final goal of the reading of poetry. Chow complains, rightly I think, that we have recently witnessed "the methodological subordination of literature to other disciplinary controls in such a way that the instrumentalist, reflectionist assumptions about language and representation, which literature challenges as part of its critical project, remain entirely unexamined. Instead, such assumptions often accompany the use of literature—now for simply one type of discourse among others—and become normative ways of reading" (132). Atkins's poetry, in contrast, foregrounds the work that literature performs on readers. Readers who approach Atkins's texts with normative modes of instrumental reception will be as taken off guard as those who approach the body of his work with normative expectations of what constitutes black consciousness. Atkins's works answer Chow's call, again before she issues it, for critical work in which "the very instability of cultural identity itself becomes a combative critical base" (140).

One scene of this combative critique is the traditions of poetry and reading themselves. Atkins anticipates the resistance attendant on his tactic of taking up critical residence within English language verse traditions. If art is a house that desires its own haunting, then Atkins is a poet who haunts the specters in the house of art. He enters into Poe and Whitman and inhabits them *as* a black writer. He uncovers those silent places within the canon where black people have been absented and replaced with white language's signifiers of darkness:

> After-twelve                    darkly comes back full stop,
>                                         hush about slumberers.
> There's an accompanying negating
>                                 intelligence:
> some other will.          Take the cupboards:
> in them, resistances, odd assortments,
> Bruegel spiteful in the dishes;
> next, autonomous hands in the fragile ether,
> a frolicking of silences: (*Whichever* 4)

The poem is not about Poe or Whitman or Brueghel or William Carlos Williams, but it asks a critical question. How would "The Sleepers" read differently if Whitman were joined by "some other will," by the black presence he occasionally summoned in his imagination? How does Williams read differently when read with an "accompanying negating / intelligence"? Whitman called for us to remove the doors, hinges, and jambs from the American dwelling. Russell Atkins invites us to a frolic among the resistances and odd assortments of our cupboards.

In his poem "While Waiting for a Friend to Come to Visit a Friend in a Mental Hospital" Atkins's persona knows that his body, and its location, signify. The black body and the African American mind are among the most persistently present/absent signifiers of American discourse. The African body was brought to America to build capital and to be capital, and it was then obscured behind capital. Black people's minds were made to disappear from American literature by the moving hand of white American writing, but black people's minds had to be present to do the work of building America. The mind of Russell Atkins engages in a transformative rewriting of American consciousness, but his writings have suffered a critical disappearance. While Adelaide Simon spoke of the gothic nature of Atkins's writings, a characterization aptly linking him to the romance of early American literary tradition, a still more useful description for Atkins's critical poetics may be found in Vera Kutzinski's accounting of a "New World (Neo)Baroque." Kutzinski follows the Cuban critic and poet Severo Sarduy in his description of this neobaroque as "an uncontrolled proliferation of meanings in the space of, or around, an absent signifier" (Kutzinski 173). This is not to say, as Kirby Congdon might have it, that Atkins has no control over what he is doing in his work but to posit the ultimate uncontrollability of meanings. The frolic of silences Atkins finds in the cupboard of American texts is a proliferation of meanings in the space where blackness has been absented. The neobaroque, as Kutzinski defines it, "manifests itself in New World literature as a deliberate and truly 'monstrous' proliferation of identities" (174). Atkins's poems are the polyphonic whisperings from that monstrous cabinet where black history has been shut away. They are the monstrous birth of American history, and in them we can read the portents of a history that will not be shut up. The neobaroque of Atkins's writing is imbricated in a proliferation of signifying styles, but it is that very persistence of signifying that separates it from the pastiche of some postmodern art. Atkins's is a path not taken by very many other writers of his time, the most interesting of whom frequently took those very examples of William Carlos Williams's American idiom that Atkins so vehemently rejected. Still, Atkins, too, represents a set of American idioms, and his works bear a distant relation to those of Jay Wright and Leon Forrest. Atkins remains, despite his tireless efforts as an editor and considerable assistance to other writers, a party of one, with no disciples to keep his reputation alive. Yet, as Atkins's poem "Changing Season" says, "there's no getting around it: / he has the last word" (*Whichever* 11). It is a word whose audience, as is so often the case for African American invention, has a belated look about it. Blues musicians sing, "Looked for you yesterday / and here you come today." Atkins writes "Irritable Songs." They are neobaroque polyphonic settings of everyday use. One shouldn't be surprised that a black man who spent his life in Cleveland writing about deconstruction as composition should evidence a modicum of irritability. Perhaps, though, as we sift through the debris of our canon battles and culture wars, among the "lapsed books" and "newspapers / lying like recoil" (*Here* 23), we might follow the examples of Marianne Moore, Edith Sitwell, and Langston Hughes and undertake a correspondence with Russell Atkins. Hughes had believed that his anthology of American Negro poetry would be outdated by 1950 if he didn't include the poetry of a Russell Atkins. In 1950 Arna Bontemps wrote to tell Atkins, "[S]omething tells me you will have to reconcile yourself to being considered an experimental poet" (qtd. in "Russell Atkins" 12). Now, more than a half century later, Atkins's texts increasingly give an aspect of Nathaniel Mackey's "Irritable Mystic" (*School* 25). Atkins continues to inscribe his own letter to the world:

some meaning rain
between by-walls
where woebegone
and ashcans misery
thunder's refrain
(lung's phlegm
for a gutter):
        in the wan room
of afternoon
                one feels,
intuitively, the refragible
        too late (*Here* 22)

# 2
## *No Saints in Three Acts: Stephen Jonas*

When God created
  the world he stood
    on the negro
  hence the price
    of beans in China
  thereafter
    —Stephen Jonas, *Selected Poems* (1994)

In what may have been the last poem Stephen Jonas ever wrote, a notebook entry Joseph Torra dates to early 1970, Jonas had in mind the social position of blackness, the Negro as both fundament and despised other in a racially defined world of human commodities. As Jonas says of Charles Olson, the Norseman-Gloucesterman whose passing is memorialized in the poem, "the remains are in his / writings" (*Selected Poems* 1994, 249). It seems characteristic of Jonas's life and works that as we read the characters spelling out his remains, we find ourselves feeling that we are not really much closer to any center of racial, sexual, or class identity around which some contemporary readers might ordinarily organize an understanding of the man than we were at the beginning. Jonas, whose "body kept changing" during the 1950s, as he experimented "with different diets or fasting" (De Gruttola 29), seemed never to find a stable position, or even body, from which to speak or write. Robert Kelly's moving tribute poem "Llanto for Steve Jonas," a poem that appeared appropriately enough in *Hearse* in 1970 (before being reprinted in Kelly's volume *The Mill of Particulars*), says of Jonas, "He was black but could / pass for silence" (n.p.). More recently (and perhaps even more mysteriously), Geoff Ward, comparing Jonas to Allen Ginsberg, has said, "It might be tempting to suggest that Allen Ginsberg strained for what Stephen Jonas was, though what Jonas was itself begs questions" (176). Joseph Torra's introduction to the recently published *Stephen Jonas Selected*

*Poems* remarks that "Jonas often passed as Hispanic or Portuguese and didn't feel comfortable when someone referred to him as black" (2). In her notes to the republication of the newsletter *Floating Bear,* Diane Di Prima described Jonas as "a very fine Puerto Rican poet from Boston" (Baraka and Di Prima 567). In Jonas's poem "Cante Jondo" the poet exclaims, "Spanish? christ, i don't even speak English!" (*Selected Poems* 1994, 161).

When Rafael De Gruttola edited the first posthumous *Selected Poems* of Jonas in 1973, he quoted Jonas himself on the matter of his origins. According to the "Personae" (appropriately plural) offered by the poet, Stephen Jonas ("ne Stephen Manuel Jonas Edwards y Perreira Santos") was "born New Bedford, Mass., 1927. adopted, at age 4, by a curious American combination of Mrs. Eddy's metaphysics and the American Friends" (*Selected Poems* 1973, n.p.). David Rattray, who believes that "a big part of the craziness" exhibited by Jonas "was a distorted reflection of the American racism he had grown up with," says that "Steve was born a mulatto in Post–World War One rural Georgia, a world where lynchings and fiery crosses and gunshots fired from passing cars in the night were a commonplace. His original name was Rufus Jones" (38–39). A letter Jonas wrote to De Gruttola has Jonas/Jones remarking about his Latin blood that "as far as I can make out, my mother was Spanish—(i think Creole i.e. French-Spanish) her mother's people settled in San Juan & later, i suppose to New Bedford where she met & married my father who was Portuguese—what else, i donno" (qtd. in *Selected Poems* 1994, 1–2). There are other reports of his having been born in Georgia, with conflicting birth dates given in 1920, 1925, and 1927 (*Selected Poems* 1994, 1), although recordings of the poet evidence a clear Massachusetts accent that must have been acquired at an early age. Jonas says he never knew his birth parents. His adoptive parents were, as he puts it, "American," the father being of Scotch-Dutch extraction. Though he says that his family was named Jonas (*Selected Poems* 1994, 1), there is apparently no evidence that he ever legally changed his name from "Jones." Judging from Jonas's first-person narrative "What Made Maud Hum" (which may not be a good basis for judgment, but what else is there at hand?), there may have been considerable confusions about race and nationality within the adoptive household of his youth. In one conversation hilariously narrated, the author recalls from childhood:

> uncle Ed said Maud had bad nigger blood and wasn't like mrs. Homan who went to the Health Society and her husband was a dentist in the colored section of the Army but when Captain Homan came home from the Army he wasn't colored at all he had blue eyes and fair skin like aunt Lizzy said I had and I didn't because I went back in my fathers people and everybody talked a good deal about the Homans but after a while they stopped and started talking about the Germans and then miss Olga came to us and everybody started talking about miss Olga and said she was German but miss Olga was not German miss Olga was Swiss. (*Selected Poems* 1994, 132)

In a society whose members placed the greatest importance on delineating one another's racial pasts, all the while clinging to the dream of an American character, Jonas found delicious ironies in the constantly shifting identifications and denials around him. In a portion of "What Made Maud Hum" that doesn't appear in the most recent *Selected Poems,* but which survives among papers Jonas mailed to Amiri Baraka, these confusions take an even more comic turn:

> Maud told me how the italians and their Il Duce was mistreating the Ethiopians and wouldn't give Mr. Sallaisse back his palace and I felt very bad for Maud feeling bad and Mr. Sallaisse that Maud said was her own flesh and blood and I told Maud I would think very much for her own flesh and blood mistreated by that mr. Il Duce but mother said she wasn't sure that Maud and the Ethiopians were the same people and aunt Loretta said she was sure they weren't and uncle Ed said Maud was just plain American like the rest of us and wasnt Ethiopian like she said at all and uncle Ed said a lots more about Maud and her get up and uncle Ed was right Maud didn't get up as she used to get up sometimes. (6)

Evidently Uncle Ed was possessed of sufficient negative capability to be able to believe simultaneously that Maud had "bad nigger blood in her" and that she was "American just like the rest of us," and maybe Ed was right.

According to Lewis Ellingham and Kevin Killian's biography of

Jack Spicer, Jonas was "[t]he first black man whom Spicer knew well" (41), and Jonas was the prototype for the black character Washington Jones, who figures in Spicer's detective novel *The Tower of Babel.* Jonas's poem "Cante Jondo for Soul Brother Jack Spicer" recalls that Spicer once said Jonas was

> . . . John Randolph
> of American poetry, a Spanish soul brother confused by
> adoption
> w/northern Europe, the American Friends & the Science &
> Health Book.
> I thanked him ("sir") for myself and for my ancestors.
> (*Selected Poems* 1994, 160).

Amiri Baraka remembers that when John Wieners came to visit him in New York, "He had a crazy half-black (maybe Cape Verdian) friend, poet Steve Jonas, who plagued him. Jonas rambled nonstop about Pound. Blacks and Jews and Poundians, all scrambled by talk of Art" (*Autobiography* 238). When Stephen Jonas, or whatever his name really was, died on February 10, 1970, apparently from a drug overdose, his death certificate identified him as a white man, parents unknown, born in Georgia (*Selected Poems* 1994, 12).

Small wonder, then, that critics and historians of American postmodernism don't know who Stephen Jonas was. In America, where the "one drop" rule has, since the last century at least, classified anyone with any African heritage as a black person, and in which, during the period of slavery, a child's legal status followed that of the mother precisely so that white fathers could sire and sell legally black children, what do we who read Jonas now, who read the remains that are in his writings, make of this poet who may have been born black Rufus Jones and who died as white Stephen Jonas? One clear conclusion to be drawn from a thorough reading of Jonas's texts is that he seems to have had an extensive and intimate knowledge of African American expressive culture to have been a white man from New Bedford. While his writings are a virtual casebook for the study of multiply directed racisms, they also provide a site from which to survey the continually intersecting lines of race and culture that so trouble the politics of American identities. For his part Jonas advises us in the poem "Orgasm XXXVI–Second Series":

I join no groups
I am a bastard
obligated to all
you Americans

Love me
as I do
you but IN THE FIRST PLACE

I vow to never ditch you and go fer
the gold. (4)

David Rattray says that "[f]or all the years that he lived in Boston, Steve passed as a white of mixed, let us say Mediterranean, background verging upon what is called on Cape Cod a Portugee" (39). This raises the odd prospect of a poet "of color" who lets it be known widely among white people that he is passing for white, a strange addition indeed to the history of passing in America. Still, all his friends seem to have known that whatever Jonas at a particular moment chose to call his racial mixture, it obviously included Africa, and according to Joseph Torra, Jonas, who "aligned himself closer to Malcolm X than to Martin Luther King, . . . in some ways liked his 'blackness'" ("Introduction" 2). Jonas's friends were mostly white, according to Jonas's white friends, but Torra also reports that Jonas liked "the fact that he could travel in circles not immediately open to whites" (2). In a country where one's race was itself a commodity, where color determined so much socially, Jonas relished the ironies his own ambiguity brought to the fore. In 1968 Jonas sent to Robert Kelly the third poem of an untitled series, reporting one such double take:

this radical imbalance
walking towards me
w/eyes for white hostility
stopped on a dime

for momentarily saw
his wife's face on
a caucasian store dummy
2 piece low cut

something 'o r'other
that don't care a that fer
the color of your money ("III")

No doubt similar shifts of racial identification and commercial distractions await potential readers of Jonas's poems. In the end it may prove to be the case that, after decades of identity politics in the academy, Jonas's unwillingness to adopt a stable racial identity or to accept the one America wanted to assign to him will prove nearly as great an obstacle to reconsiderations of his life's work as the unrelenting anti-Semitism and bigotry that forms a depressingly familiar drone throughout his writings. (Jonas is usually missing from anthologies and histories of the "New American Poetries" and from studies of African American writing. He is not named, for example, in Eugene Redmond's exhaustive history of black poetry.) There is much accounting to do if we are to form useful readings of this homosexual, convicted criminal, anti-Semitic, occasional resident of mental wards, self-proclaimed bastard poet who appears forever evasive on the matter of his own race. Amiri Baraka, one of the very few black writers even to mention Jonas, says of the early days of their relationship, "We'd look at all the 'kikes' and 'niggers' in his work, gloss it, look over it, justify it, and right on, Pound, right on!" (*Autobiography* 238). Baraka writes now as one who is no longer willing to gloss and justify such egregious effusions of bigotry, and it is important to keep in mind that the pronoun *we* in Baraka's sentence encompasses a fair number of white poets. In his second autobiographical novel, *Six Persons,* Baraka sees Jonas's anti-Semitism as linked irrevocably to racial self-hatred. Baraka portrays Jonas as characteristic of a specific social type familiar on the bohemian scene: "Anything totally esoteric they dug. And even the fact that Pound was sposed to have thot niggers simple barbarians. there was even dudes like light skinned steve j in bostown who was absolutely poundian and wrote exactly, even letters, like him, and echoed the same exact anti-nigra tone, it was weird to see and hear that, listen to them run it" (*Fiction* 322).

To think of Jonas's anti-Jewish writings under the contemporary media rubric of "black anti-Semitism" would be an enormity of use only to those whose interests are served by convincing African Americans and Jews that they are each other's real problems. Further, to do so without taking into account, as Baraka did, the abusive comments about black people that often appear in his writings would be hypocritical. Likewise, it would be a mistake to attribute Jonas's anti-Semitism entirely to his fascination with Ezra Pound and his theories of political economy. Geoff Ward proffers his guess, "though it would only be a guess, that a self-hatred stemming as much from his sexual orientation as his race caused Jonas to hallucinate agents of oppression in what he mistakenly took to be the outside world" (173). Ward goes on to argue that people have romanticized and forgotten "the paranoia of the 1960s" (173). One presumes that it is not the same people who have both romanticized and forgotten 1960s-era paranoia, but paranoia does, as Stephen Stills sang at the time, strike deep, and one of the more insidious aspects of the Federal Bureau of Investigation's COINTELPRO program involved deliberately stoking the fires of animosity between African American and Jewish communities. I doubt that Jonas was ever the object of such interference, as his correspondent Amiri Baraka was, nor do I think it wise, despite evident signs of mental imbalance in Jonas's history, to ascribe his hatreds entirely to a paranoia rooted in self-hatred. As criticism of his work proceeds in the future, it will be necessary to examine Jonas's anti-Semitism in the wider context of the anti-Semitism and other bigotries that formed a common conversational vocabulary for many of the poets, black and white, who were changing the face of American literature in the decades following the Second World War. While the anti-Semitism of Baraka's cultural nationalist period has been acknowledged and frequently dissected (most powerfully, it must be said, in his own writings), few writers have spent any time examining the anti-Semitism of many of Baraka's Caucasian fellow poets. Ed Dorn, for example, wrote a letter to Baraka in 1964 offering an intense apology for a phone call made to Baraka's home during a day of drinking, drug abuse, and what Dorn's wife told him was Jew-baiting (Baraka papers, UCLA). More disturbing yet, because entirely unapologetic, is a violently anti-Semitic poem by Jack Spicer, "A Gentle Warning from One Martian to Another," that Kevin Killian has discovered among Spicer's papers from his Boston years, a time when Spicer had been close to Jonas. It is important for our understandings of the history of American literary movements that we one day anatomize the function of ethnic insult in the circles that included poets like Jonas and Dorn in the 1950s and 1960s. Jonas was also one of Dorn's correspondents. In another letter to Baraka Dorn tells of receiving a fan letter from Jonas in which Jonas said of Dorn's aesthetic accomplishments, "In this wise you stand shoulder to shoulder with Amadeus Mozart." Dorn closes his letter by wondering what happened to the "superqueen" Jonas had been with when they last met (Baraka papers, UCLA). My own sense is that if we can find ways to continue reading and learning from Edgar Allan Poe and T. S. Eliot, we can surely find ways, while suppressing none of our outrage, to begin reading Stephen Jonas and to learn from our experiences of reading him, to learn, among other things, how aesthetic as well as political associations are so often formed with the glue of bigotry.

One thing these readings will reveal is that Jonas was in frequent contact with black poets searching for a new poetics, particularly Baraka and A. B. Spellman in the early years, despite the fact that most of his poet friends were whites, especially his Boston circle. A far more important discovery still is that throughout his work Jonas cast aesthetic questions and his own poetics in racial terms. One of the most unabashedly joyful aesthetic statements of our time, one that profoundly echoes William Carlos Williams's *Paterson,* is the twenty-sixth segment of Jonas's *Exercises for Ear,* a segment that had previously been titled "Axel Point" and "O'" before becoming one of the "Exercises":

when the old
measure's gone

            & the new
      stresses feet

tho' the heart
      stagger & the head

      be still
            let the feet go

                  black and bare
                  let 'em go
                        black and bare
                        let 'em go

                              & etc. (*Selected Poems* 1994, 32)

This moment re-echoes in Jonas's "One of Three Musicians" a poem in which Jonas's first hearing of the music of Ornette Coleman calls to mind Picasso's "Three Musicians." Jonas, like the *Dasein* poets and like Melvin B. Tolson, finds a black vernacular referent in the paradigmatic modernist master. Paul Gilroy has argued, following W. E. B. Du Bois and C. L. R. James, that African Americans, through the experience of Middle Passage and their creative responses to the mass subjection to slavery, became the first modern people. For Gilroy black concepts of modernity "were founded on the rupture of middle passage . . . [and] were punctuated by the processes of acculturation and terror that followed that catastrophe and by the countercultural aspirations towards freedom, citizenship, and autonomy that developed after it among slaves and their descendants" (197). I have suggested that one of the ruptures marking black postmodernity is the opening up of modernism by African American artists to reveal the seldom spoken Africanity and black precedence in the modern. Such a moment occurs here when Jonas, attending to the revolution by which Ornette Coleman's band reoriented jazz away from traditional conceptions of harmony and chord progressions, makes the connection to Picasso's African-influenced cubist musicians. Further, for Jonas Picasso's Afro-Iberian modernity represents a fundamentally different moment from earlier northern European sites of rupture. Jonas writes, perhaps thinking of both Brueghel and William Carlos Williams:

these are not the

shoed peasant feet out of Brueghel's
painting *The Kermess,* these are
bare black feet pounding
delta clay (*Selected Poems* 1994, 128)

Along with tracing the intertextual relationships of these lines to Williams's Brueghel poems it might prove instructive to think through the relationships between Jacques Derrida's discussions of Heidegger's meditations on the Van Gogh painting *A Pair of Boots;* Fredric Jameson's subsequent reflections on Derrida, Heidegger, Van Gogh, and Andy Warhol's *Diamond Dust Shoes;* and this striking poem of Jonas's. Jameson wishes to privilege the cultural productions of the oppressed over the postmodern depthlessness of much contemporary painting, poetry, and theory. Nonetheless, the Jonas poem may very well prove resistant to Jamesonian attempts to "reconstruct some initial situation out of which the finished work emerges" (Jameson 7), for Jonas will continually remove himself and his initial situation beyond the horizons of such reconstructions. Jonas's poem will bring the question home to the blues of delta clay but not to insist on the embodied presence in art; indeed, Jonas will refuse to embody himself as the native son of that delta clay. What Jonas attempts to do instead is to locate modernity in Congo Square, where "a theater is any place / free associates come in / to play" (128). Much as Ornette Coleman reasserted traditions of collective improvisation within an after-modern context (a revisionist invention paralleled in part by the album art on *Free Jazz,* a reproduction of a Jackson Pollack work), Jonas's spectacular punning here gives us the free play of the signifier in the context of evolving black musical traditions, rooting his form of postmodernity not in the transcendent soil of recoverable experience but in the blues tradition of shifty signifiers, that same southern blues improvisatory tradition that both spawned and sometimes spurned Coleman. Moreover, Jonas's "Exercise" tropes the political struggle for black freedom of association, what Gilroy terms countercultural aspirations toward freedom and autonomy, against a backbeat of struggle for freedom and autonomy of practice within modernism. Like so many formally innovative black writings, Jonas's poem stages a struggle of usurpation over the corpus and the corpse of Euro-American modernism. Stephen Jonas, frequent host of "Magic Evenings" in his Boston homes, was interested in alchemy and pastiche, but his poems practice neither magic realism nor the depthless, ahistoric pastiche Jameson describes as postmodern style. Instead, Jonas produces the polyphonic mulatto intertextuality of Congo Square's free associations. He is under no illusions about the oppressive structures and commodity economies that arrange for a Congo Square to exist as a means, by allowing a locatable and subvertable space for transgressive performance, to maintain their own dominance. And as a practical and punished transgressor (he was convicted of a form of mail fraud that involved subscribing, under innumerable aliases, to record and book clubs), Jonas knew the laws of cultural constraint firsthand. It appears, however, that Jonas was able to locate in the poem a textual space, *within* an oppressive modernity, for a freer reopening of the questions of agency and institutions.

Jonas was as likely to practice such a parodic reopening of tradition on black materials as on the canonical artifacts of Euro-American modernism. The first stanza of the eighty-ninth "Exercise for Ear" is just such a recasting of canonical black expressivity:

> take my hand
>         o gentle christ
> & lead me to
>         the boneyard (*Exercises* 46)

What Jonas accomplishes in the space of this small lyric is to return Thomas Dorsey to the blues he had for the most part left behind when he turned to gospel. If there is a supercanonical text in the canon of Thomas Dorsey's sacred songs, it is the song that begins, "Precious Lord, take my hand, lead me on . . . " This song, one of the most beautiful in the literature, is written out of a moment of deep loss and makes an at-least-sometimes ironic appeal for strength in a time of tribulation. It is a song that no one forgets having once heard it. Jonas's "Exercise" could well join Stephen Henderson's other exhibits in *Understanding the New Black Poetry* illustrating the technique in black poetry of "forcing the reader to incorporate into the poem his memory of a specific song, or even of a specific delivery technique" (52–53). Jonas's stanza is a moment of black experiential saturation that turns the ironic hope of the sacred song back toward the yet more ironic fatalism of its secular source in the blues. For many black audiences this would be seen as a far more audacious act than Jonas's redirection of a Picasso masterpiece. Jonas redraws the lines joining blues and gospel in the same black bodies. His parodic rupture of Dorsey's gospel message is not a means of putting tradition behind us or of replacing tradition in a position of authority over us. Rather, Jonas embodies the archetrace of enabling tradition that inevitably comes forward in the person of the antiphonal, countertraditional poet. It is not the substance of the tradition that Jonas asserts but the substantive modes of invention tradition has made available.

In letters to his colleagues it is evident that Jonas was most interested in the specifically written nexus of orality and literature. A 1965 letter to Gerrit Lansing completes a typically American intertextual circuit in which Jonas rediscovers one tradition of African American writing in the company of his white modernist predecessors: "I also got a copy of Paul Lawrence [*sic*] Dunbars (Negro dialect verse & song from back at the turn of the century) I have a first edition—have there been others? I recall William C. Williams Autobiography, mentioning him as one of his early childhood memories of his ,ithink, his father, reading Dunbar to him. His music (tho' like most of the Blues, is iambic pentameter. But it has its moments and the rhythms are eyeopeners to to [*sic*] vistas,—new" (*Four Letters* 5).

Again punning on tradition as both garb and drag, Jonas promises in one of his poems:

amidst an
        erudition of stoned
compatriots
              i'll wear
tradition out (46)

This overironized wearing out of tradition is visible again in Jonas's epigraph to "Complainte De L'Oubli Des Morts." In this epigraph, as in "One of Three Musicians," Jonas discovers blackness in the reading of a European source, this time hearing black vernacular stylings in the symbolist poetry of Jules Laforgue. As it happens, Laforgue was something of a transatlantic poet, having been born in Montevideo, and he, like Jonas after him, sought a new poetics. Speaking of his own works in 1886 Laforgue said: "I forget to rhyme, I forget the number of syllables, my lines begin at the margin, like prose. . . . This is the only kind of poetry I shall write in the future" (8). Finding a kindred aesthetic in the Uruguayan French poet, Jonas signs Laforgue's name to his signifying translation. He signs the blackness of symbolist irony by signing Duke Ellington's name in French verse:

. . . man the dead
's in the boneyard
they don't get around
much anymore.
    J. Laforgue (*Selected Poems* 1994, 117)

This 1965 poem brings the symbolist aesthetic to Congo Square, detaching the symbols from their referents and making them available for free association in a colored context. What we see in *Exercises* and in "Complainte De L'Oubli" is that Jonas works from black signifying traditions no matter what his source materials may be. His starting and ending points are American, blues-based foci, no matter what his public stance about race might have been at the moment.

By June of 1960, when Stephen Jonas wrote for the first time to LeRoi Jones (Amiri Baraka), Jonas was already a self-assured poet possessed of an original style and part of a steadily expanding group of poets centered in Boston who shared common interests in projective verse, linguistics, and the paranormal. Jonas's meeting with Jack Spicer had already taken place, and Spicer, Robin Blaser, and John Wieners were helping to spread the word of this poet's distinctive early works. But Jonas as yet had published only one slender chapbook, *Love, the Poem, the Sea, and Other Pieces Examined,* printed by White Rabbit Press in 1957. Baraka had not yet published a full book (*Preface to a Twenty Volume Suicide Note* would appear in 1962), but he was already publishing the influential magazine *Yugen,* the first issue of which had appeared two years earlier, and Baraka was widely known in circles that overlapped with the Blaser-Spicer-Jonas crew, one particular point of intersection being Robert Duncan. Jonas had attended Charles Olson's mid-1950s reading at the Charles Street Meeting House and was already familiar with the Black Mountain contingent. Baraka, like another Boston colleague of Jonas's, Cid Corman, had been a loyal publisher and correspondent of Charles Olson and published Robert Creeley, as well; so the two correspondents had much in common in terms of their shared interests in what came to be called the "New American Writing." Jonas's first letter is a simple letter of submission, striking an air of humility largely absent from later letters. Without salutation Jonas instructs Jones/Baraka: "Be pleased to—if you can find the enclosed to be of use—use. For then what are they to me if nobody else can use them" (Baraka papers, UCLA). By way of bona fides Jonas mentions his chapbook and a 1958 appearance in the magazine *Measure*. There wasn't much else to mention that year, just ten years before his death, but Jonas also indicates in this letter that he has already completed three "books" of what was to become his life's major sustained work, the *Orgasms* sequence, which he here describes as "a long journey poem." It wasn't to be the usual quest motif.

By the following February Jonas feels that he is on a much more familiar footing with Baraka, addressing him as "my dear Leroi," though Baraka had not yet published any of Jonas's work. (He would place two Jonas poems in the second issue of *Floating Bear,* and Jonas would publish five more poems in the *Bear* during the newsletter's publishing life, including the important poems "Subway Haiku" and "A Poem for Tony Sherrod.") Baraka had given Jonas reason to feel encouraged, though. He had written to ask that Jonas submit some poems like those that had appeared in *Measure*. Five important Jonas poems were included in *Yugen*'s final issue in 1962, among them "Orgasms IV" and "A Long Poem for Jack Spicer." Jonas's February 1961 letter also gives a good indication of the difficulties attendant on editing Jonas. Writing to withdraw a manuscript he had already given to Baraka, Jonas explains: "I sent on to you, some weeks back, a very long thing that I have been working on. Please forgive me, in asking this, but would you destroy it. You see that is the 4th book of a long poem that I was working on when I had a nervous breakdown in Oct., The thing is not yet completed, and that 4th book I sent you is certainly not in any shape to be offered up for publication. In sending it on to you, I was making a hasty decision. Too hasty" (Baraka papers, UCLA). It is in this February letter that a discussion of poetics begins between the two young writers that will stretch across their correspondence for the next two years. Throughout, Jonas emphasizes a music-based poetics over what he sees as a showy, content-based orientation. "I cannot go along with the young poets I read in the little mags that come into me," Jonas complains. "I shall not name NAMES but the people seem to be *too too* concerned with what they are saying—so much so in fack that they have forgot to make Poems of their things. MY MY, as I read, I think, how philosophical we Poets have become." In contrast to the attitude he thinks characteristic of so many younger poets, he is trying, as he tells Baraka, "to work out a Measure" that will "return the Poem to its former position close to that Art—Music." It is in an August 14 letter that Jonas makes his fullest statement of his aesthetics to Baraka. Expressing some irritation that George Stanley had not forwarded a copy of Jonas's "verse essay" to Baraka as requested, Jonas proceeded to quote extensively from a letter he had written to Stanley tracking his evolving aesthetic. Jonas's statements have an aphoristic quality to them, and while they give no more specific guidance to his actual practice in prosody than do William Carlos Williams's many similar exhortations, they give a good indication of how Jonas conceived of his own efforts, and they once more show him to be an artist who has a particularly African American touchstone in mind:

> Music rots when it gets too far from dance. Poetry atrophies when it gets too far from the music.
>
> . . .
>
> More to home: the gospel music cum handclapping and spontaneous footwork is remembered in the music of the MJQ [Modern Jazz Quartet].
>
> Jazz is to be listened to by an American Poet. Interesting to note how they refresh the medium—returning to "roots" of foot, hand and body movement.
>
> . . .
>
> Melody is the most artificial thing in music. Song (lyric) is that most artificial equivocal language (Poetry).
>
> . . .
>
> American speech is mostly articulation—most of the Prose we read is so much dialogue.
>
> . . .
>
> Music can still be made in poetry without doing violence to the natural habits of speech.

Like Charles Olson, Jonas envisions a poetics that is intimately associated with the workings of the body, a speech that takes its rhythms from the motion of limbs and breath. But for Jonas, significantly, the return of poetry to the state of music is to be accomplished in a decidedly black mode, to the handclaps of gospel and the fancy footwork of jazz. Jonas closes his letter on another, more personal note, promising an extended visit. "Last time I was there in Oct.," he recalls, "I flipped and ended up in the nut house for the second time. No reflection on NYC, mind you."

By July of the following year the relationship had advanced to the stage where Jonas could joke about their growing familiarity. Addressing his letter to Baraka using the shortened nickname Baraka was known by to Ginsberg, Creeley, Dorn, and others, Jonas asks his "Dear Roi": "I may, maynt I—Roi you?" Jonas includes a copy of his "Orgasm o," a poem that remains unpublished to this day, joking about the lack of the customary Roman numeral in the title. In his letter Jonas describes the mode of composition of the *Orgasms* series as a matter of using "'hot' experience as woof to INNER warp / Poem on some old tapestry / Wherein to trap the / Unikorn," and he sends "Orgasm o" to Baraka so that Baraka may note the technique firsthand. Another reason for sending the poem, we find on reading it, is that Baraka figures prominently in the poem as a sort of turning point between the Poundian vortices both poets have learned from and the black musical referents that were at the core of each poet's poetics:

> like Joe Williams (I
> like the old music)
> and Roi, oh Le Roi
> at that would be *parfait*
> at the *Wu* court. Elegant in Court dress
> to receive the Royal guests . . .
> bowing at the lower end, (eh, Roi?)
> / . . . / Like
> this is the "niew day" etc as
> "every day I get the blues"
>
> (Baraka papers, UCLA)

Thus this segment begins and ends with Joe Williams, whose "Every Day I Have the Blues" was one of his best known songs [though it's possible that Jonas makes a double allusion here, simultaneously invoking the jazzy Joe Williams and the folk blues of Mississippi Joe Williams, a singer important to both Amiri Baraka and Bob Dylan], detouring through Pound's version of China along the route. A. B. Spellman, another New York acquaintance of Jonas's among black poets, also figures in "Orgasm o," as he does in the now collected "Orgasm XII." Here Spellman is a response to the poet's rhetorical question: "POETRY? Yess.—- and the *best* (A. B. Spellman) NOT bazeball & / POOL?—Heavens to Betsy."

Jonas, however, was still facing personal setbacks, though facing them with rare humor. Before signing off with greetings to Spellman, Joel Oppenheimer, and others, Jonas reveals, "When you get this I should be once again in Brockton, Mass looney Bin—where they want to check mah marbles—So let 'em—Hope to be in N.Y. in August. Will see you—if I may so presume."

The next Jonas letter, dated February 14, 1963, indicates just how much trouble the poet was routinely getting himself into. He announces with a certain flourish: "Great news: in the latest case of Comm. Vs. S. Jonas et al—S. Jonas was found "Not Guilty". However, my "husband" being "et al", was found guilty of 22 counts of assaults with intent to kill. However, considering his tender years and the hardship endured by his wife—his absence as provider and such other material essentials—they give 'im 2 yrs in State Prison. But I must carry on—and all that jazz, y'kno wh'a I mean, honey?" Jonas's work was proceeding well in the midst of all this turmoil, nonetheless, and he was discussing with Baraka the possibility of publishing a collected Jonas volume in the Totem/Corinth Press series that was to include volumes by Baraka, Dorn, Ginsberg, Kerouac, Sorrentino, O'Hara, and others. The Jonas book never did make it to press, but Jonas mailed Baraka a substantial collection of manuscripts for possible inclusion (Jonas said the poems would "cause some eyebrow elevation") and a suggested format. Jonas's working title for the book was *Pot Handles with Lid Covers,* and his mock-up of a title page included a dedicatory poem, "Movin' Out," that closes with an appeal to Homer and, by way of Ralph Ellison, to Louis Armstrong and the origins of jazz: "Oh Odysseus / what have I done / to be so black and blue?"

A degree of personal tension becomes apparent in the correspondence at this point, although its immediate cause is not evident. On March 6 Jonas sent a not-entirely-tongue-in-cheek letter to Baraka, noting that the letter itself was submitted for publication. The letter demands that Baraka redeem himself by publishing a review of Jack Spicer, whom Jonas terms "America's greatest living poet." Calling the works appearing in Totem/Corinth "freshman antics of nothing but absolutely nothing but sheer non-sense surrounded by a whole host of gophers with probable evasions of pussy-noms like it was avant garde bill of fare," Jonas implores Baraka: "Do the decent thing before you abandon (like ditch) the 'duke' and go fer the gold; either publish this 'Review' of Jack Spicer's new book quick as you can see to, or I don't care, get another 'Reviewer' / and or 'Critic' with he-she head where it properly belongs (but few do/have) to surpass me in acute judgement." The accompanying review, which Baraka did not run in either *Yugen* or *Floating Bear,* titled "'I' BEFORE E-quality OR I THE FEW, YOU THE MINNIE-SINGERS," is as oddly put together and parodic as the letter of submission. The "review" turns out to be a proposal to review *The Heads of the Town Up to the Aether*. Jonas declares, "since nobody is at home anymore in the heads of the real world. 'ceptin meybee U 'N mee. *und so weiter*. I therefore propose 'A Review', as I have read Mr. Spicer's book."

It was probably inevitable that Baraka and Jonas would move away from each other eventually, despite their commonality of interests in a revolutionary poetics merging the lessons of Olson's projective verse with the aesthetic possibilities offered by black American speech and music. As Baraka moved increasingly in the direction of a revolutionary cultural nationalism, eventually articulated in the Black Arts Movement, he would have little patience with the always evasive and often reactionary postures Jonas assumed with regard to race. Jonas, for his part, recorded his growing disapproval of Baraka's direction in stanzas as scathing as any Baraka has ever written. In "Orgasm XXI," written in 1966, Jonas turns his reaction to Baraka's course into a Poundian denunciation. The ground is laid in an undated earlier letter Jonas sent to Baraka following a visit to Baraka's Cooper Square home:

> Roi
> I too busy studying Electronics, Computers and Special Theory (Relativity) in its broader Scope. What with writing & other studies "the which I don't talk of"—I have no time for Revolutionist & "guerilla writing" indeed. . . . Who're you publishing to? Nobody reads anymore—Its a lost art. I don't like "kikes," "niggars" & "pore" "white trash" a sample of each I encountered at yr. pad. None of which has to do with racial prejudice—its cognitions. You are a Poet & a gentleman.

By the time Jonas was composing "Orgasm XXI" Baraka had left the Village bohemian scene behind and committed himself irrevocably to life as an activist writer. It was a move that left Jonas behind as well. In his "Orgasm" Jonas attributes the most banal motivations to Baraka and, curiously, criticizes Baraka for not adopting the yet more mystified and disabling politico-economic theories that held Jonas in thrall:

> & I thot I wuz among poets (Cooper Sq. N.Y. 1962) but found a nest of intrigue & all bent on circumnavigation of the what's tried & found not wanting and frankly informed me he had no liking for his (E. P.'s) economic theories and went on subse-

> quently to stage "The Toilet" and wrote in *Esquire* (which oughtta tell ya) white man obsolete thus leaving me to ponder who'll dig up their bauxite in Africa (but of course under the *nom de plume:* "improving their standards of living") and all of it i suppose to the applause of the peanut gallery or ultimately hurray for anything— (*Selected Poems* 1994, 224–25)

And so ended, with sardonic nostalgia on Jonas's part, what was probably the longest and most productive interchange Jonas was ever to have with another black poet. In a poem that bore the title "Orgasm XXVIIII: First Series" when he mailed it to Baraka (it is not, however, the "Orgasm XXIX" in the current publications of the series), Jonas waves good-bye to Baraka, and to the aesthetics of nationalism, in terms that would be echoed by Kenneth Rexroth when he lamented the "loss" of LeRoi Jones to literature. Jonas writes:

> So that "we" have lost LeRoi
> to a new rising muddle-class (black)
> wanting to, too be told
> and in poetry, they're
> beautiful.
> (Baraka papers, UCLA)

Jonas reprises this moment in "Orgasm 52," this time adding to the satiric comment on the liberal media's brief flirtation with the image of black militance that he had hinted at with the reference to *Esquire* in "Orgasm XXVIIII": "they wanna take our Roi away from cooper sq. and / make him muddleclass jiggerboo on satreview f.m. educational / help!" (Baraka papers, UCLA). While Jonas may have been on to something about the true class affiliations of some in the Black Arts Movement (Baraka would level much the same charge about the class loyalties of cultural nationalism following his move to a Marxist critique), Jonas's farewell, like Rexroth's, is both bigoted and self-serving. Many might argue, in fact, that Jonas's own inability to wear his skin comfortably and honestly, to come to grips fully with the political implications of his color, was the direct result of his involvement in the dominant, racialist discourse that Baraka and others were seeking to destroy.

Like Charles Olson, Stephen Jonas perceived himself as a poet in the tradition of Ezra Pound, attempting to work through the lessons of modernism for post–World War II poetics, and like Olson, Jonas saw this project as necessitating a break with the dominant modes of modernist expression that took their model from an academic, formalist reading of T. S. Eliot. This attempt at a break required revisiting a moment of bifurcation in modernism itself, a moment when the more radical experimentation of writers such as William Carlos Williams and Gertrude Stein had been subjugated to what Williams saw as the reactionary ethos of Eliot. For Olson and Jonas there was a crossroads in Pound where the stultifying ennui and conservative traditionalism of Eliot's modernity paved a path more traveled, while the more significant departure from the metronomic heave of verse conventions was the rougher pathway forged in their quite different ways by Williams and Stein. Further, Jonas shared with Olson a questioning of modernist epistemologies and of humanist subjectivity that once more found the radiant gist of its expression in the texts of Williams. In a letter to Robert Kelly dated September 14, 1967, Jonas complains:

> reason the "new" scientists can't reconcile these finer particles—protons, neutrons & mesons etc., is because they are watching (or rather watching the effects of thru their artificial instruments for studying "finer states of matter") the INSIDES OF THEIR HEADS!! & because of "∞" WCW told them in, i think it was, *Journey to Love:*
>
> ". . yr rocket ships shd be
> directed *in*
> ..but then i'm an old man
> & i have seen enuf."
> (not accurate quote of WCW) (
> but the gist of it, anyway
>
> [Jonas, Letters to Robert Kelly B66F3]

But, like Amiri Baraka, in his efforts to use the rhythms of the American idiom to make the language of his verse new for his era Jonas turned to the examples of black music and speech far more consistently than did the white writers of the New American Poetries, who turned for inspiration to jazz and to black culture generally far more frequently, though still problematically, than any other white writers of their time.

As had been true of so many poets of his generation, Jonas found a point of entry into literature by way of an early and intense experience of the cloudy spirituality of late Eliot. In the poem "Gloucester" Jonas remembers:

> there was
> the studio in Pigeon Cove where Eleanor
> (divine name) declaimed me
> "The Four Quartets."
> I was brought to my knees
> and so it was that I decided for poetry.
> (*Selected Poems* 1994, 137)

Yet Jonas quickly grew dissatisfied with Eliot, coming to take Williams's side of the dispute with Eliot's Anglophilia that Williams carried on so perpetually and violently and so nearly alone. There was, for Jonas, a triteness about Eliot's diction that took itself too seriously to be wholly camp, coupled with a withdrawal from the physicality of direct treatment. In "A Poet's Word to a Blue Painter" Jonas takes a line against the commodification of primitivism associated with high modernism and against early Eliotic angst and form. After railing against the prostituting reproduction of Benin masks and "high toned Ife headgears," Jonas warns:

> So do not ask
> if I've seen afternoons
> like coffee spoons
> I use a pencil
> but what I have seen has been
> a black knife tearing into
> the full canvas belly of light
> from the open wound nothing gushes like so much blood
> (Baraka papers, UCLA)

Rejecting both Eliot's careful sense of measure and the measured artifactualism of the high moderns, Jonas urges the provisional (writing in pencil) and immediacy (the metaphorical gush of blood). More than that, though, Jonas rejects the racial politics of Eliot (despite their shared anti-Semitism), finding in Eliot's racism a portent for the future of Eurocentric modernity. At the close of a draft fragment dated 1962 we find Jonas once more issuing a warning: "Attend to the business of Ceremony or the black African will / point with Eliot's *Cocktail Party*, as finger, back at you" (Baraka papers, UCLA). Jonas's imagery is more than usually telling here, for what more fitting end could be imagined for the Western course of imperial racism than that it meet its most violent of imagined terrors unceremoniously in the wholly fantasized Kinkanja of Eliot's cannibalistic Africa?

Similarly, although the symbolist aesthetic that had informed imagism had been a productive influence for Jonas early in his self-education, he came to reject this mode as well, again linking the rejection to a racial politics. Jonas had in common with the Objectivists a severe epistemology (in a 1967 letter to Robert Kelly he terms American neglect of Louis Zukofsky the "fuckin' crime of the century" [Letters to Robert Kelly B66F3]), but for Jonas both Wallace Stevens's symbolist-influenced forms of phenomenology and abstract expressionist severity proved finally inadequate. His "A Poet's Word to a Blue Painter" begins:

to see things as they are<br>
                    is to see in that Kline thing<br>
                    the fucking blacks<br>
                    fucking themselves out ov the picture<br>
There you can see<br>
                    how it is here with us<br>
               we do not see it<br>
     Not<br>
     certainly not Stevens'<br>
                              Blue Guitar<br>
               out of the mauve vagaries—1902<br>
     that insurance man's decor<br>
     —soothing the cool walls<br>
                         of an executive suite—1952<br>
                              (Baraka papers, UCLA)

Again Jonas wants a still more immediate expression:

Sing<br>
     goddamn you, sing<br>
               as you paint in the landlord<br>
     trying to stop the music

Jonas is no doubt unfair both to Stevens and to other insurance executives, but he writes from the other end of a history that began with modernist art as irreconcilable antithesis to bourgeois things as they were and ended with modernism as official culture, indeed as the very sign of culture in itself; witness the National Gallery's East Wing as national tourist mecca, or the *Life* magazine layouts of late Picasso. In the same way that Einstein's "$E = MC^2$," a formula many citizens still cannot gloss, became the public signifier of progressive science, modernist art became, in Jonas's view, the bourgeoisie's elevation of its own lack of comprehension to the level of sacred object. Though Jonas could revisit the site of Picasso's breach of the privileged point of view of classical perspective in the company of a later provocateur such as Ornette Coleman, the poet seems to have felt that the cool reserve of Stevens's florid mundo and the colorist formalism of abstract expressionism had become the commodity props of bourgeois sensibilities rather than the interrogations of them that avant-garde art had once been. Jonas's poem includes a "*POSTLUDE OF THE BLUE GUITAR*" that turns to a dadaesque irrationalism as antidote to prevailing forms of high modernism:

> The guitar is white
> Man, if he is anything he is more
>               the Rose of Gertrude Stein
>                              which is grey

In the absence of punctuation at the end of the first line we can read another of Jonas's racial puns. Either the blue guitar *is* white man, or we are being addressed informally in a typical American idiom. Last, we can read these lines as simply stating that man is the gray rose of Gertrude Stein. With these antiphonal readings setting up an oscillating signification, Jonas's lines destabilize the poem as they destabilize the racially exclusive modernity of Stevens (and of the commercial art world of the day).

Of course, despite her acquaintances with and encouragement of some black artists, Gertrude Stein's textual world is just as racially exclusionary as that of Stevens. But Jonas has much different reasons for distancing himself from her aesthetics. Stein had brought a great deal of value to the diction of American verse, and in her case Jonas was more interested in contemporizing her approach than in breaking from it. Viewing himself and Stein as Whitman's children, Jonas still believed that the poet must adopt the idioms of his or her own epoch. He writes in "About the Poem and about Measure for George Stanley," which didn't appear in a book until the posthumously published chapbook *Three Poems* was published in 1989:

> Whitman's ear
> is not the ear,
> since Stein and Williams,
> We have come
> to hear with.
> / . . . /
> —hear
> the cry of children
> measured    to the wants
> of our own times.

In some of the most beautiful and direct lines of his career Jonas appears to practice effectively a form of Williams's measurable (according to Williams) variable foot. More important, the lines record Jonas's sense not just that the modern idioms of American speech have evolved since Whitman's day, and have been made central to modernist poetics by Williams and Stein, but that Williams and Stein have taught us to hear American English differently and hence to take its measure differently. Later, Jonas will liken the breaking up of the Whitmanian long line into the shorter measures of Williams's modernism to the elliptic phrases surrounded by silence of Miles Davis. That same evolution away from the cadences of Whitman's long line may explain in part Jonas's frequent signs of disapproval directed at Ginsberg, who Jonas called "the whale mouth." A corollary to what Jonas states directly in these lines is that Williams and Stein have helped to bring about changes in the measures of our speech as well as in our attending to our speech. It is the attention to the materials of the American idiom that Jonas most wants to celebrate in this poem. Gertrude Stein, he claims, warning the reader not to laugh at the audacity of the claim, knew a great deal more than might be suspected by "uncareful readers"

about the way
the private way
an American gets a thing said.
with his 'thing a 'majigs' and his
'well ahs' etceteras
coming back to repeat
and repeat as we all do
repeating
trying to get across to you
trying to span
as Hart Crane tried to span
that tremendous gap
the gap between
in each of our own
desolate
and daily lives. ("About the Poem")

Williams was not the only American obsessed with the question of how to begin to begin again to find the language. But Jonas does not intend that we leave the past of our prior speech entirely behind. For him, to take the measure of one's own time is to improvise from a previously given line. Thus, invoking Williams's *The Desert Music* and bringing into play the arts of jazz too often overlooked by the children of the Jazz Age generation, Jonas offers two analogies to illustrate his imperative:

the music Casals gets
measuring Bach
to the stresses of
his own times,
or the M.J.Q., learning again
learning from what has been
trampled upon
discarded and lost. ("About the Poem")

Jonas's use of his modernist models was never imitative; he was never one of those traditionalists of plagiarism Williams condemned. His rejection of what had come to be the academically correct aesthetic of high modernism, particularly as practiced by those of his contemporaries who were grouped together in anthologies as "academic" poets, was nearly total, but he also knew, as did Olson and Baraka, that the more unruly modernism of those poets he believed he could still learn from must be adapted and interrogated in its turn. Even his beloved Pound was a model to work off of, not to mimic. Following a suggestion of Jack Spicer's, Jonas often referred to his *Orgasms/Dominations* series as "anti-cantos" (Letters to Robert Kelly B66F4). His was an effort, then, to learn from that which had been trampled on in the reception of modernism, the antiphonal stylistic radicalism of Williams and Stein, and to wed the structures thus discovered to what he learned from that which had been trampled on by the progress of American cultural history, the antiphonal signifying practices of African American invention. Invariably, Jonas's instinct is to prefer American vernacular traditions, no matter that they have been diluted or inverted, to European. Of Marianne Moore's translations of fables he says in "Word on Measure," "I didn't like [them] because we have our own things going / here uncle Remus and little black sambo you know push the / home products . . . " (*Selected Poems* 1994, 111). These lines' reappropriation of the colonialist and orientalist "little black sambo" as home product mark a paradigmatic moment in racial remaking, marking the discursive site where Sambo ceased to be Indian and became an American Africanist trope (and an atavistically named restaurant chain). Like pianist Cecil Taylor, who studied at the conservatory on his way to remaking jazz in newer forms, Jonas was out to begin to begin again to make it new.

Jonas's own estimations of his strengths and weaknesses, as represented by his widely scattered notes, is unusually acute. He had a clear sense, for instance, of the offensiveness of his own bigotry. Writing in 1968, just two years before his death, to apologize to Robert Kelly for not giving him certain poems for publication, Jonas remarks of his verses that "they . . . have 'Racist' overtones!! lets hope they don't shoot us, eh?" (Letters to Robert Kelly B66F5). Possible reader response critique in the form of shooting, however, apparently was never enough to cause Jonas to rethink his hatreds. On a more benign subject, his abilities as a writer and what he had to contribute to American prosody, he was equally self-aware. At the end of the manuscript of his poem "distend" there is a handwritten note that reads like the notes on contributors often found in little magazines and poetry anthologies. The note is revealing both for Jonas's sense of what he was up to in poetry and for his sense of where he stood in relationship to the poetry he had taken for his master texts:

About my things I can say
that I have found to allay [sic]
the syntactical vigor of Pound
to the latin sense of the ironic
which is W. C. Williams
the rhythms lifted from local
—sometimes low—speech habits,
are my only original virtue
to say more at this point
would be merely piling on points
a real drag (Baraka papers, UCLA)

In the rhythms lifted from the local Jonas again found a politics that might have moved him closer to Baraka's activist position had it not been for Jonas's continued unwillingness to be more than a caustic observer of racial division. Working in Boston, a city whose ethnic politics have always been engraved in its accents, Jonas could hear the workings of ethnic difference in the air around him. "Orgasm X" observes that "[i]n Boston the Irish use phonetics for tools and dangerous weapons. As tho' the 'rr"s were files pulld across your metallic ear" (Baraka papers, UCLA). Both Baraka and Jonas conceived of linguistic sound as instrument and weapon, and both did their woodshedding as carefully listening students of the changing same in American talk (what Jonas liked to call the yak-yak). To Jonas's ear the second half of the twentieth century continued the first half's fascination with speed, while moving in the direction of greater concision and compression. Olson's prescription for the poet to move instantly from one perception to the next seemed, to Jonas, simply to put into practice on the page what was going on generally in American conversation. He again links this to jazz aesthetics in a particularly assonant section of "Orgasm XXVIII":

Speed
's the word for it & at the
                    expense of sentence.

we're hearing less today
that's all.
mind works by shorthand
(flash) . . . . . mind
& poem all
ov one piece.
saddle the verb
'n ride
eliminate plunder
(parts of speech)
like Cannonball sd. of Miles:
"he's playing less." (*Selected Poems* 1994, 226–27)

It may well be that this perception was shared by mainstream and avant-garde alike at the time, but poets whose typeset pages appeared to take the idea seriously were unlikely to appear in the *New Yorker*. Jonas records his take on literary reception in the same poem: "oh they complained abt cummings & later Ornette Coleman" (227). Jonas always goes to black music when he is searching out ways to explain what he believes poetry should do, so when we read Jonas's contextualizations and expressions of poetic desire, we must always listen to our memories of the music he invokes. In the midst of "Cante Jondo's" explorations of African Iberian archetraces in the poetics of both Lorca and Spicer we have to go to the nightclub and to church. We have to hear Charlie Parker inside the flamenco of Manitas de Plata and Lorca alike. We have to enter into the poem as into a church because "The 'amen corner' is as close as we can come to cuadro flamenco" (*Selected Poems* 1994, 160). Most important, if we are to register the analogies Jonas makes between black American modernism, the black African-influenced modernism of Picasso, and the "post-" to which Jonas wishes to direct the modernity of his verse, we have to hear Horace Silver's sides while listening to Manitas de Plata, and we have to place a "Jug" in our own slovenly wilderness:

Spicer, we want a big round sound in poetry
like Ammons gets from a horn,
or Picasso's high voltage line
execution of a picador.
(*Selected Poems* 1994, 161–62)

Jonas tells the reader that "Miles heard it (*Sketches of Spain*) like Casals like / de Falla." Lorca had to explain *duende* by analogy and metaphor, and when Jonas wants to explore the *duende* and *cante jondo* in his turn, it is always black soul that comes into his verses.

Often the technique employed is a direct allusion to commonly available instances of black musical experiment brought into the context of Jonas's thinking through of his relationship to modernist experiment in verse. The opening passages of Part IV of "Chorale and Hymn" are one of the most immediately graspable demonstrations of that technique. The poem commences with a prose statement: "CHORUS invocation key sentiment in the manner of the north american pop ballad—searching after the manner of Blue Miles number to close in on a jubilant choral hymn shouted as would a congregation of american 'nigger' foot washers" (*Selected Poems* 1994, 106). Typically, Jonas here joins together allusions to pop, jazz, and gospel, pointing the way to the syncretic continuum he will elaborate in the following verse lines. The prose opening is an opening of the text that begins and ends in the idea of communal spirituality and invention, and it acts as the "head" chart or initial statement of the choral theme on which the remainder of the poem improvises. Jonas summons Western literary tradition going back to Greek tragedy, a tradition with African antecedents in which the chorus serves as representative voice of the community, and the poet runs that tradition into the African American Amen Corner, the black spiritual chorus communally responding to and interacting with the thematic statements lined out by the leader of the congregation. The head chart establishes the key and thematic material, and in alluding to that tradition Jonas places it in the place where Western poetic tradition might call for an invocation of the muse. Appropriately for his purposes, the muse of much jazz is found in the suggestive passages of the popular song; one thinks of what Miles Davis does with the materials of "Someday My Prince Will Come," of what Coltrane accomplishes with "My Favorite Things" (or the even less expected "Chim Chim Cheree"), or, in an example Jonas might have appreciated had he lived to hear it, of the manner in which Sonny Sharrock took a black spiritual tradition that had been rendered into pop music during the folk music revivals of the 1950s and 1960s and deconstructed it as a reformulated masterwork of black improvisation on his recording of "All My Trials, Lord." The jazz improviser, like the black preacher and the gospel soloist, takes his text and takes his time, returning at the end to the restatement that is never repetition per se in jubilant choral shouting.

Jazz and pop ballads often include as counterstatement a "bridge" passage moving out of and back into the major theme. Sonny Rollins literalized the name of this compositional technique by removing himself to a New York bridge to practice his craft before returning with a reformed and transformed mastery to performances on the public stage. (It was an act reenacted with no small irony for a television commercial years later.) Following Jonas's prose opening, his page records a break in whose duration we might now imagine that we hear James Brown shouting "Take it to the bridge!"; and afterward Jonas both literally and figuratively enters his own bridge passage:

> . . . some
> men are
> born to horns.
> I waited for you the
> Bridge one
> Cranes from
> all over America
> 'Round about Midnite'
> waited
> and still
> waited by who
> frames the
> picture who
> the great
> Blue Miles. (106)

Among the overdeterminations of this passage may also be figured an inscription of Jonas's homosexuality, for he knows that Hart Crane's furtive assignations sometimes occurred under the same Brooklyn Bridge that gave its arc to Crane's epic poem. In his waiting under the bridgework of America 'round midnight, Jonas solos, meditating on his place as artist before the waters that have engulfed so many. He awaits the calling horn that brings in the chorus, and he is led to a statement of a "post-" aesthetic for those who come after the instigations of Cranes and Davises, Pounds and Williamses (Carlos and Big Joe). Jonas supplies a name for this aesthetic, and it turns out to be a name much like that which Nathaniel Mackey was later to construct. In Jonas's "Chorale and Hymn" we find lined out the "Discrepant Engagement" Mackey theorizes. Making use of techniques Mackey describes as "dissection" and "jamming," Jonas composes a score of texts in which "[d]iscrepant engagement, rather than suppressing resonance, dissonance, noise, seeks to remain open to them. Its admission of resonances contends with resolution. It worries resolute identity and demarcation, resolute boundary lines, resolute definition, obeying a vibrational rather than a corpuscular sense of being" (Mackey 20).

Jonas's discrepant engagement is one that fingers the jagged edges of literary, musical, and folk traditions, figuring in its very line breaks the movement from one statement of the theme to the next, figuring in its spaces its own difference from the predecessors embedded in its text:

From<br>
        the Bridge to<br>
the broken span and now<br>
comes the failure of the Poem as<br>
a Reconstructed<br>
                        Disconnection (*Selected Poems* 1994, 107)

It is once more important to remind ourselves that Jonas is writing *before* those critics' texts that have provided the vocabularies of postmodernity now so familiar to us had become widely available; his poem was written in 1955 and 1956. Jonas's "Reconstructed Disconnection" is a term derived from his encounters with the textual and musical traditions that formed his materials, not from any reading of poststructuralist criticisms. "Reconstructed Disconnection" might also serve as an apt descriptor of Jonas's own consciousness of race and sexuality. It is simply not the case that poststructuralist vocabularies of multiplicity and instability are an imposition on the "purer," more "authentic" texts of "minority" or "gay" writings, a pretext mashed down on a resistant body of "real" experiences. "Reconstructed Disconnection" *was* Jonas's authentic experience as it came to serve as the term he constructed for his aesthetics. Elsewhere in his poetry Jonas manipulates text on the field of the page, offering a visual analogue of such "Reconstructed Disconnections" as he brings folk materials into his stanzas. The twenty-third part of an untitled series, having already invoked the spirits of Jimmy Witherspoon and Gerry Mulligan, incorporates the lyrics of "Corinna Corinna" but unhooks the lyric lines from one another, both to suggest something of a possible mode of oral performance and to open spaces within the surface of the song for further improvisation. Jonas then appends a bluer comment to an already blue lyric:

> Corinna Corinna where'd you stay las nite?
>
> ya hair's a mess &
> yr clothes don't fit you rite
> tell me 'cause i wanna kno
> what makes yr head so hard
>
> oh the blues is all i got when
> i lost all my cash (*Selected Poems* 1994, 167)

Perhaps a paradigmatic episode of "Reconstructed Disconnection" is this eruption of one blues text *inside* another, followed by a third written into the song by the poet. In the very act of repeating and transfiguring "Corinna Corinna," Jonas interpolates an altered line from "Caldonia," as if a metonymic association between these two legendary, difficult women were signaled by a phonetic similarity in their names, as if Corinna were replicated and mutated within Caldonia (as if Joe Turner were unexpectedly joined by an antiphonal Louis Jordan). The poem, then, doesn't just appropriate a blues lyric; it actively interprets the tradition represented in a blues lyric by evolving it, working changes on it, signifying upon it, disconnecting and reconstructing it in a seemingly endless chain of blues meaning.

Jonas's reliance on the received materials of black speech and music, his rootedness in African American improvisatory aesthetics of antiphonal response, and his transmogrification of his materials in a sometimes failing process of "Reconstructed Disconnection" are most systematically enacted in his *Exercises for Ear,* a sequence in which he continually measures American language to produce what he calls "a formal rack / et in time" (*Selected Poems* 1994, 36). In these poems we witness Jonas's marking of time and linguistic space as graphic processes. Like the visual texts of Williams and the projective verse of

Olson, Jonas's poems must be seen as well as heard and thus serve as proof-texts of the aesthetic that finds its inspiration both in the song and speech practices of African American culture and in the inscription practices of African American spirit writing. The 118th poem of the sequence announces an immediate inspiration for its aesthetic in the person of Lester Young, at the same time hinting at a nineteenth-century predecessor for the marked departures from traditional metrical stanzaic patterns made by modernist verse and then revisited and revised by postmodern writers:

> & there was "Pres"
> horn horizontal aslant
> blowing nothin' but
> free verse (*Selected Poems* 1994, 76)

In Lester Young's curious signature posture, a truly eccentric physical approach to the saxophone, Jonas reads a precursor text for the form of the poem in which his tribute occurs. Further, as "Prez" so often can be heard alluding to other players with the solo lines he emitted from his slanting horn, Jonas seems to be embedding the eccentric forms of Emily Dickinson as a precursor for the formal feeling of his own free verse. He tells the truth, but he tells it slant, completing a successful circuit of literary and musical reference in stepping lines whose shape calls to mind the late stanzas of William Carlos Williams. The carefully orchestrated metrics of the opening quartet also show a Williams-like eye for lineation and rhythm as a means of guiding the attention, a concern clearly shared by Lester Young. The first four lines form a grammatical unit in which the first and the fourth lines each contain two strong stresses. The first line, with its opening "& there," achieves a syncopated, swinging feel, while the fourth line's two hard and even beats feel like a drummer's punctuation of a melody. The second and third lines are equal in measure, though composed of differing forms of feet, and the rhythm causes a reader's emphasis to fall naturally on the word *but,* bringing out an urban, colloquial usage: "blowing nothin' *but* free verse." The grammatical unit following this quartet of lines again begins with a conjunctive iamb, "& all," and again shows how an initial iamb can be jazzed: "& all them jitterbugs." Such measured movement of material in the poetic line seems to be what Jonas had in mind when describing the work as a formal racket in time. What might, to a more "academic" ear, appear to be noise is the measured soundscape, the racket, of jazz and free verse in the American idiom.

This "Exercise" is preceded immediately in the series by a tribute to Charlie Parker and to his death-defying ability to be right on time:

> once i saw Bird so high
>       that he came wingin'
> over from the apple
> w/a busted foot & a gig
>       to make at roll-a-way
> he came in on the chorus
>       from a wheelchair &
>       just made the bridge
> on one wheel (*Selected Poems* 1994, 76)

Many of the "Exercises" seem to arrive on the page with just this sense of breathless, near-failing perfection. What often have the look and feel of quotidian journal jottings and casual descriptions (one section begins, "say home / hear you / caught / the number" [78]) have, in fact, clearly been carefully constructed as sonic and visual experiments testing the limits of speech and writing as surely as Parker tested the limits of harmony and rhythm. In this, too, the *Exercises for Ear* resemble Williams's machines made with words, like the infamous poem containing a red wheelbarrow, which, once we start counting syllables and looking at the vowel sounds, turns out not to be such an artless, spontaneous note after all. The "Exercises" are like test pieces a musician attempts to see just how far a tune can be carried. Such experimentation was a lonely practice in the 1950s. In "Exercise X" Jonas declares:

> a hollow
>             victory
> you celebrate
> bird singing alone
>
> in this cold (*Selected Poems* 1994, 25)

This remarkable calibrated lyric is as resonant as Pound's "In a Station of the Metro." The "charged detail" is the bird itself. Even those few readers who do not already know that Charlie Parker was the legendary "Yard Bird" of bebop will probably look back to this poem from the vantage point of "Exercise CXVII's" jubilant celebration of Bird's last-minute Boston arrival and recognize that the yard bird of "Exercise X" is a natural analogue for the avant-garde enterprises of Jonas and Parker both.

Other exercises invoke specific music rather than individual musicians, both to celebrate the inventiveness of American popular song and to disconnect those lyrics from their traditional reception and reconstruct them in another context. "Exercise CVII" closes with the speaker, who is not the poet, offering an overironized put-down of the poet's vocation and sexuality:

> and you kan jus' kool-it
> on th' poeTREE the which you
> can save fer henry jones
> 'cause he doan
> eat noe greek (*Selected Poems* 1994, 72)

(Our bone-loving friend, Henry Jones, reappears in "Orgasm XXV," but there it is the more familiar "meat," not "Greek," that Henry don't eat [*Selected Poems* 1994, 244].) This method of ironically shifting the sense of songs so popular as to be recognized by most readers is a favorite tool of Jonas's. In "Exercise XXXIV" part of the humor derives from the fact that the poem appropriates an ancient (at least in American terms) lyric and vernacular cliché to signify quite differently from its usual usage. When we say or sing "Looked for you yesterday and here you come today," the usual sense, already heavy-laden with irony, is that the person addressed lacks Charlie Parker's ability to appear triumphantly just when we had about given up hope. But in Jonas's poem the lyric is turned against the addressee in a far different manner, for here the sense is that the speaker was seeking to avoid meeting up with the addressee. Hoping to stave off "the mediocre," the poem's persona has studiously set out to "omit" the poems of the addressee from his reading:

but here
in a yester-
day antholo-
gy

here
you come to-
day (*Selected Poems* 1994, 36)

The disconnection of the traditional lyric from its normative sense is never, of course, complete, and its reconstruction in a new, closely related, sense derives much of its irony from the continued resonance in our minds of that former directedness of meaning. Jonas's formal analogue for that lyric-reconstructed disconnection is the typographic separation of parts of words across the line breaks and blank page space, a technique practiced more radically and consistently in the *Orgasms* series. Jonas's formal racket in time is, as he puts it in "Exercise XXXV," "a means / of talkin' back" (36) in which he "back-talks" not only the individual addressee of a statement but also tradition and language themselves. The reconstructed disconnection of Jonas's visual text is a means by which he can reopen the overnaturalized relationships between words, and between words and things. Jonas writes against that privileging of oral tradition that has the effect of privileging a view of speech as transparent and unmediated. His poems, in contrast, participate in the modernist and postmodernist attempts to foreground the materiality of signifiers and the slipperiness of their significations. Like so many other early postmoderns, Olson and Ginsberg for example, he wants a poetics that renews emphasis on the embodiment of speech and the poem, but his is a poetics that refuses to see the written as a secondary and merely imitative recording of the oral. The graphic texture of the written poem, in Jonas's view, has the power to redirect speech and to retrain the ear. "Exercise LXIV," dedicated to Gerrit Lansing, begins:

the set-up of a poem
may not always please
the eye;
but the ear can be
led

conducted along
surprising causeways
where the hither- to un-
expected
(one might even venture un-
suspected)
comes in-
to prominence. (*Selected Poems* 1994, 51)

Jonas's *Exercises for Ear* is just such a leading of the ear along less-traveled causeways by means of the graphic. His poems use typography to apportion aural *and* visual space in much the same way that Miles Davis used silences to shape and underscore the causeways of his music.

For all Jonas's reliance on the materials and traditions of African American expressive cultures, it will always remain problematic to speak of someone who had such a contorted relationship to his own race as a black poet. Jean Toomer is now routinely included in collections of African American writing despite his having decided to live his life allowing people (mostly white) to take him for whatever they might assume he was (realizing, as he surely did, that they would take him for white); Stephen Jonas, who seems to have presented his race and ethnicity in a shifting pattern of identifications to suit his purposes of the moment, has just as routinely been omitted from collections and histories of recent black and white verse. It may be that no one looked for him yesterday and that he still won't come today. Unlike Toomer's, Jonas's texts are riddled with racisms and prejudices that will make his critical reception difficult, confusing, and distasteful. It would serve no useful purpose to evade the problems presented by Jonas's racism and anti-Semitism, but neither is it in the interests of literary history to leave Jonas's poems languishing in a world where our inability to fit him into America's racial cosmology as anything other than a traitor to whatever race we might assign him leaves the texts unread in a realm of unreading beyond black and white.

Jonas's writings will not easily be taken as the tragically warped posturings of a tragic mulatto. And while it is true that he rejected the activist poet's stance adopted by Baraka, it is also true that Jonas's writings do not back away from the revolutionary implications of racial politics in America. In "Orgasm XXXVI–Second Series," for example, a poem that is a working through of questions of political economy, Jonas pronounces an analysis that could have been written by Baraka:

> Piling up wealth with no out-put (useful) is adding woe
> unto woe.
>
> or the black haird people will
>
> and with premeditated fires
>
> burn the slums down . . . until local money INVEST to
>
> change your local lanscape. (Baraka papers, UCLA)

At certain places in his work it is evident that Jonas had thought through the fluidity of racial and racist definitions and had seen, as Baraka was to see when he rejected cultural nationalism in favor of Marxism, that color is no guarantee of a progressive politics. In "A Poet's Word to a Blue Painter" the poet delineates the false logic of reified color as predictive of morality or politics:

> (Bill,
> a nordic head,
> speaks, naturally
> with disgust of the white race
> for their impositions.
> what
> can you tell me , today
> kind of sense that makes
> as 'tho in the rat race
> shades could make differences
> Rats change their colors
> all like chameleons (Baraka papers, UCLA)

This, of course, makes a great deal of sense (one only has to think of a Clarence Thomas or a Hugo Black), and it is clearly as well as poetically expressed. But in the end, as in the end of this poem, Jonas's life experiences of American racial structures led him to a deep-seated misanthropy that can be as ugly as it is clever. As a result,

Jonas's poems will continue to offer the strongest resistance to any who may one day wish to enlist his work in even the most complicated of identity politics. For in the end Jonas saw even the most provisional of identifications as chameleon-like disguises. The concluding six lines of this poem read:

—black
    yellow,
        white
            homosexual or Jew—all
    of them the spew
                of the universe!

Such statements will not recommend Jonas to the new canonizers of multicultural studies (even those who might read them as a democratic sort of misanthropy), and they may finally render him as marginal a figure as the now marginalized Robinson Jeffers (who at least, white poet that he is, is still anthologized). One can't help wondering while reading Jonas's caustic and often beautiful works whether this poet who didn't like to be called black, but who enjoyed going places his blackness could take him away from whites, might be found, if racial conflagration came to him as it continually comes to us in America, shouting with the speaker of "Exercise CVI," "hey, / waitaminette / ahm kullood tu" (*Selected Poems* 1994, 71). (One can't help noticing a possibly incidental pun here on the Spanish informal mode of address, *tu*.)

There remains a great distance to be traveled in our attempts to understand the critical significance of Stephen Jonas's poetry, to understand his places in the recent history of American poetics, to understand all that he might mean to us now, and even to understand who Stephen Jonas in fact might have been. In 1966 Jonas himself inscribed an "Envoi" to his *Transmutations:*

travel far my things
til strange ears
            celebrate you
                in a prose Jamesian
for such is
        the delicate lacework
I have fashiond 'on (n.p.)

# 3
# *The Largest Ocean in the World: Amiri Baraka*

"You're too erudite." . . . What that mean?
—Amiri Baraka, *Fiction*

Ask Baraka.
—Bob Perelman, *Marginalization*

There is no reason any intelligent man should have it easy in America—especially not any intelligent black man.
—Amiri Baraka, *Home*

Perhaps LeRoi Jones could explain the pain
He knew some in Newark . . .
—John Wieners (255)

## I. FUGITIVE FICTIONS

In the aftermath of the artistic and popular success of his play *Dutchman,* Amiri Baraka felt the full force of white America's still regnant "one-at-a-time" reputation-manufacturing apparatus trained on him. The "Great White Way," as he puts it, began to flow, albeit briefly, in his direction, some other black artists resented his new opportunity to play the part of "that noble savage in the buttermilk," and, as he was to recall decades later in his *Autobiography,* "it was as if the door to the American dream had just swung open, and despite accounts that I was wild and crazy, I could look directly inside and—there—money bags stacked up high as the eye could fly!" (*Autobiography* 276). While most readers are aware today of the fact that Baraka's response had been to close that door tightly, not entirely politely, few are fully aware of the particular inducements that Baraka refused in the wake of all that buttermilk and whiteness. The gathering of metaphors in Baraka's reminiscences of those days is an indication of just how far the American language has had to reach for adequate representations of a racialized predicament that no white writer has ever really felt, but Baraka's unpublished papers indicate just how much he denied himself materially as a result of his decisions to guard the integrity of his artistic explorations. What was at stake was no less than Baraka's commitment to an aesthetics of innovation. Writing in *Cricket* in 1969, Baraka argued that "what is necessary is constant effort at achieving a total. At achieving something new" ("Notes" 46). What he was offered by America's commercial publishing establishment following the success of *Dutchman* (a work in which he had indeed achieved something new), and his subsequent media notoriety, was an opportunity to abandon that achievement, to achieve something not so new, in return for more money than he had ever before seen.

Just how much it was worth to corporate publishing to divert Baraka into its stable is apparent from correspondence with his agent. It was worth $75,000 to at least one editor, a significant sum even in 1970s-era currency. Among Baraka's unpublished papers that he has deposited at Howard University's Moorland-Spingarn collection are letters from William Targ, then editor-in-chief at Putnam, to Ronald Hobbs, Baraka's literary agent at the time. The subject of the correspondence is a fiction manuscript in progress that Targ hoped to publish. At one point Targ suggests a possible advance against royalties in the area of $75,000, a clear indication that Targ expected to sell a substantial number of copies of a second novel by Baraka. On April 9, 1974, Targ wrote to Hobbs to ask how Baraka's work on the book was progressing. By September of that year the staff at Putnams had read a draft of the novel; they did not like what they read. After reviewing Targ's earlier description of what he expected from this second novel, one has to wonder seriously if anyone at Putnams had read *The System of Dante's Hell,* Baraka's first novel, published by Grove Press.

What Putnams hoped to get from the author of *Dutchman, Black Magic,* and *Raise Race Rays Raze* was a sort of black version of *The Godfather,* a book that Targ had a hand in publishing. Mario Puzo's wildly successful commercial novel comes up more than once in Targ's letters to Baraka's agent; perhaps visions of movie tie-ins danced in Targ's head in those post-*Shaft* years. Targ reminds Hobbs in one letter of a manuscript conference that must have been a study in mutual misapprehension. On April 3 he writes to Hobbs: "You'll recall that I referred to *The Godfather* in our talks, and that we all agreed that the assigned novel should try for the same kind of strong plotting, and that we were in fact, striving for a popular novel that would be a successor to *The Godfather*." Targ goes on to urge that such a book must be structured in the "traditional or classic form," a form of "romantic realism," and warns specifically against the very hallmarks of Baraka's prose style: "At all costs scenario-notebook, surreal and symbolic techniques should be avoided" (Baraka papers, Howard University, Box 3). It is difficult to imagine what sort of "romantic realism" an editor might have expected to get from Baraka's pen, and Targ's conflation of romantic and social realism in this same letter must have been confusing to any author. In the end, at the cost of at least $75,000, Baraka submitted a novel that was often nonlinear in form, sometimes included imagery as surreal as the pages of *The System of Dante's Hell,* was constructed around a series of autobiographical scenarios, and was highly symbolic. That manuscript, titled *Six Persons,* never was published by Putnams. Its first chapter was resurrected a few years later for Baraka's *Selected Plays and Prose,* but the complete novel sat, unpublished, in a cardboard box in the basement of Howard University's Founders Library until the year 2000, when it finally appeared in Baraka's volume of collected fictions.

As the advocate of a "populist modernism," Baraka had no real objections to his work's becoming popular. Nor did he have any principled objection to being paid well for his work, which is why he had a literary agent in the first place. But when, in his introduction to *The Moderns,* Baraka proclaimed his dedication to writing that becomes "an event in itself" (xv), he did not have in mind the public event of a novel/movie such as *The Godfather* but rather a literature in which the writing *itself* is regarded as eventful—not simply because it narrates events but because something of true interest is happening *on* the page. All writing is *about* something, even such writing as takes nothing for its subject, but what Putnams wanted from Baraka was a novel that would be of interest primarily because of what it was about and who wrote it. William Targ wanted a book that would be for its readers a window onto a foreign (to *them*) world, a world of a certain racial authenticity or flavor. Baraka's words get in the way of such tourism, and he increasingly addressed himself to potential audiences for whom his world was not foreign turf. In the end it was not the novel's content, its perceived level of racial testament, or even its politics that disturbed Putnams. It was the writing itself that was rejected.

In the absence of a published volume of fiction in the years after *Tales,* many have erroneously concluded that Baraka had turned his back on the writing of fiction in the 1970s. In fact, he has continued to compose stories in varied forms throughout his career, and recent contributions to the short story anthology *Streetlights* and to the journal *Fertile Ground* indicate that Baraka's prose work has continued in the experimental directions visible in the earlier *Tales* and *The System of Dante's Hell.* Though he showed the manuscript of his second autobiographical novel to other publishers after it had been rejected by Putnams (*Conversations* 101), that book remained unpublished for a quarter of a century, and Baraka never undertook the publication of his works of fiction himself, as he has often done with poetry projects that commercial presses did not care to bring out for both aesthetic and political reasons. If the only things at stake in this aspect of Baraka's public reception history were amusing anecdotes about the ways of white editors, or even a lack of knowledge of the full extent of Baraka's prolific body of works, there might be less cause for critical concern. But too often critics have built elaborate suppositions on the basis of this absence, this lack of published narrative prose after *Tales.* At the close of his examination of Baraka's fiction in *Amiri Baraka/ LeRoi Jones: The Quest for a "Populist Modernism,"* for one example, Werner Sollors argues that already in *Tales* can be discerned a movement "from fiction to reality" (171). Projecting from his interpretation of Baraka's late-1960s collection of short stories, Sollors proceeds to an astonishing performance, the interpretation of a nonappearance: "Baraka has not published prose fiction in the years since *Tales;* and *Tales* may be considered the logbook of a fiction writer who, under the social pressures of the 1960s, catapulted himself out of writing fictions while writing a swan-song to telling tales. Baraka's concern for 'theories of government or prose' yielded to a predominant interest in government at the expense of prose fiction. As the voice of Baraka the story-teller retreated, the scream of the agitating poet-playwright-essayist of Black cultural nationalism reached its peak" (171).

This portrait is entirely too pat, however, playing as it does all too easily into media descriptions of Baraka as an artist who abandoned art for agit-prop. More important still, though, is the fact that even as Sollors was conducting the impressive research that went into his groundbreaking study of Baraka, Baraka himself was singing another sort of swan song entirely to the representatives of Putnams and other publishers; he had written another work like *The System of Dante's Hell,* a poetic narrative rooted in the realities of his own life that refused to represent itself as the mendacious social-romantic realism of the commercial publishing establishment. Baraka the storyteller had not sounded a final retreat and did not retreat even on the rejection of that second novel. Baraka the tale-teller has been among us all along. Like the character in his recently published tale "Rhythm Travel," he has been able to "disappear & reappear wherever and whenever that music played" (244); it is as if he had "turned into some Sun Ra and hung out inside gravity" while awaiting the proper opportunity to play his piece before a more willing audience.

Not only was Baraka writing fiction after *Tales;* he was writing fiction while Sollors was publishing his conclusions about Baraka's supposed renunciation of fiction. Among the several unpublished pieces among Baraka's manuscripts there is much of interest. There are three notebooks that contain preliminary work toward Baraka's published autobiography. One of these notebooks, titled *A Burning Mirror = Memoirs,* begins as a surreal jailhouse interrogation, a futuristic scenario in which "B/403" has been detained for violating the fictive "Publishing Act of 1990" (68). As the imprisoned B/403 looks back over his life, he recalls elements from *Six Persons* (49), demonstrating both the continued importance of that manuscript to Baraka's work and his continued mingling of the fictional with the autobiographical, despite Sollors's assumptions that would have driven a critical and authorial wedge between the realms of fact and fiction around 1970. At one point in *Burning Mirror* Baraka imagines the thought processes of B/403's captors, and it may be that we can read here a fictionalized version of Baraka's assessment of the thinking at Putnams a few years earlier: "Wouldn't it be great if they cd get one of the fat mouths of extremism to come clean . . . & give a big ol' public confession and media soaked announcement that he'd—wdnt it?—seen the light . . . Seen it, embraced it & was going to be part of it" (68–69). What Baraka rejected was the part designed for him by American commerce, a chance to be part of the traffic in ethnic confessionals, a part in the drama of a show trial of the 1960s; he did not reject the forms of fiction themselves.

There is much that *is* confessional about *Six Persons*. The narrator is particularly hard on the earlier versions of himself. Of his first name change (from "Leroy" to "LeRoi") the narrator says, "thas when he changed his name that first year in colored school, from english to french. why? it seemed cooler" (281). At one point in the version of the first chapter that appears in Baraka's *Selected Plays and Prose* Baraka underscores the book's connectedness to his own life: "This is my story. The story of I who was born in north east america. An African youth, hid under cotton futures. Hid under slavery, oppression." But the lines preceding this statement remind us that this is a life reshaped in memory and reformed in the telling of the tale: "This is my story. I. I tell it like I want to. Follow the eye, and you'll see" (203). Baraka's play on the "eye/I" homophony also restates a part of his developing aesthetics. More than a decade earlier he had said of Robert Creeley that the poet strikes "with his fiercest weapons first: SYNTAX. Creeley is always forcing you to rearrange your own eye, to disregard, or abandon any 'gestalt' you bring to merely reading a poem" ("A Form" 82). Baraka's prose is designed to effect a similar rearrangement of the eye, and thus of the consciousness, using the features of the rearranged language of his writing. The rearrangement of the eye is always also a rearrangement of the "I," as the title of *Six Persons*' first chapter indicates. This is not the kind of ghetto confessional Putnams required. The six persons of the book's title are the shifting grammatical and historic points of view from which Baraka constructs the ever-shifting narrative of his book and of himself. The chapter that was first published, "I," certainly would appear a less problematic form, more familiar to readers of popular autobiography and *The Godfather* alike than the later chapters narrated from the point of view of "Yall" or of "We & All," but even the very singular first person of Baraka's first chapter is a teeming congress. Just here we can see what Baraka might share with other authors of the postmodern and where he differs from them. *Six Persons* is as good a critique of Western humanism's idealized individual subject as any to be found. Witness the novel's comic critique of the Cartesian subject: "Descartes there on his back chortling like a baby, i i i i i i think i i i i i think i i i i i i think, therefo i is" (271). This passage echoes the ending of Baraka's 1965 essay "New Black Music," an ending that sounds perhaps a little more Eliotic than we might expect (but isn't that part of what it means to be *post*modern), where the poet remarks that "New Black Music is this: Find the self, then kill it" (*Black Music* 176). The relationship between the late-1960s Black Arts assault on Western individualism and the simultaneous questioning of subjectivity among the more radical Western philosophers is a phenomenon that is too often ignored. Baraka had clearly not been perusing Derrida or Foucault just before penning these lines, nor had these French philosophers read Baraka's unpublished novel. Baraka's book, though, also demonstrates his ongoing search for totality, something that would set him apart from most postmodern philosophy. The "total" that Baraka spoke of achieving in his early essays and notes, the same total that he still seeks in such late poems as "Allah Mean Everything," appears in *Six Persons* as "all the reality, its multiple addresses, and parallel appearances. Awash in a see of others" (200). Baraka has not put fiction behind him in order to govern the real. Rather he has recognized that a writing of the real must make multiple addresses and parallel appearances. If one is to present the real it must be shown as a simultaneous apparition of these faces in a crowd, multiple viewpoints, not the linear plodding of the traditional first-person plot so desired by Putnams' editors. In *Burning Mirror* B/403 says to his interrogators: "Baraka thats my name. You want LeRoi Jones? You want Everett Jones?" (16). His tormentors, unlike some of Baraka's publishers, want it all: "We want you to tell us all your names. We see them as realities" (16). For Baraka, to interrogate even oneself is to look for a subject "awash in a see of others."

Theodore R. Hudson, in *From LeRoi Jones to Amiri Baraka,* remarks that "one may read *Tales* to see what it is possible to do with language" (123), a comment so commonsensical that its importance might be overlooked. Hudson's critique of Baraka's prose, published five years prior to that of Sollors, does not anticipate a future disappearance from published fiction by Baraka and thus does not offer assumptions about political and aesthetic motivations for any turn away from tale-telling. It is doubtful that Hudson would have made such an assumption in any event, not only because he recognized, as did Sollors, that Baraka was a prolific artist drawn to multiple genres but also because he understood that Baraka would not likely close the door on such a productive laboratory as prose narrative had proved for him. In 1991 Baraka told Charlie Reilly that the manuscript of *Six Persons* was "a very ambitious book stylistically" (*Conversations* 241). He remembers that the proposed publisher "absolutely hated it" and that he had been asked by his editor, "why don't you do it over in a simple style, something like *The System of Dante's Hell*?" (241), advice that crystallizes Putnams' conception of the book while once again raising the question of whether anyone at the publisher's office had actually read that earlier novel. Baraka was interested in writing that directly addresses the real, but he knew the difference between the simple and the simplistic. In the fourth chapter of *Six Persons*, titled "They (Them Theeirs Theyres &C)," Baraka writes of a time, parallel to his own Village days, when "they ran into some straight out aesthetes from [Black] Mountain College, who said, shave all that extraneous sensuality outta the shit and get down to the flat bizness of creating a new academia" (*Fiction* 320). The key here is that in writing, as in bringing into being a new academia, it was the *extraneous* that was to be stripped away. To strip further would be to tear away the necessary, and that truly would be simple, and that Baraka refused to do.

At the opening of her essay "Anonymous in America," an essay that closed the 1978 special supplement on Baraka in the journal *boundary 2*, Sherley Anne Williams worried that in the future Baraka's literary accomplishment might be reduced to a black footnote to white bohemia, that he will be presented only as someone who "was at the cutting edge of mid-twentieth century American literature. Black Arts and Black Consciousness and Black Liberation will be explained away in a footnote like Harlem (a Negro area in New York) in the *Norton Anthology of Literature*" (435). She ends her essay with the admonition that "we won't have Baraka remembered as just another of the old (white) boys" (441). To judge from some of the published evaluations of Baraka there may be some justification for Williams's worries. Many college anthologies continue to present Baraka's post-Village poetry, particularly his post–cultural nationalism, Marxist works, as bizarre footnotes to his earlier work, and most such anthologies studiously avoid the reprinting of Baraka's prose. But a return to Baraka's long uncollected and fugitive fictions might make such reductive treatments more difficult to sustain (they should already be an embarrassment to any who present themselves as careful readers), for in those works, as indeed in his better-known publications, we can see just how strongly Baraka has resisted such reduction all along. Reading Baraka's fiction alongside the mass of his collected works should make even more evident the fact that Baraka, from the outset, was placing himself as a black artist in the position simultaneously of precedent to the white avant-garde and as a significant post- to their postmodernity.

In his 1963 review of E. U. Essien-Udom's *Black Nationalism* Baraka denounced those who are "impressed with what it is to be an exotic minstrel in this strange deadly time" ("Uncle" 89). Though Baraka learned much from his white colleagues in the artistic underground of the late 1950s and early 1960s, he was no more willing then than he was ten years later to serve as anyone's exotic minstrel. His early ambitions, as he explained in a 1962 letter to Rosey Pool, were quite different:

> To write beautiful poems full of mystical sociology and abstract politics.
> To show America it is ugly and full of middleclass toads (black & white).
> To become a great political agitator and invade Britain.

And although he was to welcome the sense he got from reading Ginsberg and others that here was the possibility of a united front for a truly popular aesthetic rebellion, Baraka would always stake a claim for modernity's black origins. In the third-person-plural chapter of *Six Persons* Baraka is scathing in his descriptions of those who only valued black innovation when it had been covered and played back to them in the authorizing redactions of white mimicry, those who "only dig they soul watered down" (321). Baraka describes the ludicrous sight of those who "stood and listened to ag [Allen Ginsberg] be them in a yarmulka, and put on the mammy jammin yarmulka and imitated him being them" (322). Anyone listening to the career-spanning collection of recordings of Ginsberg's readings, *Holy Soul Jelly Roll* (whose very title is a borrowing from African American musical traditions), will note a decided change in Ginsberg's mode of verbal performance very early on, and it is a transformation that appears to have much to do with Ginsberg's own renderings of the styles of blackness as he perceived them in his experience, at least as much as it has to do with his appropriations of the modes of the Jewish cantor and of Hindu and Buddhist chants. This is one reason that Baraka may have felt that he was meeting himself coming and going as he read the work of the Beats.

In *Six Persons'* second-person chapter, Baraka remembers that "you cd sit copyin ee cummings meticulously out of some absolutely unun-derstood text. Tho you must have understood, something. Something of what beyond the instant lesson, it 'meant'" (254). A young Baraka learned, though, that this was simply "the facade of a culture" that he had consumed, and that the danger was always thus: "What you eat, gets a chance to eat you. From the inside!" (254). Baraka consumed reading matter the way a famished Wimpy consumes burgers, and he had thoroughly absorbed the lessons of Pound, Williams, Eliot, and the other moderns he shared as a common heritage with the Beats, the New York School, and the Black Mountain group. He also knew that each of these moderns had taken a turn at poetic blackface, had spoken the white man's black English. So an encounter with Allen Ginsberg's "Howl," while liberating, was for Baraka like a trip to the hall of mirrors, "awash in a see of others." Still, Baraka had a strong sense of the immense resources of black modernisms. "They were them-selves," he writes of himself in the third-person plural, "like black ice-bergs rising out the underwater American reality" (*Fiction* 349).

This last is an especially powerful image in Baraka's manuscripts, which are themselves like those metaphorical depths supporting the visible promontories of his published books, and in its doubleness it figures the specific contours of the African American postmodern that Baraka was bringing into being in his writing. In *Six Persons* he sees the looming heights of black culture afloat in a sea of whiteness, supported by the immense volume of things unseen. This is also a trope for African American history, still, at the time of his writing, inadequately charted but evident in the consciousness of the visible subjects of contemporary America, the historical and political uncon-scious of the nation itself. The doubleness of the image, the towering peaks and the voluminous depth, again embodies for Baraka the largely unsung black base of historical and cultural modernity and the black contemporaneity rising above the smothering covering of its surroundings. That doubleness is refigured at the end of a 1967 essay in *Negro Digest,* a text that began as a letter to editor Hoyt Fuller, where Baraka calls for an art that encompasses "the first learnings of man. While we fly into the next epoch." As Baraka viewed things in 1967, the goal was to achieve "a post-American form. An afterwhite-ness color and re-erect the strength of the primitive" (*Raise* 34). Just as he desired a drama that would at once tear down and build up,

Baraka wanted an art that was simultaneously futuristic and primitive. As William Carlos Williams wanted to rescue the rose from its history of use and abuse so that it could once more be used to write of love, Baraka sought to tear away the wrappings of Euro-modernist primitiv*ism* to bring a primitive to light, so that the first and last learnings of humanity could be conjoined in a post-American, postmodern, after-whiteness.

Baraka was far from the first to have posited that the superstructures of Western modernity rested uneasily on a historic base of slavery and of black cultural invention. Historians including C. L. R. James and W. E. B. Du Bois had established that argument during the decade of Baraka's birth. Critics such as Alain Locke and Sterling Brown (one of Baraka's most memorable professors during his time at Howard University) had outlined the contributions of black artists in the New World and in Africa to modernisms high and low. Poets, among them Melvin B. Tolson, had made the black strata of modernism a theme of major works and had structured their epic forms around the shapes of that history. Amiri Baraka, however, constructed his modes of contemporaneity around a yet more audacious claim to simultaneous pre- and postmodernity, bringing into being a form of the future anterior more daring than anything previously seen in African American letters. Baraka wrote of a "post-prebirth enlightenment" (*Fiction* 3), an enlightened critique of the Enlightenment delivered from the possible-impossible double posture of one who writes both before and after the avant-garde of his own generation.

It is in another of Baraka's fugitive fictions that we can most readily sight his simultaneous appearing and disappearing act, a story titled "Suppose Sorrow Was a Time Machine" that was printed in the second issue of Baraka's own magazine *Yugen,* a journal he coedited with Hettie Jones. Both the title and the Victorian-looking illustration that accompanied the tale on its first appearance repeat that trope of doubleness and the future anterior (it is an old-fashioned futurism that Baraka alludes to here), Baraka's intent mingling of the untold past with the unforeseen (at least by white America) future. The story joins together Baraka's youthful enthusiasm for science fiction and popular culture with his dedication to reconnecting the black past to its cultural future, a joining Baraka continues to thematize in such recent fictions as "Rhythm Travel." It also previews the techniques of *Six Persons* with its use of second-person point of view. The story's

second paragraph introduces you to the "you" of the narration in midsupposition, enacting the odd grammatical tense of the title. We read, "Say that you are Tom Russ" (*Fiction* 1), and are thus asked by way of this second-person mode of address to occupy the imagined historical ground of Baraka's predecessor, his grandfather, who also figures prominently in more frequently read works such as "Black Dada Nihilismus" and *The System of Dante's Hell.* Talking to himself and to us on paper, Baraka transports us, or "you" to be precise, to the Dothan, Alabama, of 1898: "You are a Negro who has felt the ground vibrate, and you are trying to interpret the vibration. You are trying to interpret the vibration, and what it means in 1898 Dothan. I know you Tom. You are my grandfather. I am not born yet but I have felt the ground vibrate too" (*Fiction* 1).

By means of the displacement writing affords as time machine, the author becomes the not-yet-born. He opens a passage between himself and his absent grandfather, a passage along which the same vibration travels from one generation to another. It is a passage in which the body of the present is translated into the past to interpret, from its source, the ominous vibrations the unborn child senses through the womb, the maternal passage connecting grandfather and grandson. "Let your unborn grandchild know what his dead, whistling grandfather thought." Tom Russ was a shopkeeper whose store was burned down by racists. He rebuilt it, "knelt back down in those ashes and scraped the black off again, and built again" (2). Black ash and the brilliance of flame, these once more doubled images of brilliance and savagery form a dialectic that works its way through all of Baraka's works. He asks rhetorically, "How obscure is enlightenment?" just before retelling his grandmother's explanation of Tom Russ's final years. Baraka's grandmother told him that "They" dropped a streetlight on Russ's head and scattered his brains. There is an obvious parallel between Baraka's question and his grandmother's narrative. The modernity produced by the Enlightenment made the darkness darker, produced the black ash to which Russ's neighbors reduced his labors. In the iconography of cartoons, enlightenment is signified by a lightbulb going on over a character's head. In the ironic iconography of grandmother Russ the visible sign of the modern, the electric streetlight, puts out the brilliant light of her husband's mind. (The ironies rebound decades later when Baraka appears in a fiction anthology titled *Streetlights,* whose editors choose their title to symbolize the illumination that black people bring.)

Baraka imagines that he can advise his grandfather across the boundaries of place, space, and time, that he can convince Tom Russ to carry himself to the North. More than that, he speaks out of the future *to* his grandfather's tormentors, the leading (as opposed to the leaving) citizens of Dothan, the white representatives of the modernizing South at century's turning: "Goodbye, crackers, Tom Russ is leaving your town. His grandson'll be back to correct your grammar and throw stones in your well. Fifty years ain't so long" (2). And sure enough, a half century or so later, here is Baraka's prose narrative published in fulfillment of prophecy.

There is yet another turn in this timeless story, as Baraka once more displaces his own words into his family's past. As he imagines his grandfather transplanted to the Newark of 1925, he translates his own poetry into the past he has himself inherited. He imagines "Tom Russ, standing there trying to remember some of his unborn grandson's poems" (2). What better example of the "always already" could be conjured than this writing of the past as prologue in which that prologue is afterward to the writing, in which the prologue has been transported back in time, after the fact, to precede itself. As Baraka travels along the fold in time, tracking past and promise, he arrives at the birth of black modernism. Whichever definitions of African American modernity we might deploy, Houston Baker's as well as that of David Levering Lewis, the Great Migration of southern blacks to the urban, industrial North is a defining feature. Baraka writes himself into the past as precedent so that in "Suppose Sorrow Was a Time Machine" he appears both as big-eyed boy anxiously awaiting his grandfather's tale and as author of that tale. "Have you got time, Tom?" Baraka asks the ghost of his grandfather. "Can you remember any of those lines, Tom? Tell the saucereyed boy at your feet. Maybe they'll do him some good" (11).

Hence in this telling Baraka's lines come to him with the authorizing imprimatur of his family's past, in the authenticating form of his African American cultural legacies, but at the same time he is the author of his own inheritance. The poetry that Tom Russ recalls, that verse he will contribute to his grandson's repertoire of cultural knowledge, is the not yet written poetry of Amiri Baraka, the poetry that Baraka will build out of the vibrations he has sensed emanating out of that same past, that futuristic, projective, postmodern poetry he will construe with the black consciousness willed to him in his grandfather's narrative. Baraka's "post-prebirth enlightenment" projects from that fold in historical consciousness that Baraka traces in memory and in prose fiction. His writing is a time machine by means of which, like the blues themselves, he memorializes and at the same time transforms sorrow into art. (In his *Autobiography* Baraka recalls that his grandmother, though she didn't live to see a full book of his, had seen and liked this early tale commemorating her husband [21–22].)

This story, in which the child is grandfather to the man, is not *The Godfather,* is not the simple social romance of realism that Putnams dreamed of selling on their auction block. It is an effort to explore fully the possibilities offered to the present by the past that we now imagine. The narrative's fluid point of view points to Baraka's early and sustained efforts to renew experience in the crucible of art. In a 1976 letter Baraka makes clear just how the metamorphosed perspectives of time mark the distinctions among the personal narratives he is writing. Still trying to interest a commercial publisher in the manuscript of *Six Persons* (at exactly the time Werner Sollors believed Baraka was making a politically determined choice against prose fiction), Baraka writes on September 21, 1976, responding to queries from Ken Stuart in the midst of attempts to place the book with Macmillan, and distinguishing his new text from his first novel: "What you say about seeing the past from the perspective of the present is true. I don't want to write the book I wd have written when those events were happening. That wd be Dante pt 2."

*Six Persons* is neither the second part of *The System of Dante's Hell* nor the first part of *The Autobiography of LeRoi Jones/Amiri Baraka*. It is a work in which "a see of others" defines the multiplying perspectives of the writing as Baraka attempts to achieve the new that emerges from its place within the old. The text is an instrument of that "sensitivity to the world total, to the American Total," that Baraka addresses in his introduction to David Henderson's first book of poetry. It is one of those "local epics with the breadth that the emotional consciousness of a culture can make" (*Raise* 35–36). Baraka took this local epic to America's mainstream publishers, but they wanted none of it. "You went to the main stream," he writes in the second-person-plural chapter, "& found it sluggish & unmoving—reflecting blackness, repetition, blind follies, mirrors" (174).

The future that Baraka renounced in the early 1970s comes into view in his own rejected book, in the brown face of the fictive Harris Sullivan, glimpsed near the book's conclusion, "the noted black poet, . . . now poet in residence to this largest insurance company in the world he explains. He rises & reads his latest epic, 'Whitey Better Increase The Stock Options'" (461). The past on which his own epic rests, the route traveled again in his poem *Wise, Why's, Y's*, is also visible in *Six Persons*. But as in "Suppose Sorrow Was a Time Machine," here the past is confronted coming and going at the crossroads of the narrative present: "Hawkins stares through night using the moon as a crystal outlined against the sea. He barely sees these words scrawled in a ledger crossing the ocean the other way. The Jesus bulks its prow toward America—Afrikans turning to niggers just below the water line. He will not warn them" (*Fiction* 396). When he went down to the crossroads, Baraka relinquished the chance to become the Godfather of the Black Arts, to impersonate a commodity fetish. By choosing "not to take up the ankh instead of the cross, but to pull down all invisibilities" (457) he nearly became the invisible poet, and he did become the invisible man of America's fiction industry. But the achievement of Baraka's fictions remains, a massive form joining the visible promontories afloat in, to take the title of one of his *Tales,* "The Largest Ocean in the World."

## II. "THE A, B, C's"

I'm saying that the short story always exists as water dipped for drinking from an unlimited water, a big sea . . . the story wants to make sense. The poetry is what sense is made out of.

—Amiri Baraka, "*Northern Iowa*"

Inherence
is black

—Charles Olson, *Nation*

Olson died!

—Amiri Baraka, *Fiction*

More than three decades after Baraka published "Suppose Sorrow Was a Time Machine," M. Nourbese Philip suggested that memory "is the activity that fuels the imagining of the past and the remembrance of the future" (21), a suggestion that could have grown directly from the future anterior of Baraka's early time machine. Baraka's readers have also constructed historic imaginaries of Baraka's past. Some among his critics have been content to suppose what that past must have been without troubling very much about reading in the textual record. A stunning example is Lewis Turco's 1994 essay, "Amiri Baraka's Black Mountain," published in the *Hollins Critic,* in which Turco supplies a date, 1954, for the BA degree that Baraka did not in fact receive, despite Baraka's having firmly set the record straight on this count in his 1984 *Autobiography*. Turco's error on this point is repeated in *The Cambridge History of American Literature,* despite that volume's promise to "provide the fullest and most up-to-date biographical information available to scholarly analyses" and the citation of the very *Autobiography* in which Baraka makes clear that he did not receive a BA during his Howard years (von Hallberg 111, 236). Lewis Turco also renders Baraka's changed name as "Amimu" instead of "Imamu"

Amiri Baraka and asserts that Baraka's early poems "were not greatly different from Lowell's" (4). Turco's essay is accompanied by a bibliography, evidently prepared by an editorial assistant, in which the title of Baraka's play *Jello* becomes simply "Jell" and Baraka's more recent volume *Wise* is identified as *Shy's* (10). The overt purpose of Turco's essay is to separate Baraka from earlier African American lyric modes and to identify his verse as an unfortunate replication of Olson, which was an unfortunate replication of Pound's most unfortunate poetics. According to Turco, what Baraka writes and has always written is lined prose. (Perhaps Sollors, by this account, simply had not recognized that Baraka had taken to writing prose fiction in lines rather than paragraphs.) In Turco's rendering of Baraka, "there is little of Hughes's blues to be found here" (7). Turco wishes to divide Baraka entirely from poets writing metered, stanzaic verses. In his view: "Baraka did not transform either the academic confessional period style of the 1960s, or Olson's prosodic peculiarities into his own style any more successfully than Olson transformed Pound's, or as successfully as Hughes, Hayden and Brooks combined black ethnic traditions with English formal techniques to make a poetry as effective as any written during the period of protest and after" (8). Turco, who isn't sure of Baraka's name, who thinks there was a discrete "period of protest" (now well behind us it would seem), and who can't seem to see to it that Baraka's titles are correctly reproduced, is absolutely sure that the real place to look for the successful poetic representation of "black ethnic traditions" is in poems guided by "English formal techniques."

Where some African American critics have been concerned to distance Baraka from early white colleagues in the artistic bohemia, Turco wants to glue Baraka to them as an exemplar of the nonpoetic. While Turco's essay is an extreme instance, other writers have practiced a similar reimagining of Baraka's past. Stephen Henderson singles out a singularly egregious example in Robert F. Moss's "The Arts in Black America." Moss writes: "Perhaps the last important 'accommodationist' was Baraka, a competent beat poet who was beached by the receding currents of that short-lived movement in the early Sixties. Taking the techniques of Ginsberg & Co.—a declamatory voice, deliberate formlessness, street language—and fusing them to virulent outbursts of racial protest, Baraka was able to found a new school of black poetry" (qtd. in Henderson, "Black Poetry" 152). Decades later, as we witness the remarkable continued popularity of Beat writing and the succession of anniversary tributes and conferences organized around varied Beat figures, Moss's remarks about the "short-lived" Beat movement seem as curious as his identification of Baraka as an "accommodationist" black artist. The evidence of Baraka essays written prior to his cultural nationalist period, some of which appear in the collection *Home,* should provide ample evidence to Moss or anybody else that the younger LeRoi Jones was far from being anybody's accommodationist. Stranger still is Moss's suggestion that Baraka had founded "a new school of black poetry" on a repertoire of techniques entirely derived from white writers, an assertion that can only be made in a critical vacuum, in a self-induced ignorance of the multitude of statements made by white Beats attesting to the importance of black culture to their own aesthetic development.

Far from being an accommodationist, Baraka has declared, with his accustomed air of certainty, that "disassociation from the mainstream—that is, what is said to be real by the white American image makers—is a very great virtue" ("Philistinism" 55). That comment was delivered to an audience at a conference titled "The Negro Writer in the United States" sponsored by the University of California Extension in August of 1964. Tape recordings made at the conference reveal embryonic versions of the positions taken by such later critics as Moss and Turco, criticisms that try in one way or another to redefine Baraka's relationships to black life and white artists in such a manner as to confirm the presuppositions of the critic. The major essays presented at the conference were subsequently published in revised form in the collection *Anger and Beyond,* edited by Herbert Hill, who had served as the conference director. But for a fuller sense of the discussions that took place before and after the papers and readings at this conference one must turn to other sources.

In his *Autobiography* Baraka recalls that the celebrity suddenly thrust upon him after the success of *Dutchman* made him "the bull's-eye of the joint" (280). On the tape recording of Baraka's poetry reading at the conference later circulated by Pacifica Radio, an eerily familiar debate takes place at the close of Baraka's presentation. In the course of that debate a parade of white critics, including Robert Bone (whose analysis of James Baldwin had produced one of the most explosive sessions at the conference), took the microphone in attempts to pry Baraka from, or glue him to, varied aesthetic positions they had staked out in advance. The white critics can be heard to mount a concerted effort to get Baraka and Gwendolyn Brooks, who was also reading at the conference, to disavow one another. Brooks and Baraka, though, proved unwilling to play that game, and it was left to the critics themselves to drive a wedge between them. Kenneth Rexroth, chair for the evening's readings, closed the debate by announcing that the audience would just have to learn to "dig" Baraka's work. Judging from contemporary accounts of the conference, not much digging went on. Poet Adam David Miller, who attended as a Berkeley graduate student, wrote in his review of the encounters at Asilomar over the weekend that, "faced with a body of literate Negroes possessing some knowledge, who are not anxious to please, whites are nonplussed" (11). Perhaps the most thoroughly nonplussed was Robert Bone. When a few black people in the audience during his essay on Baldwin dared to demur from his conclusions, he blurted out, according to witness Miller: "You Negroes should grow up and learn to take criticism" (10). Capturing moments of consummate miscommunication that characterized the age, Miller observes that white intellectuals too often "simply refuse to believe it when a Negro tells them he knows more about himself than they do; and Negroes insist on feeling that the fact of their uniqueness makes real communication with them by whites impossible" (11).

The aesthetic divisions that came into view at the California conference in 1964 were not purely racial, but they were given a racial turn. Many of the white critics in attendance seemed intent on playing a perverse game of "good Negro—bad Negro." The poet selected for the role of good Negro was our Miss Brooks, whose poetry till then had featured the very formal fittings later so highly praised by Turco. The bad Negro was to be bad, bad LeRoi Jones; he who consorted with Beats, Baraka. In his review of the conference for the *Nation* Kenneth Rexroth reported that "any attempt to create a literary antagonism or schism between Miss Brooks and Mr. Jones was fiercely resisted by ordinary people in the audience. This was not just 'defending our own.' It revealed a degree of understanding of how poetry works that would be very unlikely in an all-white audience" ("Panelizing" 98). The critics' attempted division was thrown into confusion momentarily when Brooks refused her role and remarked that she had learned much from the then still young LeRoi. Baraka's riposte was already written in his conference presentation, later published as

"Philistinism and the Negro Writer": "The Negro writer can only survive by refusing to become a white man" (56), hardly an accommodationist position. However, Baraka continued to insist on his prerogative to accommodate within his own work that which he found to have real use value within the poetries of white writers: "So that if T. S. Eliot says something about the essential strength of language as image, I take it to mean me. If Pound says something about image as emotional and intellectual complex, I take it to mean me. If Apolinaire says something about space-time relationship or sense-drama or philosophical abstracts, that is my reality . . . something that I can use, where I am, in my ghetto or outside of that ghetto, but available as air is, or love is. It's there. You know it" (60). Baraka believed that no black writer could accomplish art in America by trying to be white, nor could any black writer who wrote out of a motivation to please white people expect to create original art. Some white people hearing this message were not pleased, were nonplussed, perhaps because they recognized here a turn in the discourse, the passing of a post; it wasn't about them.

When we leave behind the kind of presuppositions that have so often marked criticism of Baraka's career and return to reading Baraka's early texts, it becomes clear that the poet's work is more of a piece than has generally been credited. His totalizing impulse was already evident long before he became a Marxist, before his period of cultural nationalism, as can be seen in the early nonfiction works of *Home*. His commitment to a poetics in the tradition of African American cultural innovation was not birthed in the moment of his break with the Beats and his change of name, nor did he leave Appolinaire behind in the Village when he returned to his native Newark. In his sixth decade, as in his third, what Baraka valued was "not the writing that reflected those tired white lives again, but necessarily those people, those white and black people who were talking about a side of America that was more valuable because it hadn't been talked about" ("Philistinism" 60).

"Has the story of Allen Ginsberg, Peter Orlovsky, Ray Bremser, Greg Corso, Philip Lamantia, and even mad ½ black Bob Kaufman been told?" Baraka asks himself in *Six Persons* (*Fiction* 336). "Well somebody'll tell it," he answers himself. The tale of the Beats has too often been half a tale, albeit full of sound and fury, and the stories of such innovative black artists as Stephen Jonas, Bob Kaufman, Harold

Carrington, Gloria Tropp, even Baraka himself have yet to get adequately told. The major biographies of Ginsberg give only scant space to Baraka, who was a crucial colleague. Critics such as Moss and Turco would have us believe that half of the tale of American poetry and culture, casually and inaccurately rendered, is the whole story. Allen Ginsberg knew better.

In an interview included in St. Clair Bourne's film documentary about Baraka, *In Motion,* Ginsberg remembers that the one and only time he ever met Langston Hughes was in Amiri Baraka's living room, underscoring the fact that Baraka has always been a nexus for the modern and the post. But then Baraka, by theorizing the "changing same" in *Blues People* and elsewhere, had, even while calling himself one of *The Moderns,* brought into full view a postmodern that had been there before Olson had used the term, a blacker postmodern than ever contemplated by Toynbee, the African diasporic postmodernity that had been prefigured by C. L. R. James and W. E. B. Du Bois.

By the time Allen Ginsberg returned to the United States from Paris in the late 1950s, Baraka was already active at the heart of an ever-expanding group of artists intent on the creation of what would shortly come to be known as the New American Poetry. Gordon Ball, in his notes to Ginsberg's mid-1950s journals, reports that it was Peter Orlovsky "who introduced him to LeRoi Jones and his circle of younger poets" (347). In fact, though, this was a reintroduction of sorts, as the two poets had already exchanged letters following Baraka's first reading of "Howl" (Baraka, *Autobiography* 219–20). Baraka recalls that Orlovsky, Ginsberg, and he "even hung out one night at a place on Seventh Avenue South, where Kerouac was reading with Phillip Lamantia and Howard Hart. There was a sense of community growing among some of the young writers, and I was one of them as well as the editor of one of their magazines" (*Autobiography* 225). What has been striking in the literary histories written in the years since has been how often critics and historians, even historians of the community Baraka describes, have proven unwilling to acknowledge the significance of what must be seen in retrospect as America's first racially integrated avant-garde. While it is true that this community was not free of racial prejudice and tension, some of which is described in Baraka's memoirs of his movement toward the Black Arts period, only the Depression-era radical social movements had seen as extensive interaction between black and white writers, and never before in

American literary history had black artists exercised such far-reaching influence on white writers. Within a very short time Baraka had established contacts with Gary Snyder, William Burroughs, Ted Joans, Philip Whalen, Robert Duncan, Gilbert Sorrentino, Ray Bremser, Stephen Jonas, Diane Di Prima, Tom Postell, Jack Micheline, Ron Loewinsohn, Allen Polite, Gregory Corso, and Bobb Hamilton. He met Leroy McLucas, briefly manager of a Village jazz club, who was later to figure in the Umbra group, whose photographs appeared on the covers of many important jazz albums, and who became an important friend and traveling companion of Ed Dorn's. The Black Mountain artists became a core grouping within Baraka's early community, and he numbered among his friends both Ed Dorn and Fielding Dawson.

In 1959 Baraka participated in a marathon reading (the source of that now famous picture of Jack Kerouac reading, arms stretched out, from a stepladder) that included Kerouac, Ginsberg, Corso, Joans, and Jose Garcia Villa. Kerouac particularly valued Baraka's work as an editor, predicting in a letter to Allen Ginsberg of *Kulchur, Yugen,* and *Beatitude,* "all those lil things will grow into big DIALS in time—" (*Letters* 219). One of the many things to remark about this list of little magazines is that, unlike the *Dial* of a previous generation's avant-garde, all three of these publications were in large part the result of the efforts of black poet/editors Baraka and Bob Kaufman. Elsewhere, Kerouac calls Baraka, then known as LeRoi Jones, a "[h]istoric publisher, secret hipster of the trade." This description appears in *Lonesome Traveler,* as Kerouac recounts a party at the Jones home at the time of publication of a new *Yugen* issue, a recounting that both underscores the sense of community among these writers and hints at some of the tensions that would lead to later ruptures: "he's got a new issue of Yugen Magazine which he printed himself on a little cranky machine and everybody's poems are in it, from San Francisco on to Gloucester, and costs only 50 cents. . . . —Leroi's getting sick of parties, everyone's always taking off his shirt and dancing, three sentimental girls are crooning over poet Raymond Bremser, my buddy Gregory Corso is arguing with a New York *Post* reporter . . . " (115).

When the 1958 *Partisan Review* published an attack on Kerouac's writing, Baraka challenged the assumptions of the review in a letter to the editors. Even here we can see that Baraka was already positioning himself as far more than a follower of the Beat scene. "As with

Dada," he writes, "Beat represents a line of departure rather than a concrete doctrine" (qtd. in Kerouac, *Selected Letters* 121). Not only literary critics but some of the artists who participated in these communities contemporaneously seem unable in memory to reconstruct the full extent of the contributions of black writers. Even Joyce Johnson, who remembers Hettie and LeRoi Jones as the first interracial couple she had ever met, forgets how interracial their small press magazine was. In a recent note she lists writers that Baraka and his first wife published in *Yugen*, which she describes as "a little magazine with two hundred readers and a big impact. Kerouac, Ginsberg, Corso, Diane Di Prima, Gilbert Sorrentino, Robert Creeley, Barbara Guest, Charles Olson, and Frank O'Hara were among the writers Hettie and LeRoi published" (68). This is, of course, an all-white list. Overlooked by Johnson are other writers who appeared in *Yugen:* Tom Postell, Steve Korret, Bobb Hamilton, Oliver Pitcher, Stephen Jonas, and Baraka's college friend A. B. Spellman.

Both the silliness of Lewis Turco's efforts to separate Baraka from his black poetic forebears and the more serious but still misleading efforts of others to separate Baraka's history from those of the now old, and sometimes dead, white males of the New American Poetry serve to segregate the house of American letters far more effectively than the Black Arts ever did. A far more accurate, and moving, view of Baraka's relationships with other avant-garde poets, black and white, is afforded in the poem "One Night Stand." This poem, which appeared in Baraka's first collection, *Preface to a Twenty Volume Suicide Note . . .*, and bears a dedication to Ginsberg, commemorates a particularly prodigious prodigal's return. Baraka, who, as his *Autobiography* makes clear enough, even if Lewis Turco cannot get it right, never graduated from Howard University, returned not that many years later as a published poet in the company of a delegation of "Beat" writers. At a time when most university departments of English remained segregated by law or by practice, Baraka led a band of poetic revolutionaries through the gates that guard the Howard Hilltop. "We roared through the old gates," Baraka writes (21). These were the same gates that figure in a Howard story that Baraka himself always allowed might be apocryphal, the gates that guard the campus from the passing eyes of white travelers. In "Philistinism and the Negro Writer" Baraka again told the tale of the alarm expressed by the Dean of Men when he discovered the young LeRoi Jones casually eating a watermelon. "Do you realize that you're compromising the Negro?"

asks the shocked dean (52). Baraka was later to represent his ungraduated departure from Howard in his novel *Six Persons:* "Yes, Colored School, goodbye, we'll see you again—some way" (*Fiction* 272). Now, like the grandson who returned to Dothan, Alabama, to correct the grammar of those crackers who had tormented his grandfather, here was the young man who had changed his name (from "Leroy" to "LeRoi"), returning to campus with several of the chief talents of Beat poetry in tow, introducing them to the campus where he had once studied Dante and learned about the blues from Sterling Brown. "We came in, with our incredulousness, from the North," Baraka writes in the tercets of Dante's *Divine Comedy*. "We *are* foreign seeming persons" (*Preface* 22). They were only foreign seeming because they were so American. Looking back at his editorial policy when publishing *Yugen,* Baraka says that he published that which he found most valuable, "those white and black people who were talking about a side of America that was more valuable because it hadn't been talked about" ("Philistinism" 60). The integrated carload of bohemian artists roaring down from New York into the streets of Northwest Washington, DC, were the embodiment of that which had not yet been really talked about, that which remains too little talked about even today. When we read what these artists actually have written with and to one another, a far more complex and interesting seascape comes into view.

Baraka writes in his *Autobiography* that Olson's "Projective Verse" had been a bible for him "because it seemed to give voice to feelings I had about poetry and about society." But just as the younger writer, in his *Partisan Review* defense of Kerouac, was careful to make clear that he was no mere follower of the Beat prophets, Baraka points to the influence he had on Olson's evolving art. "When Charles came down to Cooper Square," Baraka remembers, "there was another sense that what we were doing he could use, that it was something he thought useful and correct" (*Autobiography* 282). There is evidence enough of what Baraka sensed in Olson's own poetry:

I don't think there is anywhere
but where I am
which can bring me closer

to what I shall look like
when if I do look

as I would look
      out of my eyes
into John Cronin's
or yours (Olson, *Nation* 138)

This may be an unprecedented moment in the record of American poetry. A white poet takes his measure, within his poem, as he would appear in the eyes of a black poet; for it is Amiri Baraka, then still LeRoi Jones, who is the addressee of Charles Olson's second person in these lines from "The Hustings," the poem Olson composed in answer to an election year letter from the younger poet, a letter seizing on the accession to power of a new generation, as represented by John F. Kennedy, to raise the deepest of questions of the politics and morality of the practice of poetry. Or, to be more exact in our measure of the moment, Olson, hovering between the exactings of *shall* and *will,* imagines how he should look from his present stance when looking into the challenging eyes of LeRoi Jones. In another draft of the poem Olson addresses himself:

> what do you have to say, Poet? what do you have to say What do you have to say What do you have to say to Leroi Jones (*Collected Poems* 532)

What Baraka had pressed him about was at the heart of Charles Olson's conception of himself as poet, the constitution of polis, his relationship to all those other eyes looking out of heads. Baraka was asking Olson, How can we be poets, here, against the terrors of the given, against what lies told by our presidents and our press, seemingly against the very American grain? Olson's answer was a post-Whitman promise of possibility. The Whitmanian stance seemed now available only to the irretrievably naive or with the accompaniment of a studied skepticism:

Do you believe
in what has been your life?
Or in these bundles

of the promise
of the use

of human beings
en masse? democracy
en masse en
transistors? (*Nation* 134)

The imagined polis was assuredly not the McLuhanite global village, which proved instead a mass produced and delivered by the broadest powers of transistorized pejorocracy. Against the broadcast that separated transmitter from receivers, elect from preterite, Olson elected to see still the promise of America:

In the eyes
of men and women
is the race

they run, and election
is their own, demanding
that they have everything

an uncontaminated earth
shall offer them. (*Nation* 134–35)

Both poets were cognizant of the forces that alienated Americans from their putatively inalienable right to make election their own. One reason that Baraka corresponded with Olson was his sense that the older poet had not elected to alienate politics from prosody, that Olson, unlike those Baraka thought of as Olson's sycophants, refused to consign the political and the cultural to separate spheres. Olson knew just how great a distance interceded between the *shall* and the *will* of his measure. "I care," he wrote to Baraka, "that there is not enough known yet to support you / in your eyes // or myself in mine" (*Nation* 139). Nonetheless, he held, "we are whatever / the human race / can be in the imagination" (*Nation* 136). If, as he opined in "The Hustings," the New Frontier of his former tutee John Fitzgerald Kennedy was "decadence," Olson, whose imagined democracy was projected far past anything countenanced by Pound or even by Williams, wrote that "the future / is the race's future / all over the place" (*Nation* 137).

This is clearly closer kin to what Melville termed his radical democracy on all sides than to the racist elitism of the previously Agrarian among the New Critics, and Olson's interest in both the past and the future of the race "all over the place" set him apart from many of the more liberal middle generation of moderns as effectively as did any element in his aesthetics. For Olson the issues of politics and aesthetics remained always joined. Thus in *Proprioception,* much of which had been published by Amiri Baraka prior to its gathering together for a volume, there is the outline of a historical-poetic project that Benjamin Friedlander sees as "consonant with Martin Bernal's in *Black Athena.*" Friedlander, in a letter to Baraka, argues that "Olson appreciated the political ramifications of this project (overturning the rule of the West as constituted by Plato, by reaffirming the Afroasiatic roots of the Greeks)" (qtd. in Friedlander). The young Baraka certainly appreciated the fuller significance of Olson's opposition to what he labeled "Greekism" to distinguish post-Renaissance humanism from the actually ancient ("It is not the Greeks I blame," Olson declares in "Human Universe" [*Collected Prose* 157]). Western humanism had bent toward the diminishment of the human universe to a parochial racialism. Olson picked up from Pound the study of Frobenius, hence the appearance of the city of Wagadu in Olson's poems, and was engaged with the ancients of Africa, as well as Sumeria and Greece. Unlike Pound, Olson's universe was equally open to his contemporaries, so he was in attendance at a gathering in the still segregated Washington, DC, of 1952 to hear a black woman of his acquaintance, who had just arrived, make the memorable remark that "ONLY THE ARTIST IS ON TIME" (*Collected Prose* 251). It was just this sort of timeliness that Baraka found attractive in Olson. The artist, in Olson's view, was, in the postmodern era, "talking from a new 'double-axis': the replacement of the Classical-representational by the *primitive-abstract*" (*Collected Prose* 251). This is the same primitive that Baraka addresses later in "What the Arts Need Now," and for Olson as well as Baraka it was a primitive carefully distinguished from the primitivism of the modernists. Olson explains in the "Letter to Elaine Feinstein": "I mean of course not at all primitive in that stupid use of it as opposed to civilized. One means it now as "primary," as how one finds anything, pick it up as one does new-fresh/first. Thus one is equal across history forward and back . . . one states . . . a different space-time" (*Collected Prose* 251). For Baraka, too, the primitive was not the precivilized but rather the first learnings of man, the primary civilization.

In 1966, in the midst of his development of a culturally nationalist aesthetic, Amiri Baraka wrote that "each voice is a place in America" (*Raise* 17), a phrase that might easily describe a thesis in Charles Olson's poetry. The two poets understood the ways that race takes place in America, the way that our language racializes the space we inhabit, the placements that race effects. At an early stage in his thinking through what was to become the *Maximus* poems, Olson had contemplated a composition called *Red, White, and Black,* an exploration of the multiple ways that Indians, Europeans, and Africans had created communities on this continent, a subject of continued attention in *Maximus* itself and in numerous individual poems. At the opening of "Place; & Names," which Baraka published in the eighth issue of *Yugen,* Olson writes of "a place as a term in the order of creation" (*Collected Prose* 200), the "crucialness," as he puts it,

> being that these places or names
> be as parts of the body, common & capable
> therefore of having cells which can decant
> total experience.

The link of place and name here parallels Baraka's later usage, and Olson's conception of a totality decanted finds its response in Baraka's introduction to David Henderson's poetry chapbook, where Baraka asserts that "the animating intelligence is a total of all existence. The many registrations. Ways of making sense, of sensing" (*Raise* 35). For Olson and Baraka, race is a sort of placement serving as decanter, a way of sensing. Race is not an inherent nature but a mode of being in the world, a social relationship, a language reified.

For Olson, blackness is not inherent; inherence is black. A 1962 poem commences:

> the Mother the Negro and the Englishman
> the independence has recreated itself
> we walk away black in the encounter
> the world is full of light (*Nation* 148)

What begins sounding like a bad old joke ends in inherence. "What is our inheritance in America?" might be one way of putting the questions raised in Olson's "The Hustings." The English in America first thought of the Indians as the Americans. Indians, granted the malapropism of their English name, were inherent in America. A little later in our history, Englishmen became the Americans, in part by dressing as Indians and throwing English commodities (tea) overboard. Subsequently, whiteness came to be held as inherent to Americanness, Africans became commodities for American import (sometimes thrown overboard), and, though the Alma Mater was popularly figured as an Indian mother, and while thousands of Virginians demanded their inalienable right simultaneously to claim whiteness and descent from Pocahontas, actual Indians were reserved for the twilight status of the quasi citizen. (As explosive as the Constitution's fractional counting of black bodies for the purpose of white representation is its repeated phrase, "except non-tax-paying Indians.") Olson's poem begins the work of disentangling that particular set of placements so that other namings might take place. Were independence to recreate itself we would all walk away black in the encounter, Olson suggests. This is not the familiar primitivist wish fulfillment of Norman Mailer's "White Negro." It is instead lyric recognition of, among other things, a paradox central to American culture. In contrast to other parts of the Americas, the culture of the slave system in the United States produced an oddity of matrilineal inheritance in a patrilineal society. If white men were to continue to produce children as commodities outside the patrilineal inheritance, then a curious patriarchal reversal in the means of reckoning descent was required. Whereas ordinarily the sons of a white man were entitled to his name and legacy, the children of black women in slavery inherited their mothers' status as slaves, and alongside this evolved the "one drop rule." "Oh mighty Drop," reads Gwendolyn Brooks's *Primer for Blacks*. "One Drop / maketh a brand new black" (9). For Brooks, as for Baraka and Olson, this is a matter of language and placement: "The word Black / has geographic power, / pulls everybody in." What Baraka, Brooks, and Olson each comprehend is that America cannot simultaneously promulgate the one drop rule and constitute itself as culturally white, any more than Virginians can be at the same time legally white people and the children of Pocahontas. Given the one drop rule, we were always already black in the encounter.

Race, as Homer Plessy sought without success to impress on the Supreme Court, is a form of property. It is property because Americans gained their purchase on independence while purchasing persons. Race in America has its beginnings in the commodification of people, and as Olson wrote in "On the Shore," a poem composed at the same time as "Is Black," "there isn't any nature in distribution" (*Collected Poems* 556). Yet, as he envisioned possibility in "The Hustings," where independence has recreated itself, there "Commodity // has dwindled to itself" (*Nation* 148). Neither Olson nor Baraka was a Marxist in the early sixties, but both understood the paradoxical nature of the commodity, where the social character of human labor appears to us as an objective character stamped on the product of that labor. The product of the labor of theft was the slave. Europeans attempted a particularly brutal mode of reification, transforming the social relationship among humans into a commodity relation between a white subject and a black object. The objects objected, often and forcefully. Writing at the peak of civil rights activism, Olson recreates a postenlightenment encounter. In his world full of light, "Commodity // has dwindled to itself. Inherence // is black" (*Nation* 148).

The importance of Baraka to Olson is readily traced. As "Leroy Jones" he appears in the *Maximus Poems*. He republished Olson's seminal essay "Projective Verse" as a Totem Press pamphlet in 1959. *Yugen,* coedited by Baraka and Hettie Cohen, published Olson's "Theory of Society," "Place; & Names," "The Distances," a selection from *Maximus,* and a selection from Olson's "West" sequence titled "As of Bozeman." As coeditor with Diane Di Prima of *Floating Bear,* Baraka published "Grammar—A Book" (which demonstrated Olson's interest in both Bantu and Chinook), "A Plausible Entry for, like, Man," "A Work," and numerous individual poems. During his time as an editor of *Kulchur* Baraka saw into print Olson's "Logography," "Proprioception," "Bridge Work," "The Hinges of Civilization to Be Put Back on the Door," and the postscript to "Proprioception." When Olson spoke at the Berkeley poetry conference, he specifically credited Baraka for this editorial work and, as Ben Friedlander has recently established, Olson proposed to Donald Allen that the book publication of *Proprioception* be dedicated to Baraka as acknowledgment (Olson, *Collected Prose* 416n179). Olson's review of *The Contours of American History* was undertaken in response to a request from Baraka, and Baraka's note to Olson approving the book's "ideas on the political meanings of corporate capitalism" (qtd. in *Collected Prose* 324) prefigures the course that Baraka's thought would take as he moved beyond the cultural nationalism of the late 1960s.

In many ways Baraka as a younger poet seemed to hold a position in Olson's work similar to that Olson had filled in the writings of William Carlos Williams. Baraka was a crucial representative for Olson of a further objective for projective verse. But the politics and geographies of race were at the heart of the correspondence between Olson and Baraka. It was not simply that Baraka's wide-ranging knowledge of African American music and cultural history was of great interest to Olson; Baraka seemingly embodied, or bodied forth, many of the deepest questions that Olson essayed to examine. In a 1965 letter to Ed Dorn Olson remarked that Baraka seemed "the 'key' to that very sort of politics which goes way ahead of these obviously transposed events of the sd present" (qtd. in *Nation* 206). Though Olson and Baraka might ultimately disagree in their political analyses, both recognized, as Olson wrote to Baraka in 1964, that "the power of the Negro is in fact the power of numbers of non-whites now" (qtd. in *Nation* 207). Olson realized what many Europeans and Americans of the day refused to grant, what Malcolm X and Amiri Baraka had learned early on, that the historical forces sweeping through the colonized lands of the world could have the political effect of radically altering black Americans' conception of themselves on the world stage.

Aside from the attraction of his poetics, Olson's politics represented for Baraka about the best that might be expected to emerge from the liberal tradition at a time when, as Baraka observed in a "Revue" of a review of *The New American Poetry,* it was widely held that "the Negroes in the South cannot utilize violence to achieve their ends (whatever? schools, homes, jobs? Why bother? But if you don't want another man to *handle your life* . . . you *might,* just might, mind you, have to kill him)" (*Floating Bear* 15). In Baraka's estimation Olson had moved well beyond the "peripatetic academicism" (*Floating Bear* 15) of most American liberalism. That Charles Olson, who had worked for Roosevelt's Democratic Party, should prove considerably more progressive on matters of racial justice than Roosevelt is hardly surprising. That Olson would gravitate to Black Mountain College, which had provided refuge for the first wave of Freedom Riders attempting to desegregate Jim Crow buses engaged in interstate transport, is not surprising. Black Mountain College had also included Jacob Lawrence among its arts faculty at a time when all surrounding schools were rigidly segregated. That Olson would convene a meeting of the Black

Mountain faculty to discuss admission of black students at a time when none had yet applied is typical of Olson. That Charles Olson and Amiri Baraka would have developed such a close and fruitful relationship during this period should not be surprising. It was exceptional at the time, though, and remains little discussed to this day. It had not been that many years earlier that Allen Tate had undertaken vicious reprisals against a Vanderbilt colleague for merely suggesting that the white scholars and writers of Vanderbilt might meet socially with their colleagues at Fisk University, and that, too, remains little discussed to this day.

"I feel a place / of names" (*Floating Bear* 495), begins Baraka's poem "Indians." Published in 1968 in the thirty-fifth issue of *Floating Bear,* the poem indicates the continued confluence of interest in the political topography of naming shared by Baraka and Olson even as Baraka was moving ever farther from what he saw as the limitations of his relationships with the white artists of his Village days. Olson's anatomy of a postmodernism that rejected the whited sepulcher of Western, "Greekist" humanism for a more expansive human universe continued, and continues, to be of use to Baraka. Here too, however, Baraka apparently has out-precedented himself. As in his short story "Suppose Sorrow Was a Time Machine," he presents himself as precedent to the very traditions of expression whose legatee he is. His adaptations of Olson's postmodern critique end by positing black expression as future anterior, as at the same time pre- and post-Western.

In their writings on art and technology we can begin a local tracing of Baraka's movements through Olson's insights to a new position with its roots in an appeal to a yet earlier *techne*. In the essay "Technology & Ethos," which Baraka first published in the journal *Amistad* in 1970, the poet closes with an echo of Olson's echo of Heraclitus, asserting change as the only constant, the changing same explored earlier in *Blues People*. Baraka argues in this essay that "technology itself must represent human striving" (*Raise* 157) and develops the idea of technological evolution in terms that recall Olson and Marx: "So that a telephone is one culture's solution to the problem of sending words through space. It is political power that has allowed this technology to emerge, & seem the sole direction for the result desired" (*Raise* 156). What commodity society presents to itself as the ineluctable telos of communications, as if we could read the inevitability of the telephone in the very folds of the human vocal apparatus,

Baraka views as historically produced within specific, describable contexts. Then, in a paragraph easily read as a direct response to "Projective Verse," Baraka calls for a projective move beyond type, imagining something akin to the poetry videos he would later appear in, a new technological reality that might body forth the word in substantively new ways.

In "Projective Verse" Olson, clearly overstating his case, argued that the typewriter, "for the first time" (*Collected Prose* 245), afforded the poet the equivalent of the musical staff and bar. He saw the machine as enabling poets to record more effectively than ever before the exact voicings of their work. For Baraka in 1970, already moving toward greater emphasis on the performative in poetry, attempting to apply lessons derived from Coltrane and Rollins to the projection of verse in space-time, the typewriter already appeared an atavism:

> A typewriter?—why should it only make use of the tips of the fingers as contact points of flowing multidirectional creativity. If I invented a word placing machine, an "expression-scriber," *if you will,* then I would have a kind of instrument into which I could step & sit or sprawl or hang & use not only my fingers to make words express feelings but elbows, feet, head, behind, and all the sounds I wanted, screams, grunts, taps, itches, I'd have magnetically recorded, & at the same time, & translated into word—or perhaps even the final expressed thought/feeling wd not be merely word or sheet, but *itself,* the xpression, three dimensional—able to be touched, or tasted or felt, or entered, or heard or carried like a speaking singing constantly communicating charm. *A typewriter is corny!!* (*Raise* 156)

Olson, it should be noted, moved in similar directions, pushing Pound's ideogramic methods farther into the holographic swirl that confronts readers of his *Maximus*. Baraka sought to conjoin the ancient technologies of talking drums to the visionary musics of his contemporaries in the Free Jazz revolution. The emphasis on visual elements in Baraka's later scripts, as well as his dynamic public performances, attest to his continued search for technologies of human striving, for newer modes of hieroglyphic chant beyond speech and writing.

Olson had followed a similar arc in his relationships with Pound, and race had to do with that, too. In his essay "GrandPa, Goodbye,"

Olson recalls how Pound had attributed what he took to be Williams's confusions to biology and cultural inherence. "He's one of the reasons I make so much of race," Pound had said to Olson. "It's hard enough for a man to get things clear when he's of one race, but to be Bill!—french, spanish, anglo, some jew from saragossa" (*Collected Prose* 148). It was about this time that Olson determined he would no longer see Ezra Pound. Pound's importance to him as a poet, though, was something still to be seen to. In "This Is Yeats Speaking" Olson challenges his readers, "brief me contrary ABCs" (*Collected Prose* 144). As Baraka was to ascribe academicism to American liberalism, Olson had told Pound, "you damn well know anglosaxonism is academicism and shrieking empire" (*Collected Prose* 405–6). Olson continued to find Pound's *ABC of Reading* a convenient conveyance, a suitable speller for a postmodern poet. Olson, reconceiving the self in relation to his time and his language, would break away from the penetrating beak of Pound's ego driving through the assemblage of the *Cantos*. Still, he shared Pound's conviction "that music begins to atrophy when it departs too far from the dance; that poetry begins to atrophy when it gets too far from music; but this must not be taken as implying that all good music is dance music or all poetry lyric" (*ABC* 14). Baraka begins a poem for Olson by asking, "this bizness of dancing, how / can it suit us?" (*Transbluesency* 46). Looking to the "cruel time" surrounding his first book, Baraka knew that Pound's Old World dance would not suffice; he knew, too, that the children of this cruel time "are older / than their worlds, and / cannot dance" (47). Both Baraka and Olson found themselves going back to the basics, back to their ABCs.

With "mu-sick, mu-sick—music / worse than war" filling his ears even in the streetcars (*Poems* 174), Olson set out his ABCs beginning in 1946 and completing them in 1950. Beginning at the beginning, Olson writes, "The word forms / on the left" (*Poems* 171). The enjambment at the opening leaves readers momentarily with the possibility of taking the word *forms* as noun rather than the verb it proves to be, and in the end the poem proves to be about forms as much as it is about forming. Our alphabetic reading technologies mean that we begin on the left. Our words must, as our eyes, follow the line. The politics of queuing up comes to be as natural to us, as inherent, as a grammar. Our speech forms up at the speed of thought, but it does form along internalized lines laid before us. At the end of his earliest

ABCs, Olson draws his own line of inheritance linking the imagist aesthetics of Pound to the projective verse of Olson and Creeley:

> Words, form
> but the extension of
> content
>
> Style, est verbum
> the word
> is image, and the reverend reverse is
> Eliot
>
> Pound
> is verse (*Poems* 172)

This time the ear hears pause but not comma; therefore, a listener will hear *form* as verb, whereas the eye will find a noun. It is not that words form only the extension of content but that words and their forms are but the extension of content. The play between eye and ear here enacts the reversals offered between Eliot and Pound. Pound's ideogramic technique, in which word is image, even acoustical image as construct in time, leads to Creeley, who wrote to Baraka's *Yugen* in 1959: "I learn a frog is a frog because of its structure, not because it looks like one ('a toad'?). A poem I believe is also one by virtue of this same aspect, not because it looks like one" ("Letter" 30).

In the same way that Olson's "The Hustings" sought to answer Baraka's probings, Baraka's "The A, B, C's," dedicated to Olson and published in the sixth issue of *Yugen,* could practically stand as a fourth stage of Olson's poem. The third of Olson's "ABCs" ends with an interrogative:

> what we needed most
> was something the extension of
> claritas: what do we have
> to report? (*Poems* 175)

Baraka's poem is his report, his effort at an extension of *claritas,* structured in three cantos to parallel Olson's three poems. Baraka had rejected what Olson denounced as "the dyes / of realism" (*Poems* 174). In *Floating Bear* number six Baraka put forward his idea that "perhaps poems must sit in an *uneasy* balance between what is 'real' and what is 'ideal.' The purely real is also fantasy. There is a hinge, a colloquy of fantasias that permits of all existences. The mind, the body, the spirit are not fantasies. They are not *artifacts*, either" (51). The poem, for Baraka as he approached his thirtieth year, was no more artifactual than the body. It existed as the hinge of colloquy within the social real, which is to say that it is in the employ of language:

> It is the walls of these words protect me
> throw a fierce cordon
> around me, that I may 'signify'
> to my heart's content. ("A, B, C's" 39)

The walls of these particular words would appear particularly porous. The play of Baraka's punning permits at least these readings: He may signify that his heart is content; he may signify the contents of his heart; He may signify willfully and endlessly. He is signifying upon Olson's poem with its reference to the extension of content. And the scare quotes hovering around the word *signify* signal that he is signifying in the colloquial sense—which means, also, that while his words may justify themselves along the left margin, may line up along their ordering imaginary, they will not stay in line. "It becomes irreversible, an / ellipse," he adds in the second canto, and here I hear a play on the Eliot/Pound reversals in Olson's previous poem.

In the third canto of his poem Baraka writes:

> From the street, across from where
> they are tearing down the old church,
> you can peer into the windows
> of the very poor. The rich have
> (more) propriety, and the gorgeous plants
> that make shadows
> on the ruins. (39)

These lines cast out in one direction toward the Situationists' parodically playful recasting of Marx (propriety is theft). The rich have propriety at least in part because they have more. In another direction these lines indict an everyday Eliotism (these gorgeous plants I shore against the ruin).

As he concludes, Baraka swirls in the very uncertainties of Olson's ending:

> Because I am standing among the ruins
> of ourselves. The sun is still
> where we can see it (you know what happens
> when it moves . . . ) You
>
> cannot even say . . .
>                                         or
> It is
> close to me
> and
> uncaring. It
> stands
> in my chest
> cavity. It
> is unmindful,
> & has no name. (40)

"No name in the street" would be James Baldwin's formulation. Against the placement afforded us in the name of our state, Baraka details an ultimate alienation that he will later attempt to bridge, the power of commodity structure to divide us as subject and object, to part us from our own song. "You've taken my blues and gone," would be Langston Hughes's formulation.

Like Olson, Baraka sought a way past the deathly division of human labors that parts us from our own capacities. In "Human Universe" Olson insists that we be, ourselves, "both the instrument of discovery and the instrument of definition" (*Collected Prose* 155). For Amiri Baraka, even in his early works, blacks in America were peculiarly instituted in a way that left them best suited to point up the crisis of our divisions and the possibility of a way out. "And this is not necessarily racial," Baraka argued at the Asilomar conference in 1964. "It's scientific in a certain sense. . . . We've lived here, which is what everyone else has done, and we have memories of our particular and specific ways of living here, and that is valuable as statement not only about this place but about the nature of the world" ("Philistinism" 56–57). Baraka had once described David Henderson's poems as "local epics with the breadth that the emotional consciousness of a culture can make" (*Raise* 36). To use Baraka's analogy from the Asilomar speech, "Philistinism and the Negro Writer": "[I]f you live in a big house and you keep me locked in a room and you never go in that room, you don't know anything about that room. If I come out of that room to clean many other things in the rest of the house, then I know about the whole house, and if I want to talk, I can talk about the whole house" (56–57). However local this imagined "house" poet's epic might be, it will have a great deal to tell us of our own emotional registrations and consciousness.

America didn't really want to go there in the early 1960s. Perhaps, Baraka conjectured to his audience at Asilomar, "one way Negroes could force institutionalized dishonesty to crumble, and its apologizers to break and run, would be to turn crazy, to bring out a little American Dada, Ornette Coleman style" ("Philistinism" 53). While this was a prospect that greatly interested Charles Olson, it was not his project. Baraka appreciated Olson's efforts to reach past the impositions of humanist historians to the record of humanity's first learnings, but Baraka was also following trails forged by Cheikh Anta Diop, J. A. Rodgers, Arthur Schomburg, and Carter G. Woodson. Before Baraka had ever heard of Olson, before he had become LeRoi rather than Leroy, he had spent hours with Sterling Brown listening to the projective ensembles of Duke Ellington and the innovative linings of Ma Rainey. At Howard University he had already seen how America's racialized class structures had intervened to divide him from his own song. As he writes in *Six Persons,* "the school bourgeois dictatorship made sterling brown teach us jazz in the dormitory. it was not really music after all" (*Fiction* 262).

When Baraka stirred to his discovery of Charles Olson and Robert Creeley, he was entering into colloquy with two poets who, whatever their substantive understanding of the music, had spent hours listening to the same Charlie Parker records he had lived with. In his encounter with Charles Olson's mode of postmodernity Baraka found impetus for his own rejection of post-Agrarian modernist lyric. In his own essays Baraka told his readers to "[s]ee everything fresh and 'without form'—then make forms that will express us truthfully and totally" (*Raise* 157). In science as in art such new forms would achieve new morality. "But what is our spirit, what will it project?" Baraka asks. "What machines will it produce? What will they achieve? What will be their morality?" (*Raise* 157). A part of Olson's appeal for Baraka had been his willingness to engage in the poem with the politics of technology and the moralities of our histories. For his part Olson had found in Baraka not a younger disciple but a disciplined respondent whose hearing provided him a measure of himself. Benjamin Friedlander reports that Olson noted on the outside of a 1960 letter from Baraka: "the only man I know who's hearing me / is a brother under the skin" (qtd. in Friedlander), and Olson added a characteristic bracket in the middle of that second line, bracketing the question of color by raising it in the poem.

Baraka found in his soundings of Olson a postmodern that arose from America's congress of red, black, and white, a postmodern whose condition of possibility was black inherence. And while he joined Charles Olson in the hands-on search for an actual past to oppose to the massa narrative of triumphalist Americanism, the yet-more American post-American postwhiteness that Baraka discerned was a further future anterior with its roots in the first learnings of the race. Or, as Baraka writes in "Technology & Ethos," "[t]he actual *beginnings* of our expression are post Western (just as they are certainly pre-western)" (*Raise* 157).

## III. ATLANTIS

The next day the spaceships landed. Art Blakey records was what they were looking for.

—Amiri Baraka, *Fiction*

Our name is magnetism.

—Amiri Baraka, *Fiction*

The several pathways of Baraka's poetics propose themselves most powerfully and straightforwardly in a poem from the collection combining his and his wife, Amina's, reflections on jazz and blues, *The Music*. Like the definite article of the book's title, the title of the poem, "The Aesthetic," points to a particularity, a singularity, though a particularly munificent one. The form of the poem places in practice the free verse prosody of Baraka's modernist predecessors. Its rhetorical structure is itself an allusion, calling to mind that passage where William Carlos Williams announces that he had wanted to write a poem that we could understand. It proposes itself, too, as a sort of postcolonial coming-of-age greeting. Where Kipling's "If" wondered if we could keep our heads, Baraka's "The Aesthetic" offers a conjecture about what might be inside them. These formal and rhetorical allusions to a past of white writings turn, though, around a direct insistence on a black continuity. Like Melvin B. Tolson before him, Baraka links the complex abstractions of traditional African arts to "the tense ambiguities / of Black Blues" (70). If "you" can understand that, the poet promises, if "you" can understand that which animates both Picasso and Negritude, both Louis Armstrong and Igor Stravinsky, "then my work should be clear / to you, what I say / easily understood."

There is an inkling in these lines of the forward-looking historicism that marks Baraka's post position in the race from modernism. "We hum / to anticipate, more history, every day," he writes in "The Rare Birds" (*Music* 80). That interracial conjoining of forms and rhetorics legible in "The Aesthetic" motivates this poem's title and dedication. The rarest bird was, of course, Charlie Parker, whose ornithology was an alto science of the blues' "tense ambiguities." Langston Hughes is among the literary birds of these lines, which are dedicated to the late Ted Berrigan, a second-generation New York School poet who shared Baraka's love of the music and his admiration for Frank O'Hara. Who, before Baraka, has linked Langston Hughes to Ted Berrigan? These birds, in Baraka's delineation, are "angular / like sculpture," like, in fact, the fabled bird of Brancusi, that bird that takes its angle of ascent again from the complexity of an angular, African art. As he linked Hughes to Berrigan, Baraka brings Brancusi together with the "more tangible" hues of Jacob Lawrence. What Baraka is unfolding in his stanzas is the wrapt embrace of modernism and Africa. "You / remember the eyes of that guy Pablo, and his perfect trace of / life's austere overflowings." We might remember as well the "austere offices" of love, as Robert Hayden, author of another ascending angel, had described them.

William Carlos Williams reappears in the final stanza of "The Rare Birds," a stanza that proffers a veritable tour of Baraka's aesthetic and political inheritance:

Williams writes to us
of the smallness of this American century, that it splinters into
worlds it cannot live in. And having given birth to the mystery
splits unfolds like gold shattered in daylight's beautiful
[hurricane.
(praying Sambos blown apart) out of which a rainbow of
anything
[you need.
I heard these guys. These lovely ladies, on the road to Timbuctoo
waiting for Tu Fu to register on the Richter scale. It was called
*Impressions,* and it was a message, from like a very rare bird.
(*The Music* 80)

The splitting mysteries of this stanza recall those passages of *Paterson* wherein Williams returns again and again to the significance of the newly split atom and to the image of the scientists staring intently into the new world open before them. To this Baraka adds the element that Tolson termed ethnic ambiguity, splitting open the question of race raised, but never fully addressed, in *Paterson,* the poem set in a town neighboring Baraka's Newark. But "The Rare Birds" also performs the paradoxical feat of metaphoric time travel read out of "Suppose Sorrow Was a Time Machine," finding a post-Williams, post–Black Arts Baraka footing the path toward a science more ancient than Williams's variable feet had danced around. On the road to Timbuctoo, ancient seat of learning and precolonial college town, Baraka places himself at the intersection of all poetic genealogies and aesthetic traditions. In "Suppose Sorrow Was a Time Machine" Baraka's mid-twentieth-century writing is a complex vehicle for the transmission forward and backward of vibrations between the Alabama of 1898 and the postwar present of an America that remained wracked with racial torment. In the Africa shaking with the temblors of post-independence continental movements Baraka's poem serves as a sounding box registering the simultaneous arrival of the vibrations set in motion by ancient Chinese poetry and the vibrations of the postcontemporary "New Thing" in American black music. The *Impressions* Baraka imprints on the scene are the legacy of John Coltrane, who shared Baraka's interest in Eastern arts and African wisdom.

These are visionary registrations that Baraka records. In the note he had published in the sixth issue of *Floating Bear* (a note responding to a cycle of poems by George Stanley that begins, coincidentally, with the invocation of black and white birds), Baraka, remember, declared: "There is a hinge, a colloquy of fantasias that permits of all existences" ("A Note" 51). The poem is material colloquy, the place where the ideal is realized and bodied forth. It is a historical space in which time folds over on itself, crossroads as existential hinge. This is the crossroads logic of temporality in "Suppose Sorrow Was a Time Machine," the aesthetic hinge joining *Impressions,* the tense ambiguity of the Yoruba Ogun and of the blues.

Sun Ra's concerts frequently featured a chant whose rhetoric forwards just such a colloquy of fantasias. Singer June Tyson would lead the musicians of the Sun Ra Arkestra in a verse that alternated declaration with interrogative: "It's after the end of the world. Don't you know that yet?" What question can be more patently rhetorical than "Don't you know that yet?" since the questioner has just revealed to "you" the knowledge that is the subject of the inquiry. The second person of this chant is every bit as slippery as the pronouns of Baraka's second-person chapters in *Six Persons*. Who is this "you" addressed in the question? As members of the audience join in with the Arkestra, reiterating the question in a call and response that becomes all call, who remains as the referent of these repeating pronouns? How are audience and addressee constituted as voices joined in the chant? More important, what ideal position must we be in to ask the question at all? The declaration, not that the world will end soon but that the world *has* ended, places us in an afterworld. It is already a postworld audience that is hailed by the chant. We are already an after people when we are asked if we know yet what we have just been told. The vertiginous sense this compels is the same postcontemporaneous pastness that Baraka finds along the road to Timbuctoo.

A version of that visionary path to a future perfect of tense ambiguity graces the front cover of Baraka's Motown recording, *It's Nation Time,* released as a "Black Forum" production in 1972. A broad pathway follows the sightlines of perspective to a vanishing point that is the apex of an ancient pyramid. Because the pyramid is of a piece with the vanishing pathway that leads up to it, it is at once an ages-old architectural wonder and a wondrous brick road pointing into the flaming sun of an Afrocentric future. The road is framed by two columns supporting a titular crossbeam. Beneath the title, *It's Nation Time,* the beam bears Baraka's name and the description "African Visionary Music." Interestingly, there is no indication on the front of the album, aside from the name of Imamu Amiri Baraka, to alert potential Motown customers to the presence of poetry on this recording. That information appears among the album credits. The cover is, still, loudly inscribed with spirit script. The columns are richly overwritten with the artist's rendering of hieroglyphics, as if to reinscribe Egyptian writing in an African context from which it had been torn by post-Tut modernist Egyptomania. If H. D.'s *Helen in Egypt* is a modern opening onto an ancient Egyptian mythos, the cover of *It's Nation Time* opens a Nubian crypt to release a black anima as the ancient condition of possibility of that modernity. The buildings of the city that are spread out along the horizon line of the illustration are adorned with additional symbols reaching from the rooftops, suggesting an admixture of Islam with its predecessor spiritual systems. These signs may also be taken for wonders; they look a great deal like modern antennae. Many of these signs are echoed in the objects carried by the crowd of pilgrims approaching on the road, all of whom appear black. Sun Ra lays claim to both ancient Atlantis and to futuristic space journeys. When we finally arrive on Saturn, he assures us, we will find his footprints there before us. Similarly, on the cover to *Heliocentric Worlds* Sun Ra adds his own portrait to the pantheon of classic astronomers decorating the cosmos diagramed there. Sun Ra, like Baraka, images a colloquy of fantasias in which he is both past and future. The pyramid that points the way to the nation of Baraka's ideal finds its reincarnation in the face of the yet-to-come that rises above the pictured pilgrims to the future anterior city, the Magic City of Sun Ra's redeemed Birmingham, the "Sun building-teaching African wisdom" described in Jeledi Katibu's liner notes to Baraka's album.

Such a future anteriority is written into Baraka's reflections on black America throughout his career. "We were sitting at the edge of civilization," he writes in "God and Machine" (*Fiction* 223), where he advises that we should "Dig the ancient mss. of Sun-Ra" (225). In the third-person-singular chapter of *Six Persons* he recollects a desire "to be other than in the obscure shadows of the obscure road, listening to songs so futuristic they made no sense" (*Fiction* 293). To be other than shadowed Baraka turns to an ambiguous blackness ("The Shadow knows"), where the nonsense of the futuristic songs is played out of ancient scores. Sun Ra returns to us from the interplanetary space ways to leave us manuscripts he wrote in our prehistory. *Six Persons* details Baraka's own writing as sharing these qualities with Ra's ur-scripts: "They was thinkin' and writin' stuff down, impenetrable poems about the dizziness and confusedness of bein' black subjects readied for the defense of the subject matter" (*Fiction* 319). Black subjects themselves become the material hinge of fantasias Baraka records as he remembers artists he has known in his *Autobiography*. Gloria Tropp is one instance, though she is infrequently remembered by scholars of the post–World War II poetry scene. She often appeared with her husband, Steven Tropp, who worked as a jazz and R & B drummer, in performances that tested the boundaries between page and stage long before the term "performance poetry" had been popularized. Baraka recalls her appearance at readings "made up like in Hollywood science fiction movies about what blacks will look like in the future" (219). Of course, Hollywood had made no such movie at that time and wouldn't for more than a decade. (The seldom seen blaxploitation era Sun Ra film *Space Is the Place* is probably the earliest contender, though not exactly a Hollywood film.) If the music was so futuristic that it made no sense, it was because it was music from the other side of the real/ideal colloquy. The poets wrote out of a dizzying position as black subject, then went to the Five Spot "to watch that spectrum of black philosophy, the sound of our life before us, and our minds. We cd hear our minds each night spit back at us. As we were, Miles, then Monk" (*Fiction* 337). Gloria Tropp, who would have fit easily among Sun Ra's assembly of astral black travelers, made herself up to look like the future, Baraka remembers.

This futurity was a scriptural technology, a making manifest of an ideal. In "God and Machine" Baraka speaks of it as "the spiritual revelation of the Ujama computers" (*Fiction* 225). There is a post-Plato idealism at work here, although it is a revelation of pre-Platonic origins. In Baraka's understanding the unseen is developed "first as 'theory' then known, tho it always, like all forms, 'existed'" (*Fiction* 225). Baraka's postmodernity turns out to be nominative. It is in the Adamic act of naming that the unseen comes to be known as experienced. The act of casting the existent in names is arbitrary, but so, according to Baraka, is life. "Gatsby's Theory of Aesthetics," written in 1964, argues that "arbitrariness, or self-imposed meaning, is the only thing worth living for. It is the only thing that permits us to live" (*Transbluesency* 132). It was the experience of thinking as a black subject that brought Baraka to this spiritual revelation, not a study of poststructuralist theory. Baraka was joined in this mode of thought by many other black artists, including those who did not join him in the politics of cultural nationalism. Russell Atkins, who wrote of the arbitrariness of semantics and values in the same year as Baraka's poem, was one such ("Some Thoughts" 26). While a recognition of the arbitrariness of signification is to be found in writers as early as Saint Augustine, the contemporary association of that recognition with structuralist and poststructuralist controversies too often elides African American thought all together. But the struggle for black power was first and foremost, as James Baldwin so often suggested, the struggle for the power to define, a struggle that presupposes the role played by power in acts of language and significance (Baldwin 24). The aesthetic politics of those struggles can be located in such Black Arts–era writings as Fran Ross's recently republished novel *Oreo*. In the concluding pages of this riotous narrative the title character reaches an epiphany that closely tracks the Baraka of "Gatsby's Theory of Aesthetics." "From the beginning she had determined what each item on her list signified," readers learn in a classic instance of free, indirect discourse. "She would complete her task and ascribe meaning now, at the end" (206). Again, this assumes that meaning is something ascribed, and the Black Power of Ross's novel is the power to make that ascription for oneself, a power Ross extends to the reader of her own text. The act of naming is at once a theorizing and a making known, a mode of creating into knowledge. If, as Kenneth Burke liked to say, works of literature are names for experiences, then the name is a recording of the subject. "Our name is magnetism. As the unity forms our name is the single intelligence. It is the music itself" (*Fiction* 225), and that is why the music is a site from which our philosophy is returned to us. The music does not simply reflect the listener, but it stages a colloquy in which we "hear our minds each night spit back at us." The road from Tu Fu to Timbuctoo, the path between the ancient manuscripts of Sun Ra and the ascension of John Coltrane, is a place of post-*Impressions* modernism. It is, like Duncan's open field, a place of first permission. Like the Dixie Turnpike of Jean Toomer's *Cane* it grows out of a goat path in Africa, and like the cover illustration of *It's Nation Time* it extends beyond the reach of temporal technologies to travel the space ways with Sun Ra. This is how Baraka is able to conceive of the *beginnings* of black expression as being both "post Western" and "pre-Western" (*Raise* 157).

When Baraka calls for a dose of "American Dada, Ornette Coleman style" ("Philistinism" 53), we need to keep in mind that his vision of what is truly American is again rooted in a prior blackness that reveals a post-America. Hence, Bob Kaufman can be described by Baraka in the notes to the collection *Eulogies* as the source for something that is both modern and "Native American" (217).

Post-American form commences, like "America," like "the Negro," in neologism. Baraka's poem in memory of Bob Kaufman begins by recalling Kaufman's coinage *Frink,* a word as yet uncollected by the *OED*. The word is left unexplained on a line of its own, remarked only by the slash that follows it. The second line of the poem unfolds Kaufman's name in wordplay of Baraka's own devising, teasing out meaning by compounding a new tense, another tense ambiguity, out of the syllables of the surrealist's surname. What might a "Kauf man" mean? Baraka explains that "Kauf meant thought" (*Eulogies* 80), and we can hear another name lingering at that line's turning, the name of Thot, ancient Egyptian bringer of writing. In Baraka's rendering "Frink," like "Kaufman," is a crucible wherein "thought / & 'Freak' / collided." For much of America's history white writers held that whatever was going on inside the heads of Africans held in bondage, it was not "thought." This was in some sense a defensive insult; better perhaps to think that slaves do not think than to think of what they might be thinking. So certain was white America of black intellectual incapacity that laws were passed to prevent slaves from preserving their words in writing, from extending their thought beyond the reach of their master's voice, beyond the disciplinary ear of the white overseer. The thought of black thought was to many whites a freakish thing, to which Bob Kaufman replied with a "frink." If the worst thing Africans in America might do to unsettle the white settlers was the crime of thinking while black, Bob Kaufman was an incorrigible offender, and Amiri Baraka's eulogy to him is a sustained case of aiding and abetting.

By Baraka's lights Bob Kaufman was both the ideal and the condition of possibility for what came to be celebrated in the media as the Beat Generation. "Bob Kaufman was the prototypical beatnik before beatnik got coined," Baraka avers (*Eulogies* 217), alluding to the controversies surrounding the origins of the post-Sputnik San Francisco neologism that was coined either by or about Kaufman. Baraka's Kaufman is notable above all as the fount of a language, "the first guy to use that proto-beat jargon," word of whom first came to Baraka on the East Coast by way of the *Beatitudes* (possible prototype for the *Floating Bear*?), whose cofounders included Kaufman and Ginsberg. But just as Sherley Anne Williams voiced her concern that Baraka's legacy not be allowed to become a mere appendage to white Beat histories, Baraka worries that Kaufman's posthumous profile will go straight from neglect to assimilation. In his eulogy Baraka derides those "others" who "opportunize around / his myth" (84) and abominates "the whiteness which / Keeps his memory" (86). What was done to Kaufman in life was bad enough. Not only were his coinages appropriated without credit, but the full weight of the state's oppressive apparatus fell on him. Police officers devoted an inordinate amount of their attentions and tax-payer-supported time to the harassment of this street poet, and he was treated to the early psychedelia of electroshock personality tuning. Baraka's metaphors bring together the state's forced adjustment of Kaufman's mental state and Beat publishing's efforts to press his poems into wider circulation:

My friend drama town  
City lights will cook  
the boy  
his head, shorn, his smile,  
worn (85)

A visit to the city lights of New York led to Kaufman's confinement. Had City Lights Books in San Francisco not bound over some of Kaufman's poems for public distribution, the poet would have received even less critical ink than the too little that Baraka complains about in his note to the poem. Still, it was the daily drama of city lights that both drove Kaufman and did him in. The neighborhoods around City Lights Books, North Beach especially, seemed Kaufman's environmental niche, but it was here, too, that he was arrested over and over again. After his death, then mayor Dianne Feinstein proclaimed Bob Kaufman Day in San Francisco. There is no mention of race in Mayor Feinstein's proclamation, and one wonders if the white officers who had tormented him would find, as the mayor did, that Kaufman "shed light on the ironies and pleasures of San Francisco for over 30 years." There had been no mention of race in the film that was made of Jack Kerouac's *The Subterraneans* either, which was all the more notable since the subject matter of the novel had been an interracial love, but MGM underscored the irony of that erasure by using some of Bob Kaufman's poetry in the film's prototypical Beat cafe scenes. Thus do "others / opportunize around / his myth."

These occlusions of race are unbecoming a country whose history is rooted in the creation and commodification of race. Picking up on the pun the word affords, Baraka writes that "Race itself spells / Competition / 19th century" (87). What Mayor Feinstein and MGM did not care to spell out is the extent to which America's love affair with the myths of free market competition requires a market in unfreedom. The electroshock metered out to Kaufman in New York's Bellevue Hospital after he had been detained for disputing authority was certainly one way to deal with unregulated free competition in the marketplace of ideals. It was a "therapy" that used an apparatus uncomfortably resembling the metal braces placed over slaves' heads in earlier centuries to silence them and teach compliance. The capitalist competition of our nineteenth century was a rigged race, an economy extracted from the backs of black labor. The "Abomunism" invented by Kaufman in the late twentieth century was offered as one way we might spell ourselves, get out of the race, get away from traffic in persons. It was not at all well received by the competition, whose far-from-invisible hand struck out at this mixed-race poet chanting in public places.

As a Marxist, the later Amiri Baraka cannot approve the anarchism he finds in Kaufman's stance. Still, Baraka recognizes a kindred politics as well as racial kindred. Apostrophizing the departed Kaufman with one of the late poet's many onomastic puns, Baraka writes:

I say BombKauf, the
      Abomunists
Were
Reds
whose footprints yodeled
like pre God Pygmies (86)

In this formulation communism (Reds) has left vocal footprints that have out-precedented themselves; they are the aftertracks singing like humans who preexisted their deities. But Baraka is also laying a claim for Kaufman's Abomunist manifesto (manifesto—the making manifest as self-imposed, arbitrary meaning of the ideal, manifesto as hinge and colloquy) as a late avatar of indigenous American thought. In his note to the poem Baraka says, "I think Bob is actually one of the sources of the modern kind of American surreal imagery—Native American—rather than imported from Europe" (217). Here Baraka recalls both the long history of American Indian admixture in African American genealogies and the indigenist motifs that marked much of American modernist art, both cubist and surrealist. The African American poet is again seen as native source for a differing modernity, a modernity that contests the defining features of textbook high modernism:

Human
Beings
Bob
That's what you
Heard

A POST AMERICAN
Phenomenon (87)

As Tom Russ feels the vibrations of his grandson's memory at the end of the nineteenth century, and Baraka registers the pulsations of Tu Fu beneath his feet on the pathway to Timbuctu, Bob Kaufman senses the imprint of the human (Friday's footprints in the sand?), a form so native to America that it heralds an after-America. The human is for Baraka precedent and telos, Atlantis and future nation. The past is before us, and follows us, in this formulation, graphically projected into the field of the poem as Baraka concludes his eulogy for Bob Kaufman:

PAST US

US PAST (90)

On the page we can choose to read "U.S." in "US," giving ourselves a national collectivity in the reading that has been too often refused in our living; "Us" as colloquy between ideal community and real history. Likewise, Americans' habits of pronunciation lead us by the ear to hear "passed" where "past" has been written. The past is what we pass beyond. The shape of this couplet is a cube of cross words, field of first permission to be arbitrary, to award ourselves meaning. It is a place where we meet ourselves coming and going, nexus of cross purposes. It is an invitation to become ourselves, to make ourselves up, to turn in the language and turn ourselves into what we could have been all along. "Why don't we turn / around?" Baraka asks as he ends, a not entirely rhetorical question.

# 4
# *The Ancient Rain: Bob Kaufman*

you can be backward-looking and forward-thinking at the same time.
—Greg Tate, in Dery, "Black to the Future"

We fly ahead into the past
—Bob Kaufman, *Cranial Guitar*

Who will look to Bob Kaufman—if we don't?
—Barbara Christian

## I

*para el topo, la aguja del agua.*
*No busquéis, negros, su grieta*
*para hallar la máscara infinita.*
*Buscad el gran sol del centro*
*hechos una piña zumbadora.*
*El sol que se desliza por los bosques*
*seguro de no encontrar una ninfa,*
*el sol que destruye números y no ha cruzado nunca un sueño*
—Federico García Lorca, *Poet in New York*

In the world of Bob Kaufman's poetics Federico García Lorca and Crispus Attucks stand together in *The Ancient Rain*. Kaufman asserts a kinship with Attucks, writing "Crispus Attucks is my son, my father, my brother, I am Black" (*Ancient* 80). Where Amiri Baraka had, audaciously enough, imagined a world in which his own poems could come to him through his grandfather, Kaufman here fathers his own father. Further, he envisions an afterworld where "[t]he Negroes have gone home with Lorca" (79). The music of *The Ancient Rain* is "purely American, not European" (77), yet that pure product of the America that is shared by Kaufman with another poet whose roots are in the

Caribbean, William Carlos Williams, that purely American ancient rain "illuminates Lorca, the mystery of America" shines in Lorca's eyes (79). It is Ben Belitt's English, however, that Kaufman embeds in his poem as the representation of the "voice out of the whirlwind":

> Federico García Lorca wrote:
> Black Man, Black Man, Black Man
> For the mole and the water jet
> Stay out of the cleft.
> Seek out the great sun
> Of the center.
> The great sun gliding
>       over dryads.
> The sun that undoes
>       all the numbers,
> Yet never
>       crossed over a
>          dream. (Kaufman, *Ancient* 80)

Kaufman's incorporation of lines from Lorca is not unique to this poem. As Maria Damon has pointed out, two lines in another Kaufman poem, "Oregon," are derived "almost verbatim from 'Los Negros' in Ben Belitt's translation of Lorca's *Poet in New York*" (Damon, *Dark End* 56). We need more weight on that word *almost* as it contends with *verbatim*. The lines we read in *The Ancient Rain* turn out to be neither quite what Lorca wrote nor what Belitt translated. By conjoining Attucks and Lorca, Kaufman effects a yet more radical translation of Lorca and of modernism, conjuring a transmigration of African-inflected verbal innovation that transfigures modernism, placing Kaufman himself in the position of both father and son to the modern, temporally as well as racially miscegenated.

Still, in the chaotic chorus that has accompanied that turning, Kaufman's audacity has fallen into a silence deeper and longer-lasting than his own legendary periods of self-imposed or self-inflicted silence. Kaufman's rewriting (perhaps rewiring) of the program of the modern became one of those "Beat Occlusions" that Maria Damon speaks of in her essay in *Beat Culture and the New America*. From the time of Barbara Christian's 1972 essay "Whatever Happened to Bob

Kaufman?" to the recent appearance of studies by Kathryne Lindberg, Mona Lisa Saloy, Mark Reid, and Damon herself, few American critics have broken the silence surrounding what must be seen in retrospect as a veritable transubstantiation whereby Kaufman raised the body of black arts from within the entombment of modernity, retaking at the same time the terrain of the American cultural future anterior. "Beat Occlusions"? In *The Portable Beat Reader* editor Ann Charters declares Philip Lamantia to be "the only American poet of his generation to embrace fully the discoveries of surrealism" (318), thus silencing the remarkable similarities between Lamantia's poem "High" and the poem titled "O-Jazz-O" by Bob Kaufman (a poet only two years older than Lamantia), a poem that appears just eleven pages later in Charters's own anthology, apparently occluding as well the work of Ted Joans, who seems to have been insufficiently potable for the *Portable Beat Reader*. Joans is not even mentioned in Charters's list of "Books for Further Reading" (623–31).

Kaufman anticipated these occlusions, not only by means of his own occlusions of himself but in the writing. Kaufman's second book, *Golden Sardine,* ends with an open letter to the *San Francisco Chronicle,* a letter with ominous historical connotations. During the period of American slavery white masters dispossessed Africans of their drums, but Kaufman, who grew up in New Orleans and must have heard the second line drumming in the streets as the backbeat of his own childhood, knew that black people had never been wholly mastered and could not be deprived of what they brought with them, themselves, their own cultural baseline. Similarly, Kaufman saw in his own lifetime the commodification of the Beats as white Negroes, as pale-face savages beating jungle drums. (One of the unremarked ironies of Ted Joans's parodic "rent-a-beatnik" advertisements was the fact of a black artist offering to rent out the bodies of those Norman Mailer declared to be white Negroes.) Already Kaufman had seen the public bleaching out of the artistic movement whose major works, including both "Howl" and *On the Road,* were inconceivable without the influence and models of black arts. Damon offers a signal instance in her essay "Triangulated Desire and Tactical Silences," in which she points out that the "wasted-looking young [white] man in the famous *Life* magazine photo accompanying its article on the Beats" is reading a copy of Kaufman's *Abomunist Manifesto* (142). The texts that tend to accompany such photos do present Beat life as dangerously interracial, but the influence of black Americans is generally presented as something that is inhaled along with music and marijuana. Seldom did contemporary representations of Beat life in the popular media underscore the *intellectual* contributions of black artists and thinkers.

In a pattern that was to repeat itself many times in the postwar years, African American writing was erased from the public history of the Beats even as the Beats themselves loudly and persistently proclaimed the centrality of black culture to their lives and works. Kaufman knew that there would be future parades of the Beats, and he knew that they would in all likelihood march through the white quarters, like Boulder's Naropa, and he knew that they would be marches to the beat of a different drummer. As he wrote to the *Chronicle* in 1963, the "silent beat makes the drumbeat, it makes the drum, it makes the beat" (*Cranial Guitar* 97). Though Kaufman anticipated his own occlusion in the parade of latter-day Beat celebrants, he knew that the silence that crowded around him was the founding ground of the parade that followed in the wake of modernism. T. J. Anderson has counted eleven times that the word *beat* appears in this missive in "its various forms, thereby establishing our recognition of the 'silent beat' that conveys an opposite and recurring rhythm as well" (331). This rhetorical effect finds its analogy in the drumming of Tony Williams on the incomparable Miles Davis collection *In a Silent Way*. Davis himself was an established master at the art of playing silence, and Williams was well schooled in the Davis ensemble. In the long work that follows the title melody on this album, "It's about That Time," Williams sets up a strong, simple beat against which the other instruments raise their voices. But there are passages in which Williams's beat continues, without Williams, for significant periods. Nothing among the surrounding instruments calls attention to this recurring absence, but it becomes something the listener anticipates and attends to. It becomes as much an organizing form as its counterpart, the head of the drumstick striking a surface. The appearing and disappearing of this beat echoes a similar technique in the album's first cut, "Shhh/Peaceful," in which a figure played on the high hat comes and goes. Williams's occasional silences on "It's about That Time" set the stage for the fuller use of his drum set that comes later in the piece, at the same time providing a jazz musician's rhetorical underscoring of the composition's title; the piece *is about* that time. Kaufman's silent beat that comes before and after every beat asserts itself in the spaces between the words of his letter, as his periods of silence and speaking presence punctuated the life of San Francisco through the decades, as the silence surrounding him punctuates Beat histories even now. The silence about Bob Kaufman has a subject; it is about that poetry. In his letter to the *Chronicle,* to which he signs himself as the hand that is not clapping, the drummer who does not beat his own drum, he predicts that his silent beat will "drown out all the noise, it comes before and after every beat, you hear it in between, its sound is / / Bob Kaufman, Poet" (*Cranial Guitar* 97). Jean-François Lyotard, a philosopher and writer who, like Jacques Derrida, spent crucial years of his life in North Africa, argues that "there is a necessity for a phrase to be linked with the event as a happening. Even a silence, being a phrase, is a way of linking. Each time there are many different ways of linking phrases, so that each moment is a beginning in the middle of time" (*Peregrinations* 8). Kaufman's silenced beat is the linking phrase, the passage through time that proves the portability of blackness, the middle passage, as the absented center of the postmodern.

Lyotard suggests, in what is by now perhaps the most overquoted phrase in his works, that postmodernism "is not modernism at its end but in the nascent state" (*Postmodern Condition* 79); thus, "*Post modern* would have to be understood according to the paradox of the future (*post*) anterior (*mode*)" (81). Far less well known is the fact of Lyotard's discussions over the course of a decade with a group of American radicals associated with the Caribbean writer and political philosopher C. L. R. James. Lyotard first became familiar with the work of James and his American colleagues through affiliation with the French Marxist group *Socialisme ou Barbarie,* but he continued his contacts with James into the 1960s. Three decades earlier James had advanced an argument regarding African Americans and Western modernity. In works such as *The Black Jacobins,* which was published in a French edition in the 1950s, James held that the experience of historic rupture represented by the Middle Passage and the new modes of labor organization in the New World meant that African Americans "from the very start lived a life that was in its essence a modern life. That is their history," he writes, "as far as I have been able to discover a unique history" (392). In subsequent years James was to advance a similar argument regarding modernism. In essays and speeches written during the same years that Kaufman was publishing his first poems, James, following in the path of Alain Locke and others, turned to a careful consideration of the Africanity that was at the very heart of Pablo Picasso's art. This much was known to Lyotard at the time that he began to frame his theses on the postmodern understood according to the logic of the future anterior.

The silenced passage leading from C. L. R. James to Kaufman leads again through Spain and through North Africa, and Kaufman is not alone as he traverses this route. The lines he lifts from Lorca's *Poet in New York* were immediately recognizable to Amiri Baraka, whose "Lines to García Lorca" had been included by Langston Hughes in his collection *New Negro Poets U.S.A.*, and they would have been recognized as well by such poets as A. B. Spellman, Ted Joans, Clarence Major, and Jayne Cortez. Also instantly recognizable was the fact of Kaufman's rephrasings of Lorca. In Lorca's "El Rey de Harlem" the refrain "Negros, Negros, Negros, Negros" is not repeated just before the lines quoted by Kaufman, but at the end of the stanza. Kaufman has transposed and altered Lorca's own phrasing. The line "No busquéis, negros, su grieta" is translated by Belitt as "Black man, never search in its cleft." Kaufman has enacted the plurality of Lorca's "Negros" and replaced Belitt's version of the refrain, "Negroes, Negroes, Negroes, Negroes," with "Black man, Black man, Black man" (80). Similarly, Kaufman has elided the reference to "la máscara infinita," dropped the lines "hechos una piña zumbadora," and has changed one of Belitt's translations in the direction of economy and compression, thus changing its meaning. Where Lorca writes of the sun gliding, "seguro de no encontrar una ninfa" (24), which Belitt translates as "with no expectation of dryads" (25), Kaufman writes of "The great sun gliding / over dryads" (80). It is precisely at Lorca's point of most intimate though often uncomprehending contact with black America that Kaufman rewrites the lines of one of international modernism's greatest poets and, perhaps even more significant, interposes himself between Lorca and the man most responsible for bringing Lorca's works to an American audience. Kaufman lays hands on the body of Lorca's texts and makes them black American signifying structures.

There is a certain poetic justice in this. Lorca's *Poet in New York* grows out of his experiences in Harlem during a summer session at Columbia University. Ensconced in a room at John Jay Hall, Lorca was ostensibly at Columbia to learn English, a task he abandoned almost immediately. Lorca laid hands on the stationery of Columbia University and wrote *Poet in New York* on the reverse of those pages in Spanish (Smith B1) rather than in the English he was busy not learning. Kaufman rewrites and misremembers, dismembers, his modernist model, reauthorizing his own poetics. In *The Ancient Rain* Kaufman takes Lorca home from Harlem to heaven, in the process translating him out from among the texts of white American intellectuals and into the heaven of black people. In so doing, Kaufman was responding to an invitation he found in the Africanity of Lorca's script, the same invitation C. L. R. James was to answer in the paintings of Picasso. The passage that linked North Africa to modernism and postmodernism passed through Spain. In the English version of Lorca's essay "The Duende," a lecture Lorca delivered in Havana on his way home from Harlem that was later appended to Belitt's 1955 translation of *Poet in New York,* Kaufman would have read that "[i]n all Andalusia . . . people constantly speak of the *duende* and find it in everything that springs out of energetic instinct" (154). He would have read further that *duende* is associated with "black sounds," with mystery, with roots, "with whatever is sustaining in art." Lorca writes that *duende* "is a power and not a construct, is a struggle and not a concept" (154). Finally, as if authorizing Kaufman's revision of the translated Lorca, Lorca observes that "often the *Duende* of the musician passes over into the *Duende* of the interpreter, and at other times, when musician and poet are not matched, the *Duende* of the interpreter—this is interesting—creates a new marvel that retains the appearance—and the appearance only—of the originating form" (159). The reappearance of Lorca's originating form, spirited away from Belitt's English, in the company of the revenant Crispus Attucks is just such a new marvel.

Kaufman has found in Lorca's *Duende* the black sound of modernism's future anterior. In a signifying act that will be repeated in the works of Baraka, Jonas, Spellman, Cortez, and others, Kaufman unveils the black strata among the founding phrases of the modern, thus revealing as in a postmortem the blackness of nascent modernism. This is starkly evident in a modernist genealogy described by Kaufman himself in his 1960 prose pamphlet *Does the Secret Mind Whisper?* This work was advertised by City Lights Books as the opening section of a novel-in-progress, but the novel appears to have vanished. According to the City Lights cover blurb, the published portion "provides the atmosphere in which the 'characters' are to appear—and disappear." The characters, then, have, as planned, become the silent beat that "is beaten by who is not beating the drum" (*Cranial Guitar* 97). It is within the prose poetry of this silenced novel that we learn from Kaufman of "that maniacal wood where sarah last egyptian first saint mother of all gypsies pumped blood of wild rose into lorca's andalusian veins where federico first sang where mithra in black spanish robes placed her sword in ignacio's groin where sweet lorca weeps bitterly yet lives in the afternoon yet loves in the afternoon that darkly loved wood where all who enter are lost yet live forevermore companion to etruscans and black mountainous shapers of mahogony african breast sucked by old lonely aesthetes" (*Cranial Guitar* 153). Here the poet not only makes a claim for a certain prior Africanity in Lorca's modernity, but he posits an African genesis of Lorca's very culture. (He seems to claim Dante as well.)

Kaufman, the author of *Solitudes Crowded with Loneliness,* reads the initial section of *Poet in New York,* titled "Poemas de la soledad en Columbia University" ("Poems of Solitude at Columbia University"), into *The Ancient Rain,* but he reads Lorca with a black American difference. "That he came from Spain of the Inquisition," Kaufman says of Lorca, recalling not only the imposition of Christian orthodoxy by violence but also the expulsion of the Moors and the Jews, "is no surprise" (81). But Kaufman's reading is a surprising rewriting that counters the racial orthodoxies of his own country: "I observed those who read him who were not Negroes and listened to all their misinterpretation of him. I thought of those who had been around him, those that were not Negro and were not in crackling blueness, those that couldn't see his wooden south wind, a tiltin' black slime that tacked down all the boat wrecks" (*Ancient* 81). In the end Lorca serves for Kaufman as a sort of spiritual underground railroad, a messianic vehicle whose second coming will be a day of absence. Like William Melvin Kelley in his novel *A Different Drummer,* Kaufman imagines a great exodus:

THE NIGHT THAT LORCA COMES
    SHALL BE A STRANGE NIGHT IN THE
    SOUTH, IT SHALL BE THE TIME WHEN NEGROES
        LEAVE THE SOUTH FOREVER,
    GREEN TRAINS SHALL ARRIVE
    FROM RED PLANET MARS

> CRACKLING BLUENESS SHALL SEND TOOTH-
> COVERED CARS FOR THEM
> TO LEAVE IN, TO GO INTO
> THE NORTH FOREVER, AND I SEE MY LITTLE
> GIRL MOTHER
> AGAIN WITH HER CROSS THAT
> IS NOT BURNING (*Ancient* 60)

The green tinge found so often seeping through Kaufman's verse flows, of course, from Lorca's "Romance Sonambulo," as the crackling blueness of his late poems derives from Lorca's "Norma y paraiso de los Negros." But Kaufman reads "Verde que te queiro verde" and imagines a gospel train, a great getting-up morning, and in a rapture that lifts the righteous bodily into heaven while leaving the Klan behind, he dreams the bodily return of his mother, her cross reclaimed from racist significations.

Kaufman's adaptations of surrealism were more historically engaged and more politically directed than were those of many among his white contemporaries. Despite the leftist and anarchist leanings of some older poets, such as Kenneth Rexroth, and younger Beats, such as Ginsberg, Ferlinghetti, and McClure, few of them were ready to confront America's racial politics as forcefully as did Kaufman and Baraka. Even a poem whose title is lifted bodily from a black poet, such as Michael McClure's "It's Nation Time," contains no reference beyond the quotation marks of its title to its origins in black art; indeed, McClure's poetry has yet to be critically examined in its interracial historical context. The sorrowful fact is that even today too few critics who read McClure also read Baraka. More important, though, Kaufman's poetry joins a radical tradition of surrealism and racial politics that reaches back through García Lorca's *Poet in New York* and Aimé Césaire's *Return to My Native Land* to the radical politics of the French Surrealist Group. Kaufman would have known, of course, of the encouragement offered to Césaire by André Breton when the two poets met in Martinique during the war (Kaufman liked to tell friends that he had Martinican heritage himself) and of the role that Breton played in circulating the texts of the Negritude poets in France. Kaufman would also have known of the anticolonial politics of the Paris Surrealist Group, including Breton, Char, Eluard, and Tanguy, perhaps best represented by their contribution to Nancy Cunard's *Negro* anthology, the essay titled "Murderous Humanitarianism." In Césaire's own writings Kaufman could locate exactly the kind of rewriting of history and language that places Césaire clearly in a critically "post" position to modern movements in French verse.

Kaufman's *Ancient Rain* is an inescapably postcolonial text, posing a post–Old World future inhabited by the Lorca of Harlem. The first paragraph of Kaufman's prose poem declares simply, "At this time, the dead nations of Europe and Asia shall cast up the corpses from the graveyards they have become" (75). The "ancient rain" that falls in the poem is not simply a reinvocation of the symbols of fertility of traditional verse, for this rain both kills and resurrects. It is a rain that redirects the course and discourse of history: "The Ancient Rain is falling on the waves of immigrants who fled their homelands to come to this home of Ancient Rain to be free of tyranny and hunger and injustice, and who now refuse to go to school with Crispus Attucks, the Ancient Rain knows they were starving in Europe" (77). These immigrants who become Americanized by replicating the injustices that drove them from their homelands, who sit in theaters that would not admit Crispus Attucks to be instructed in the racist mores of their new home, will not be raised by the rain to go home with Lorca. They are instead like the dinosaurs made extinct by the rain, their history the one dinosaur skeleton left "to remind the world that the Ancient Rain is falling again" (76).

It is the public construction of American history that Kaufman rebaptizes in his poem, much as Césaire looses the flood of his language so that he can stand in the postdiluvian air and say, as if for the first time on earth, the words *storm, tornado,* and *leaf.* Kaufman's deluge will wash away the ugliness of American historical narratives so that American history may be written again. For Kaufman American history has produced a bad movie, *The Night of the Living Dead:* "The Ancient Rain splits nations that have died in the Ancient Rain, nations so that they can see the culture of the living dead they have become, the Ancient Rain is falling on America now. It shall kill D. W. Griffith and the Ku Klux Klan; Hollywood shall die in the Ancient Rain. This nation was born in the Ancient Rain, July 4, 1776. The Ancient Rain shall cause the Continental Congress to be born again" (76). If Griffith's *Birth of a Nation* was history written in lightning, as Woodrow Wilson, college roommate of the author of Griffith's source text, *The Clansman,* claimed, then Kaufman calls forth a greater storm still that will cleanse the earth of such un-American Americans. They are like the Germans of Kaufman's poem who have entered into a secret agreement with the Klan that permits them, even after the Holocaust, to dine comfortably in Atlanta restaurants that Negroes cannot enter (78–79). The rain of apocalypse will force the South to recognize that its native son, William Faulkner, was right. "The South," Kaufman prophesies, "shall be forced to admit that we have endured" (80). Oddly enough, Shirley Temple is spared in the destruction that rains down on Griffith and Hollywood. "Shirley Temple understands the Ancient Rain and goes to Ghana, Africa, to be ambassador" (78), perhaps her reward for all that time spent at Bojangles Robinson's knee.

Lorca is not the only modernist whose life and work finds itself recast in the fun-house mirrors of Kaufman's revisionist measures. In some instances Kaufman's rewritings of the past foreground the very conjunctions between European and American modernisms that his own writing takes as its impetus. In "A Remembered Beat" he assumes the first-person plural: "We remember when Max Bodenheim remembered Lorca" (*Solitudes* 44). Past and future meet again in the San Francisco byways of Kaufman's "Harwood Alley Song." This poem follows the death by venereal disease of Atlantis with a reclamatory address to Rimbaud. Kaufman calls the French poet away from his African adventure, coaxing him back into poetry: "Rimbaud, you brilliant maniac, desert turtle. / Stop flirting with camels, turn in your pike" (*Cranial Guitar* 62). Where Kaufman wants to invite Rimbaud out of Africa, his approach to Gertrude Stein, who had once lived in his beloved Bay Area, finds him bringing her closer to blackness. Stein had a most curious relationship to black people and culture throughout her career. While she would welcome a Richard Wright into her salon, she would also presume to instruct Paul Robeson in his proper relationship to black spirituals. Where she was known at one time at least to have an African sculpture displayed on her work desk, she denied the value of African art to the emergence of modernism. Though black characters were at the heart of one of her signal early fictions, *Melanctha,* she infamously declared that the Negro suffered from "nothingness." It should surprise no one that Stein appears as both influence and subject in the writing of Bob Kaufman, but it is surprising to find him associating her with the underground railroad. This happens in at least two places in his poetry. In *Golden Sardine*

Kaufman writes of her arrival "in her private underground railroad car, surrounded by know something intellectual WITH STILL LIFES in their eyes, & no navels" (*Cranial Guitar* 36). Like Adam, the no-navel intellectual seems to have been born out of nothingness himself, though he doesn't seem to be suffering from it here. The reference to the underground railroad points in two related directions at once. In the first place it is Kaufman's humorous way of saving Stein from her own racist tendencies and making of her the ally that Wright had thought her to be. Thus when Kaufman confesses to "all the crimes committed during the month of April" in "A Terror Is More Certain . . . ," it is not only to save his own neck (and perhaps Eliot's as well) but to "save Gertrude Stein's reputation" (*Cranial Guitar* 45). Kaufman is also, however, drawing an analogy between the radical militance of the pre–Civil War abolitionists and the post–World War II Zionists. It turns out that Stein "is secretly flying model airplanes for the underground railroad stern gang of oz." Placing the gang in Oz may be a gesture in the direction of armed utopianist fantasy, or it may be a surreal undercutting of the terrorist impulse. In either reading Kaufman must be seen as conjoining the armed struggles for freedom of Jews and of Africans in America, a subject Stein gives little indication of having ever considered. The most audacious element of these passages is that Kaufman, who was not at all well known among readers of Stein at the time, presents himself as the one who will rescue Stein's reputation, which was then in far more danger from academic literary critics than from accusations of racism. Kaufman's railroad imagery also writes a link to the writings of an East Coast poet, Tom Postell, whose "Gertrude Stein Rides the Town Down El" appeared in an early issue of Baraka's *Yugen*. Kaufman had probably read that poem on its initial appearance and in any case was familiar with the landscape that serves as the poem's backdrop. His own "Demolition" remarks that the El remains the same even though it has been torn down. Both black poets place Gertrude Stein on a ghostly metaphorical vehicle, revising her past to make her more useful to their present. Kaufman's audacity takes the additional form of rewriting Stein's most notorious line. In "Come" he works by compression, tightening Stein's already compressed circle nearly to the new dimensionality of string theory: "AROSEAROSE" (*Cranial Guitar* 51).

The real Americans of Kaufman's poems remain the sons of the Revolution, not the sons of the Daughters of the American Revolution. They are "God's Angry" men (79), people like John Brown and Crispus Attucks. Attucks, whose own death by a British colonial bullet recalls Lorca's execution during the Spanish Civil War, is the black angel of America's post-Hollywood history. He is Kaufman's counterpoint to the tale told by Griffith and *Gone with the Wind* of heroically suffering racists. He *is* in death "the burning of Atlanta by the Union Army" (79), and he is the inassimilable first principle of American culture. "Crispus Attucks does not want a white mother" (79); he is the future anterior son and father of the modern nation. (We have to wonder, too, if Kaufman could have known that Charlie Parker, another in the pantheon of the poet's modernist saints and progenitors, had attended Crispus Attucks School in his youth.) In Kaufman's *Ancient Rain,* where "all symbols shall return to the realm of the symbolic and reality become the meaning again" (75), "Black angels roam the streets" protected by Ulysses S. Grant (79). It is Grant's tomb that Kaufman visits at the end of his poem, the scene of ascension, the place where, accompanied by his father and son, Crispus Attucks, he hears the voice out of the whirlwind, the voice of Lorca, who could not speak English, speaking in the mysterious black sounds of the *Duende*'s African accents: "Black Man, Black Man, for the mole and the water jet, stay out of the cleft, seek out the great Sun of the Center." Kaufman's "The Poet" repeats the common assertion that the poet lives in his poem. "The Poet" again seems to intuit the silence that will befall Kaufman:

> WHEN THE POET PROTESTS THE
> DEATH HE SEES AROUND
> HIM,
> THE DEAD WANT HIM SILENCED.
> HE DIES LIKE LORCA DID,
> YET LORCA SURVIVES IN HIS
> POEM, WOVEN INTO THE DEEPS
> OF LIFE. (*Ancient* 70)

Lorca lives in his own poems and is resurrected, like Stein, through the transubstantiation of Kaufman's recasting of the modern. Kaufman survives his poems, survives as his poems, transfigured in our reading.

## II

"I told Jesus be alright if he changed my name."
—Traditional

I am not an I.
—Bob Kaufman, *Solitudes*

The state of Bob Kaufman's corpus makes conclusions about any possible writerly intentions more than usually suspect. If I have here spoken of Kaufman's audacity in rewriting Lorca's modernity, I have done so in the knowledge that we cannot tell whether Kaufman's audacity was a matter of conscious revision, faulty memory, or even the flagging attentions of unidentified City Lights typesetters and editors. "The text of *Golden Sardine* is especially suspect," writes Gerald Nicosia, "as the early City Lights books were not free of typographical errors, and it is not known who, if anyone, actually corrected the proofs" (6). The poems that we read under Kaufman's name come to us as transcriptions from scattered tape recordings of his recitations, damaged manuscripts haphazardly retrieved, proof positive that the "author function" is a corporate phenomenon we name when we read a text, not the corporeal person to whom we attribute that reading. What Kaufman says of his own body in "All Those Ships That Never Sailed," the poem recited publicly to his wife, Eileen, on the day that he broke an avowed silence of ten years, might well be said of his body of work:

My body once covered with beauty
Is now a museum of betrayal.
This part remembered because of that one's touch
This part remembered for that one's kiss—
Today I bring it back
And let you live forever. (*Cranial Guitar* 125)

The poetry of Bob Kaufman comes to us marked by its passage through so many hands. If, as Kaufman said of Lorca, he lives in his poems, it is in the scarred, singed, and rent fabric of writing that we encounter Bob Kaufman.

Or "Bomkauf"—the punning signature appended to the "Abomunist Manifesto" shows us that Kaufman rewrote himself as readily and as significantly as he rewrote Lorca. Amiri Baraka's eulogy continues that interventionist tradition, as Baraka replaces the absent, voiced bilabial stop of Kaufman's Abomunist pseudonym. Americans tend not to pronounce the *b* at the end of the word *bomb,* a fact recorded in the title of Kaufman's "BOMS" (*Solitudes* 83). In compressing his own given and surnames, Kaufman's neologistic signature makes a sort of bomb-head of the Abomunist. One who abominates bombs may become a bomb-head. In the "Abomunist Manifesto," the missing *b* of *Bomkauf* is the specter haunting the post-Hiroshima epoch of the Beats. Baraka's eulogy reinserts the silent *b,* the silent *b* elided in the manifesting of the Beat, the silent beat that makes the Beat. At Kaufman's death, his final vow of silence, this time seemingly unbroken save by posthumous publication, Baraka makes manifest the silent *b* of Bob Kaufman's Beat signing.

This play in the field of names is among the most tense of black American ambiguities. If one of the worst sins among African Americans is to call somebody out their name, perhaps it is in part because black Americans have had to struggle across the centuries to name themselves and to have those names respected. At the same time, the nominative force that motivates a move from "Little" to "X" to "Shabazz" is ironically echoed in the shifting landscapes of Bob Kaufman's ethnic and racial self-representations (how Jewish is he, really?) and in the revisionist histories of his naming practices. Baraka's replacement of Kaufman's *b* is a resurrection and a redefinition. Where Kaufman rewrote Lorca, Baraka rewrites Kaufman's revision of himself. As he silently altered the final vowel of his own given name, from Leroy to LeRoi, Baraka orthographically alters the text of Kaufman. "[I]ts sound is / / Bob Kaufman, Poet" (*Cranial Guitar* 97)—and that starts with *P,* which rhymes with *B* and is the voiceless bilabial oppositional other to Kaufman's voiced but silent signature letter. Baraka spells the deceased by spelling things out for us. Jayne Cortez tells us that "a signature is a signal before an interruption" (Cortez and Feinstein 61). Kaufman interrupted his silence before signing off. With Baraka, we must be resigned to Kaufman's absence.

I had an encounter of my own with the historical conundrums of Kaufman's manuscripts and their names when reading the remarkable poem "The American Sun," the poem placed immediately after

"The Night That Lorca Comes" by editor Raymond Foye in assembling the book *The Ancient Rain* with, Foye tells us in his note to the volume, the author's blessings—though whether that means Kaufman had actually proofed the pages remains unclear. In one passage, Kaufman contemplates American technology and its relation to an empire of commodities:

> THE BUDDHA IS NOW STANDING
> IN FRONT OF THE AMERICAN SUN CALLED
> R.C.A. VICTOR, LISTENING TO HIS MASTER'S VOICE.
> THE BUDDHA HAS A BLACK SPOT ON ONE EAR NOW.
> THE AMERICAN SUN CALLED
> ARTHUR FARNSWORTH TELEVISION
> HAS TORN DOWN THE TEMPLE
> WALLS AND DRIVEN THE MONEY-
> LENDERS FROM THE WESTERN
> SIDE OF THE RHINE RIVER TO
> THE EASTERN SIDE OF THE RIVER
> THAT DIVIDES THE GERMAN EMPIRE
> INTO TWO SEPARATE BUT EQUAL
> STATES. (*Ancient* 64)

This is an extraordinarily rich passage, from its reincarnation of the Buddha as the R.C.A. Victor dog to its concluding allusion to *Plessy v Ferguson,* but what peculiarly puzzled me on first reading was the name "Arthur Farnsworth." I could find no likely real-world referents for this name. Finally, after I had posted a query to an online poetics discussion group, Ron Silliman suggested that the reference was most likely to Philo Farnsworth, who was memorialized on a plaque that Kaufman would have passed routinely in the course of his peregrinations along San Francisco's Sansome Street. This suggestion strikes me as plausible because of the poem's association between television and Farnsworth. Philo Farnsworth was the inventor in 1927 of the first all-electronic television. (The narrator of William Gaddis's *Agapē Agape* notes that in "the first public demonstration of television the image of the dollar sign was projected for sixty seconds by Philo Farnsworth in 1927" [6–7].) Farnsworth's rechristening as "Arthur" could simply be a matter of Kaufman's faulty recollection, transcribed from a taped recitation. Then again, it could entail associations ranging from Arthur Rimbaud to early television's Arthur Godfrey. In the absence of the poet's correction or a scholar's elucidating discovery, we are left to read the conundrum *as* a conundrum. As it happens, Philo Farnsworth was a character whose biography might well have fascinated Kaufman. Farnsworth, like a recent California poet laureate, had no college degree, but he had managed to produce a primitive picture tube by age nineteen and produced the first all-electronic picture the very next year. In the great American tradition he was a tinkerer and something of an autodidact. In the great communitarian tradition his invention was the result of intense labor by a team of colleagues dedicated to realizing his dream (Kisselhoff 33, 41). American television was to colonize the globe in Kaufman's lifetime, but it was also to shrink it. Television brought pictures from a divided Berlin to a divided America. Farnsworth's electronics also displayed America to itself, spread pictures of the brutality of southern racist oppression, of which Kaufman had personal experience, before the eyes of the whole world, which was watching. If the cinema of D. W. Griffith was an American modernism that affirmed racism globally, Farnsworth helped to usher in a postmodernism, a sphere of invisible, if licensed, ownership:

> THE ENEMIES OF
> THE AMERICAN SUN ARE SHOWN
> THEMSELVES ON TELEVISION,
> IT IS FILMED INSIDE THE CROSS
> BY THE AMERICAN SUN.
> UNLIKE BIRTH OF A NATION,
> IT IS NOT IN PUBLIC DOMAIN (*Ancient* 65)

Farnsworth, a native sun in Kaufman's eyes, also appears in *Does the Secret Mind Whisper?* as one link in a cultural lineage Kaufman traces from Socrates, through Picasso, to Whitman, a line of biblical "begats" in which Kaufman places fathers *after* sons.

Lorca is not the only modernist whose hymns are relined in Kaufman's renderings, nor is Philo Farnsworth the only subject of Kaufman's renamings. Maria Damon notes the multiple reconfigurations of the name of "Caryl Chessman," whose protracted trial and appeals, chronicled in books and a movie, became one of the more celebrated and controversial capital punishment cases in midcentury America.

In the lead piece of *Golden Sardine*—"Carl Chessman Interviews the P.T.A. In His Swank Gas Chamber Before Leaving On His Annual Inspection Of Capital, Tour of Northern California Death Universities, Happy"—Chessman's name undergoes a sort of serial derangement. In Damon's reading "Chessman, the subject of one of the most notorious and protracted capital punishment cases in the twentieth-century United States, becomes mythified through the fragmentation and dispersal of his name" (Damon, *Dark End* 41), beginning, perhaps, with the suggestion there in his family name that he had become a pawn in somebody's game. The fragmentation and dispersal begin with the suppression of the *Y* in Chessman's name in the title. (Kaufman is scrupulously accurate in other matters, however; the "Cell" number supplied for one "Caryl Melville" in "Waitun PLace" was in fact and exactly the phone number for the White House switchboard at the time of publication.) The dispersal of the name in Kaufman's writing attends the dispersal of the person, the living referent, in a California execution chamber.

"This is a poem about a / nobody" (*Cranial Guitar* 32). Emily Dickinson declares herself a nobody and asks readers if they are nobodies too. The dreariness of being somebody, in her lyric, is a bog to be bypassed. Caryl Chessman was either a nobody made terribly somebody by the state, or he was a vicious criminal celebrating himself in the public eye. In either event he was extinguished by governmental order, to be survived by his name, which lives on in infamy. Whether or not he was, as he was accused of being, the "Red Light Bandit," he was put to death in his own name, self-confessed grinning psychopath converted by writing and twelve years on death row into a celebrity victim of California's aptly named criminal justice system. When we contemplate Kaufman's professed desire to be anonymous (*Ancient* ix), we might do well to weigh it against the fate of the celebrated nobody whose name is dispersed through these paired poems in *Golden Sardine*.

Kaufman's achievement is akin to Ammiel Alcalay's description of the work of Juan Goytisolo: "By probing suppressed chapters in his personal and our collective histories, [he] interrupts the lethargy of our received assumptions in the hope of charting new itineraries along which memories of our future can be routed" (152). As much as Chessman may have become a suppressed chapter in our recent history, he is not, strictly speaking, the nobody of Kaufman's poem, and neither is Kaufman, the silent beat. Rather, "nobody" is the subject of the poem, constituted in an act of anonymous witness, dispersed through the body of the text in the endless proliferation and recasting of the name of Chessman, pawn in the postwar cold of America's ideological warfare:

> This poem is about a
> nobody, twenty something
> years old, whose parents
> sent him to a good college
> but, who instead read buddhist
> magazines & of course became god,
> he is now standing in front of his
> parents' house saying, they think I've been in school [for four
> years,
> how can I walk in and tell them I am god, I think I'll [go over
> to chessman's little studio & sleep. (*Cranial* 32)

"Nobody," e. e. cummings told us, "is altogether a queer fellow," as young as he is old (296). Nobody would seem to be the very subject contemplated by California's "Master Plan" for higher education, that modest proposal for the edification and life-preparation of California's young. Kaufman had early on recognized the symbiotic relationship that existed between California's much vaunted university system and its burgeoning collection of penal campuses. What for Chancellor Clark Kerr was to be the modern multiversity becomes in Kaufman's configuration of the far-flung system of "death universities" the place of Chessman's autoeducation, the studio of his cell, becomes the refuge for California's promising progeny, now become god.

"Now I am become death, destroyer of worlds." In testimony before Congress J. Robert Oppenheimer recollected a moving passage from Hinduism's Vedic scriptures, words that had passed through his mind as he witnessed in awe the explosion loosed on the desert that marked the success of the project he headed, named for Whitman's, and our, Manhattan. For most of us born after the Second World War this testimony was witnessed as an oddly flattened image flickering across the black and white screen of Philo Farnsworth's invention. The title of Kaufman's poem remarks the University of California's extensive entanglements in defense research even as it satirizes the state's commitments to capital punishment. It sometimes seemed that nobody could resist the state's death drive, and in Kaufman's poem "nobody" does. Nobody, announced at the poem's center, is to join Chessman in his "San Quentin word saloon" (*Cranial Guitar* 33), through which runs the armature of death and entertainment that powers both poem and state.

Caryl Chessman, albeit fading from popular memory, has played a curious role in our history and our current politics and continues to stir controversy. Ronald Reagan was carried into office as governor of California not only on the strength of his promise to contain the rebellious young on the archipelago of campuses of the university so glowingly contemplated in the Master Plan (a containment every bit as pressing for his electorate as was the containment of Soviet power) but also on the back of his backing for capital punishment. As it happened, the governor who oversaw the execution of Chessman was an outspoken opponent of the death penalty, Edmund G. Brown, father of the yet more liberal Jerry Brown, who, as a twenty-one-year-old, helped persuade his father to grant Chessman a sixty-day stay. It was, of course, exactly that sort of liberalism Reagan was determined to turn back.

The Chessman case had an immediate and lasting effect among artists. Avant-garde filmmaker and sculptor Bruce Connor began work in 1959 on a metal sculpture inspired by the impending Chessman execution. Encountering persistent difficulties in the casting process, Connor eventually determined to rework the wax model itself to produce the work that came to be known as *Child*, a provocative statement about the horror of the death penalty. Peter Byrne, in a retrospective account of Connor's life and works, reports that San Francisco newspaper columnist Herb Caen "led a chorus of public derision" (31) against Connor's *Child*. This is, at it happens, the same Herb Caen often credited with coining the word *Beatnik* to describe none other than Bob Kaufman. In tracing the subsequent peregrinations and vagaries of Connor's *Child* Byrne observes that the shape-shifting wax model came to transcend the particularities of Chessman's fate. In Byrne's estimation "a sculpture created in opposition to capital punishment evolved into a comment on the plight of all children confronted with adult sexuality, and adult values and pressures to conform to a social system" (31). Much the same process can be seen operating in Kaufman's poem as the dizzying transformations of Chessman's name race away from attachment to his individual case to propose a dark comedy of resistance to America's spectacularizations of death.

Rochelle Owens is another whose apocalyptic texts have their origins at least in part in those same modes of resistance. In recalling her own early years she traces the birth of her controversial play *Futz* to the turbulence of the war in Vietnam and the execution of Caryl Chessman. (In her memory she refers to him as "a killer" despite the historical fact that he was executed not for murder but for kidnapping [Nash 1]. Indeed, it was a belief that Chessman's crimes had not risen to a level commensurate with the ultimate penalty that so struck Governor Brown's conscience.) *Futz* was written at a time when Owens held a day job at the prestigious Sotheby-Parke Benet Galleries in New York, in wonderment that "a society could produce, simultaneously, the 'Man in the Grey Flannel Suit' and the atom bomb" (Nash 3). Here again we can read the parallel in Kaufman's text as education, entertainment, and apocalypse are all wickedly satirized, as they had been wickedly conjoined by the state. And, in yet one more ironic circuit, Fanny Howe, whose selected poems would one day be published by the same "death university" satirized in Kaufman's poem, had, soon after her arrival in California, joined with other artists and activists protesting Chessman's execution.

It was Chessman's own writings that, while infrequently read today, brought him such wide notoriety and controversy during the course of his many years on death row. Having made the fatal error of representing himself in his court case when charged at age twenty-seven as the "Red Light Bandit," an especially unwise move when one is attempting, as he did, to recant an allegedly coerced confession, Chessman, who had no funds, found himself ill-equipped to contend with the powers the prosecution could bring to bear against him. He was refused daily transcripts of the proceedings. In fact, thanks to the unfortunately timed death of a court reporter, no full trial record was ever completed, leaving news accounts and Chessman's own, quite possibly biased, memory as the historical record.

Though Chessman claimed his confession was extracted by means of police brutality, a charge not difficult to believe of 1950s-era policing in the Los Angeles region, he never gave a satisfactory account of himself, in spite of publishing four books before his execution. Still, many believed that sending someone who had not committed murder to the gas chamber was itself an instance of state-sanctioned brutality and barbarism. Always articulate, Chessman fit rather neatly, as did Kaufman, into the American literary tradition of the autodidact, reading constantly, studying law, and transforming himself into an accomplished and effective author. His book *Cell 2455, Death Row* sold half a million copies and was turned into a 1955 movie with a cast that included the young and soon to be famous Vince Edwards. (Two decades later Hollywood returned to this material with a made-for-television feature, *Kill Me If You Can,* starring Alan Alda, who was still riding his *M*A*S*H* fame.) Stung by the popular success of Chessman's writings, the state forbid him to write anything at all apart from papers for his appellate proceedings and attempted to block his access to the proceeds of his book sales. Pleas to spare his life streamed in from such strange bedfellows as Norman Mailer and Billy Graham, Christopher Isherwood and Robert Frost. Popular culture artifacts of the Chessman controversy include Roulette Records' release #4231, a 1960 recording by Ronnie Hawkins that paired the "Death of Floyd Collins" with the A-side "Ballad of Caryl Chessman." Backing Hawkins on that single were musicians later to gain fame as The Band, who also worked with the composer of songs such as "George Jackson" and "Hurricane," Bob Dylan.

Neither Billy Graham nor The Band could do what Governor Brown was unable to do, though, and notwithstanding one more dramatic stay of execution granted just two hours before his scheduled punishment, Caryl Chessman, following a legal battle of twelve years duration, heard the two pellets drop into the bucket of acid on May 2, 1960. Those final moments are fittingly recast as a movie spectacle in the first of two Chessman poems in Kaufman's *Golden Sardine:* "& now doctor von stroheim is explaining how the two miniature atom bombs set each other off in that little gray pail that the guards are putting a coat of lipstick on right now . . . " (*Cranial Guitar* 33). If, as the saying goes, you can put lipstick on a pig, but it's still a pig with lipstick on, then there is little the state can do in the way of ritual and appeals to the public welfare to disguise the essential horror of execution by gas chamber. The invocation of a German director for this scene, so soon after the Second World War and the Holocaust, places the execution of Caryl Chessman uncomfortably close in manner to the genocidal gassing of innocents in Europe. Von Stroheim's fictive explanation of the science of capital punishment, which is here laid out in a way that calls to mind the workings of fusion bombs, serves as a discomfiting reminder that just as earlier waves of German refugees created a vital community of exile talent in Hollywood, so too did postwar European refugees join in the paired American efforts to explore space and to create ever deadlier weapons of mass destruction. (Kaufman points again to the polysemous legacies of German refugees in the United States in the second of his Chessman poems, in which we witness the grand opening of the Arnold Schoenberg supermarket [recalling, it may be, Schoenberg Hall at UCLA] against a background of raining black Volkswagens [*Cranial Guitar* 36]).

And Kaufman's articulation of entertainment with nuclear weaponry in this passage is not nearly so surreally contingent as later readers may suppose. There is an intriguing news item nestled below the fold on the front page of the *Los Angeles Times* for Sunday morning, May 1, 1960, the day preceding Chessman's death. The lead story that day was the ruling expected from the California Supreme Court just two hours before the scheduled gassing. Accompanying that story is a photograph of Caryl Chessman that shows him being photographed (this is, after all, the postmodern) and questioned by journalists at San Quentin. The caption beneath the photo reads: "Last Interview?" the ominous question mark taking precedence over such other news of the day as the struggles of Nixon, Kennedy, and Humphrey for their parties' nominations. Near the bottom of the page is a three-paragraph story with a chin-dropping headline: "Underground Movies Urged for Bomb Shelters." This is not, as it turns out, an argument in favor of showing underground films such as those of Bruce Connor, Maya Deren, and Stan Brakhage to while away the hours spent in shelters during a nuclear war. Instead, it is a report of a speech delivered by a major figure in the development of the hydrogen bomb to a meeting of the New York Democratic Club in which the guest scientist proposed that "future motion picture theaters be built underground to provide ready-made bomb shelters" (*Los Angeles Times* A-1). The scientist making this modest proposal, played by von Stroheim in Kaufman's mental movie, was Edward Teller, who, in addition to his labors on behalf of what he liked to term the "Super" bomb, was a tireless political persecutor of Oppenheimer and who later was to serve as cheerleader-in-chief for Ronald Reagan's dubious and expensive Star Wars, or Strategic Defense, initiative.

But if the phone number for the president's White House rings in the "waitun place" of Chessman's cell, so, too, does one end of cold war converse find its terminus here. It is no less a personage than God who gives Chessman "A LITTLE RED DEW LINE TELEPHONE" (32). The DEW line, as millions of American school children were reassured by Civil Defense educational films, was the Defense Early Warning system of radar installations strung along northern lines of latitude for the purpose of detecting any Soviet first strike launched across the polar regions. The little red phone recalls the Hot Line, in truth a teletype but represented synecdochically in the public imagination by the red phone reputedly always at the ready for the president to reach out and touch to launch a bevy of Teller's super bombs. The Hot Line more closely attended by the real Chessman would have been the phone link at the ready to bring word from a governor or court staying his death orders. Kaufman's line here is doubly ominous, though. Representing the phone call to which all arrested suspects are presumed entitled, Chessman's little red phone suggests that it is he who holds the power over life and death, not his governor.

The prose poetry of Kaufman's imaginings echoes other "MAKESHIFT GAS CHAMBERS OF SUPPRESSED HISTORY" (39). Chessman's trial is "being held in the stomach of Junipero Serra" (31). Drivers following the coastal highway north to San Francisco will pass under a large statue facing west to the Pacific and pointing one large, stone finger out over the highway toward the horizon. This figure is a representation of Father Junipero Serra, currently a candidate for sainthood in the Catholic church. But even as the Vatican documents the requisite miracles recorded in his name, others are considerably less excited at the imminent canonization. American Indian movements have joined with revisionist historians and allied activists in protest at the prospect of Serra's posthumous elevation, noting his central role in the destruction of native civilizations and the enslavement of indigenous peoples under the mission system of early California settlement. Rather than the sanctification of narratives of Western expansion and suppression, Kaufman imagines a different import for the clichéd final scene of cartoon travelogues: "AS QUAINT LI'L' OLE WESTERN CIVILIZATION. . . . . . SINKS SLOWLY IN THE WEST, WE LEAVE FUN-LOVING CALIFORNIA WITH ALL OF ITS . . . COLORFUL DEATH FESTIVALS & SET SAIL FOR EXOTIC NEBRASKA" (37).

The "Leafless Nebraska" dreamed by Kaufman lies well to the east of Serra's lifeless statue, and, as Victor Hernández Cruz tells us in his poem "Nebraska," "In this part of Mexico / Se habla inglish" (64). Here once more is enacted a primal scene of conquest and execution. Chessman transforms into "AN AMERICAN BUFFALO, THUNDERING ACROSS CALIFORNIA'S LYING PRAIRIES" (38). These passages, though, do far more than simply link Chessman symbolically to the nearly exterminated American bison and the hunted, haunted prairie tribes of the Ghost Dance. Kaufman's attention is drawn to Nebraska (whose citizens founded Arbor Day to relieve their leafless condition) because it, too, was the scene of a recent, highly publicized execution. Charles Starkweather, whose spasm of violence in the company of his underage girlfriend (who was later the subject of her own book) galvanized the western states, was electrocuted for his criminal rampage at the conclusion of a case that drew national and international attention. Like Chessman, Starkweather's story was to become the subject of a Hollywood film, starring Martin Sheen and Sissy Spacek, and still later was recast for telling on television. While there was never the least doubt, as there was in Chessman's case, regarding Starkweather's guilt (it was the girlfriend whose precise degree of culpability was so controversial in this case), there was something still that struck a nerve in the global media coverage of this murderer's end. (Conducted to his death by electricity, Starkweather shared with Kaufman himself the experience of having electrodes clamped to his person.) There was a sense somehow that in their zeal to execute this smirking kid, the state authorities came away from their ritual of sin and expiation less cleansed of an afflicting evil than mired in it, a sense in which this was another of those "Gothic Hate Festivals of Rotted Conscience" (38) spelled out in Kaufman's movie-poem. The state was essentially made smaller by execution, its elect seen at last as those "new mirror people with no sky in their faces" described by the poet. (And these mirror people would seem to recall the mirror-faced figure in Maya Deren's *Meshes in the Afternoon,* at the same time prefiguring the mirror-faced space traveler who accompanies Sun Ra in the opening segment of *Space Is the Place*.) If Starkweather, with his strangely appropriate name (another quality he shared with Chessman), was more Custer than Crazy Horse, more killer than ever Chessman was, he was still a midcentury punk out of America's most closely drawn drama of dreaded delinquency, and there was something ultimately cannibalistic in the mass media rites of his end. His killers, like

Chessman's, were "VOMITING ASSASINS" who "KILLED HIM, & DESTROYED THEMSELVES IN THEIR REPUBLICAN-DEMOCRAT HASTE TO EXTINGUISH HIS BURNING" (39).

Kaufman is not drawing a literal equation between Starkweather and Custer's victims; he is not saying that the German extermination of Jews was identical to the extinguishing of Chessman; he is not even saying that Republicans and Democrats are the same. He is suggesting that we take on a deathly sameness in permitting the state to kill in our name. Whether it is the "GENOCIDED RED CRAZY HORSE PEOPLE," the Chessman/Buffalo "FLYING WITH ZULU KINGS TO THE BOTTOMLESS PITS OF AMERICA'S SOUL" (39), or "I. Socrates" (35), in their killing we take on a terminal similitude, become "zombie congregations of cold Nebraska people" (40). If *Night of the Living Dead* was a horror film formed in the fear of cold war–era apocalypse, Kaufman's "HORROR MOVIE TO BE SHOT WITH EYES," dedicated to the "Mothers of America" (in all the doublings of that meaning [34]) is an inferno of conquest and execution in the heart of middle America.

In Kaufman's most audacious script it is Chessman who sends death threats into our national imaginary, who reminds us of the ancient rain. Caryl (Carl, gentleman jim, Stonewall, Caul) Chessman (Ruth, Darrow, Melville) denies our "GODLY GAS BIRTHRIGHT" (31), tenders our long overdue "ENORMOUS GAS BILL" (36), calls us out our name, calls us to our proper name. In the quiet of "guilty California" we can read in the interstices of Kaufman's Chessman script "the message to all garcias everywhere, longitude people, beyond the margin" (33).

# 5
# *Capillary Currents: Jayne Cortez*

## I

at that moment of no compromise
his poetry became poetry unique to poetry
—Jayne Cortez

The music is already there. By the time the ear falls prey to the groove, the music is already multiplying, leveling monuments to expectation and erecting newer castles in the air; a layering with open work areas dangerously unguarded. This is not at all unusual these days, and never was. Still, each generation hears ellipses. Still, Jayne Cortez is already listening, present tense, as she begins "I See Chano Pozo," her praise poem for the great midcentury Cuban conguero and composer. The band is already at play. The seven minutes and thirty-one seconds of the poem's second site in Cortez's 1982 recording, *There It Is* (which, without a "whoop," intriguingly prefigures the doubled variant versions of the next decade's rap hit, "Whoop, There It Is"), open with percussive punctuation. Elliptical hand patterns on bongo and conga look ahead to what we will hear of Chano Pozo in the poem, while adverting to the backward glance at the poem's title. As the other instruments intervene, a harmolodic whirl ensues. There is a discernible tonal reference point, but we seem to be free of strict key. Bass and guitar refuse to fall into the usual gestures of accompaniment. Rather, each independently carves in air series of serious notes, selected with an ear to what the other is doing but never settling into the prefabricated chord that an audience might intuit. The "It" of *There It Is* is, in Cortez's explanation, an "example of what a poet does with music and what musicians do with poetry" (Cortez liner notes). It is, then, a sample, and as is true of all samples, it refuses coincidence with itself. The performance, as Tony Bolden remarks of Cortez's poetry generally, "exemplifies blues music's propensity for syncretism" (64). The poem takes its place at the nexus of prefigured and postproduced poetic history, and it displaces it.

Only after the musicians have begun to chart out the paths by which they will defamiliarize the territory does the human voice intrude in the mix. Familiarity is in the nature of song, but familiarity is not identity. Male voices in the recorded version of the poem commence a titular chant, but it is not until the poem's second stanza that listeners hear how the poem's very name is harmolodically deflected. The chanting musicians sing a long, North American *a* in the initial syllable of Pozo's proper name, "I see Chano [here pronounced "Chay-no"] Pozo." When Cortez follows, pronouncing the name in her own voice, she gives it a more properly Spanish inflection, "Chano Pozo," and the distance between the two accentual naming patterns names the distance traveled from the call of Pozo's Cubana bop to the harmolodic discrepancies of Ornette Coleman's response, and that of his Prime Time band members, who form the nucleus of the recording unit for *There It Is*. As Cortez intones the poem's first line, "A very fine conga of sweat" (*Coagulations* 65), it is apparent that we have been dropped in medias res, into the propulsive power point of a synesthetic difference engine. As the differing pronunciations of Chano Pozo's name might indicate, we are not so much in the middle of some most particular thing in progress as we are in the middle of progress itself, in the middle of the Middle Passage.

In the version of the poem that Cortez performs in the same year for the Ron Mann film *Poetry in Motion* there are no chanting counterpoints to the poet's pronunciation. Nonetheless, because her own voice, speaking in an interview, overlaps the performance's opening bars, leaving behind the image of poet as interview subject and leading us to the image of the poet surrounded by already performing musicians, the text of what we presume to be her poem spread on a stand before her, the same effects of difference within familiarity, figured differently, again obtain. The interviewed poet is speaking of the tradition of call and response as the film editor thrusts us into the already-in-progress jazz poem. Is the paper in front of the poet a visible sign of the difference between prose speech and jazzed poem or, more likely, moving prop against which rest all such ultimately unanswerable questions. The performance is a response to the poem, an example of what musicians do with poetry. The poem is a prior response to jazz, example of what a poet does with music. The interview statement is in response to a question, example of what an audience does with jazz poems. And there it is, the core of possibility in jazz text. All calls participate in a rhetorical logic by which they incorporate in advance the anticipation of an answer. All response is response to something and thus shapes itself to its calling while transposing it. All performances of "I See Chano Pozo," on page or staged, partake of this same shifting logic, harmolodic transposition of a calling in anticipatory response.

"A very fine conga of sweat" (65). The drum is already in play, someone sweating over it. Cortez calls us to attend to a long history of *Cubanismo* in North American discourse, a *Cubanismo* long embargoed by an aggressively consumerist politics that would prefer to have its sugared antecedents and eat them too. As I write, North America is again celebrating one of its periodic seizures of love for Cuban music. Compay Segundo, Ibrahím Ferrer, Rubén González, and other members of that ad hoc social construction known as the Buena Vista Social Club have been circulating successfully through North American venues on a seemingly endless tour whose energetic performances belie the superannuated birth certificates of the musicians. Los Van Van, one of Cuba's most popular bands, is playing to standing-room-only houses across the country, even in Miami, where anti-Castro exile activists, culturally depraved by our long dark embargo of the soul, attempted to shut down their countrymen's concerts. The way was made smoother for this most recent eruption of Cubanaphilia not only by Ry Cooder's yeoman service as cultural ambassador but by the earlier tours of virtuoso pianist Gonzalo Rubalcaba. Charlie Haden, the bassist who was at Ornette Coleman's side during the invention of harmolodics, took the Cooder role in that earlier episode, arranging recording dates and concert appearances with the astonishing young pianist. For his earliest U.S. appearances, though, Rubalcaba was forced to philanthropy by our State Department. Not permitted to play for pay, the Cuban artist played two major concert benefits on the coasts of the United States as a means of building audiences for his recordings, though his first releases widely available in the States had to be released through his American label's Japanese division in order to meet, however circuitously, the demands of the embargo. That American officials went to such lengths to keep Cuban arts out of the United States, while presumably keeping their arms wide open in welcome to any Cubans willing to permanently separate themselves from their island, is testimony to their knowledge of both the powers of Cuban cultural innovation and the willingness of an unembargoed American mind to lend an ear.

The ironies of these most recent Cuban sorties of course follow after Cortez's poem. But there had been a similar phenomenon shortly prior to her release of *There It Is*. In 1979, Irakere, among the most spectacular concentrations of Cuban music talent, had released its first Anglo album, following close on the heels of a triumphant tour of international jazz festivals. This was the first time that most American music fans were able to hear Paquito D'Rivera, Chucho Valdes, and Arturo Sandoval, names that have continued to claim the attentions of serious music lovers in the years since. The 1979 American label album was the direct result of a visit of American jazz artists to Havana in 1977. In the same way that Charlie Haden and Ry Cooder were able to introduce North Americans to art their representative government did not want them to know in the 1990s, American jazz greats constituted themselves as an advance guard for Irakere's storming of the jazz festivals at Montreaux and Newport two decades earlier. And here we come to a more direct intersection with Cortez's poem, for the American artists most responsible for bringing the good news of Irakere north were Stan Getz, who had visited Cuba in the 1950s, and Dizzy Gillespie, who was visiting Cuba for the first time despite the fact that he had been, more than any other, the man responsible for the explosion of Afro-Cuban music within the bop revolution of the 1940s. His collaborator in that fecund syncretic concoction was Chano Pozo. In 1948, just months after the historic recording sessions that produced "Cubana Be" and "Cubana Bop," the band appeared at Wrigley Field in Los Angeles, the same Wrigley Field memorialized by Jay Wright in his book *The Homecoming Singer* (*Transfigurations* 25), and Cortez was in the audience.

In his liner notes to the 1979 Irakere album Leonardo Acosta remarks as one of the group's contributions to the expansive vocabulary of Latin jazz their bringing into the popular music of Cuba of the "intricate and vigorous Yoruba and Carabalí rhythms which have been well known in Cuba but which had not been 'integrated' into the mainstream" of the music, a cultural syncretism that is matched in Cortez's poem. Acosta also makes an intriguing suggestion regarding the long history of Latin infusions into American jazz idioms. "Their affinity comes from before the existence of jazz as such," he asserts.

"We all know the history of the beginnings of jazz, but we don't always associate it with the ending of slavery in Cuba, between 1880 and 1889, and the massive immigration of black Cubans, free but jobless, to places like New Orleans." Jelly Roll Morton, he reports, once listed Cuba among the sites of origin for jazz. If Acosta is at all right in his genealogies of jazz, this means that not just Irakere's interventions in American music but Chano Pozo's initial forays as well might be marked out as a return as much as an immigration. Afro-Cuban rhythms, the subsequent additions of Yoruban and Carabalí timings to those of Congo and Dahomey, might be a reappearance within the modernity of jazz.

The bebop innovations of Parker and Gillespie revolutionized jazz, that music most intimately identified with North American modernity. Their rewritings of the rule books of harmony against the backdrop of a reinvigorated pulse within the rhythm section were radical wrinkles within the already modern. In this context Gillespie's work with Chano Pozo, identified by Cortez in her liner notes to *There It Is* as "the first conga player to play with a jazz band," must be heard as a return of an African Caribbean anterior already echoed in the structures of jazz. Similarly, the postbop renovations orchestrated by Ornette Coleman, given Coleman's experiences playing rhythm and blues in his circuit-riding youth, are a return with a difference. Bop reoriented the solo line's relationship within harmony. Coleman's jazz stripped away the usual chordal structural supports of harmony, leading through his early Free Jazz stage to his later harmolodics, while at the same time moving from bop-oriented rhythms to a further funk. All of these differential returnings are audible in the harmolodic music of Cortez's musical associates, both on *There It Is* and in the somewhat smaller-scale performance caught by *Poetry in Motion*. And this syncretic mode of renewal is heard again in Cortez's poetics.

In her *Poetry in Motion* interview Cortez says, "It's about sound; the sound of the music against the sound of the poetry." This is as true for the printed poem on the page as it is for any of its performance variants. Speaking to Sascha Feinstein about her more recent work, Cortez remarks the deadliness that can attach to an artist whose signature song is demanded by all audiences, about how "repeating something exactly as it had been recorded . . . is no longer a release" (61). One way to avoid such staleness is to vary the piece with each release, while maintaining the recognizable script of the signature itself. This is what Cortez has done with her multiple performances of "I See Chano Pozo," but it is also what she has already done in the poem's composition. The lyric's refrain alters with each reappearance, and within the semantic registers of the sounds she has elected to carry her chorus, we can reread the perpetual postmodernizings of Latin jazz's renewed incursions. Cortez's unpunctuated rhetorical question, "Is there anyone finer today" (inside of which I hear a bop-styled pop refrain from an earlier era: "Nothing could be finer . . . "), finds its respondent chorus chanting, "olé okay / Oye I say / I see Chano Pozo" (65).

Here the Spanish cheer is answered with a peculiarly American idiom. Both *olé* and *okay* pick up the internal rhyme with *today* from earlier in the line, troping the rhetorical question with the rhetoric of the idiomatic. The origins of the American *okay* are shrouded in philological controversy. This prototypical Americanism has frequently been given a West African etymological source and has also been traced to American Indian ancestry. It was without doubt widely popularized as a result of its use in early American partisan politics. In any event the appearance of its close linguistic cousin *Okeh* as the name of one of the most popular race records labels earlier in the twentieth century solidified its shadow racial connotations. The next line repeats this alternation of Spanish and English, this time following the command *Oye* with the declarative, *I say,* all the while punching percussively at that rhyme with *today*. Finally, speech turns to sight, matched by a phonic modulation from *a* to *e,* as the declaration completes itself, or finds its answer, in "I see." The grammatical ambiguity proceeds from the absence of graphic punctuation, leaving us unable ultimately to determine whether the poet is saying that she sees Chano Pozo, or if she is saying and seeing him, saying *as* seeing, an uncertainty that acts as analogue to the unresolved tonalities of the harmolodic music in the recorded versions. As it happens, that uncertainty has its audible rhyme in the contending pronunciations of Pozo's first name in the version heard on *There It Is*. The musicians pronounce *Chano* so that its initial syllable rhymes with Cortez's *olé, okay, oye,* and *I say,* but Cortez herself, marking a sort of harmolodic distinction, does not. In her reading of it the first syllable of the name rhymes with the first syllable in "Havana," the place name that immediately follows Pozo's in the poem, citing his home.

Such differences make a circle of signifying, as Pozo is lauded within the poem as "The one who made Obonu into / a circle of signifying snakes." That circle of Dickinsonian sibilance sews Pozo's name through the circuit of stanzas, reminding us of its echoes in the name *Cortez,* plaiting a sonic signature within the onomastic weave of the praise poem. This is an occasional poem, after all, first composed by Cortez for the Chano Pozo Music Festival held at Dartmouth in 1980 (a fact that might propel us to a reconsideration of New England and what we thought we knew of it). In her interview years later with Sascha Feinstein, speaking of her poem "Flying Home," Cortez distinguishes between the signature tune with which an artist might saddle herself for life and "depth or art or spontaneity." But she leaves an enticing opening in another remark she makes on that occasion: "A signature is a signal before an intermission" (61). Her literal referent is that commonly brief stretch of readily identifiable melody or theme with which musicians signal that they are about to take a break. For over two decades the melody Miles Davis used in this way was titled simply "Theme." Miles, though, never signed his theme the same way twice. One need only audition the versions heard in his mid-1960s live recordings and compare them to the torqued and retooled electric versions heard just a few years later at venues like the Fillmore auditoriums to see just how far a signature can be stretched without snapping out of legibility. Cortez's poem is her way of signing a certain history in music and letters, but she has incorporated the signatures of others as well, gathering them into a sheaf of allusion.

For "I See Chano Pozo" asserts a second genealogy alongside the melody line that follows the *Cubanismo* of jazz from its beginnings in New Orleans, through its reappearance with the advent of Chano Pozo in bop, and into the more recent figurings of Irakere and the Buena Vista Social Club. That second genealogy is literary, Afro-Spanish and again attached to the music. North Americans now are listening again to the *sonedores* of Cuba. In doing so they retrace the listenings of an earlier mode of modernism, one that found in Afro-Cuban musical forms a way to revivify the legacy of *modernismo* left by Rubén Darío. Rubén Darío, born Félix Rubén García Sarmiento in 1867 in Nicaragua, was the principal figure in the modernization of New World Spanish language poetics, bringing the breakthroughs of Whitman to bear on the traditions of Spanish verse. While Darío was profoundly influenced by his readings of American poets, his was in no way an imitative or subsidiary poetic movement. His poem addressed to Theodore Roosevelt demonstrates just how opposed he remained to imperialisms both military and cultural. But by the time of Darío's death in 1916, the aesthetics of the *modernismo* that he had championed were waning throughout Latin America. *Modernismo* lingered in a somewhat attenuated fashion in Cuba, where it had been wedded to the techniques left to that national literature by José Martí and Julián del Casal. By the time of the earliest poems of Nicolás Guillén, *modernismo* was increasingly overshadowed by the poetics of those newer artists collectively known in Cuba as *Los nuevos* (Marquez 13–29).

As international modernism seized on the imaginations of artists, the fascination with the Africanesque on display in the works of Picasso, Braque, and others found its way increasingly to places where African culture was considerably more immediate than any museum piece, awaiting ready, if tardy, reappropriation and redirection. In the Spanish-speaking New World this led to the *Negrista* poetics of such "white" writers as Luis Palés Matos and José Zacarías Tallet. Afro-Cubano writers, though, were early on seeking out other models, and they found them, as did the Negritude poets of the Francophone Caribbean, in the arts of the Harlem Renaissance. This brought into being a circle of signifying cross-influences that overlaps the musical history memorialized in "I See Chano Pozo." Poets like Césaire, Damas, and Cuba's Nicolás Guillén came to read the English language poets of the Harlem Renaissance, among whom the Caribbean influence was already powerfully apparent. In turn, as Langston Hughes's endless travels brought him frequently through the Caribbean region, he made a point of meeting with these poets, subsequently assisting in their works' appearance in English translations in North America. Along with Mercer Cook's translations of the Negritude poets he had met in his trips to France, translations that he shared with generations of students at Howard University, this marked the first recycling through North American audiences of an Afro-Caribbean, avant-garde aesthetics with its accompanying radical politics, resonant with the lingering echoes of earlier Caribbean contacts within the poetics of African American culture.

Caribbean movements emphasizing the indigenous in the arts came increasingly to revalue the African elements in their cultures, and this revaluation inevitably brought about a political reconfiguration. Although Guillén never developed as far-reaching a philosophical critique of European culture and ideology as did the Negritude of Césaire and Senghor, his version of *Negrismo,* in contrast to the works of his white predecessors (which might be seen as having more in common with Van Vechten than with Césaire), increasingly took aim at the presumptions and neocolonial aspirations of his giant neighbor to the north. Thus the romanticism of Guillén's earliest poems, published in *Camagüey Gráfico,* is soon given greater edge by the political ironies of his collections *Sones para turistas* and *West Indies, LTD.* But it is the diasporic Africanity found in the forms and language of Guillén's poetry of the 1930s and 1940s that signs itself in the poetry of Jayne Cortez decades later.

North Americans fill concert halls today listening raptly to the *sones* sung by Ibrahím Ferrer. It is an old music new to many Yankee Boomer ears. One of the ways in which Nicolás Guillén rewrote the *modernismo* of Darío more than sixty years ago was to embrace the Afro-Cuban *son* as a form in which to realign his poetic language with the languages of African America that he heard in the air all around him. It was an air already suffused with the international, the diasporic, the syncretic, for, as José Piedra has argued: "The *son* has remained loyal to its remote, nonliterate source: the Dogon *sò. Son* and *sò* are core principles of Cuban and Dogon ontologies respectively. The evolution from the latter to the former likely involved the Afro-Haitian culture and language, which from the outset of the revolution of the slaves went into exile to the eastern tip of Cuba" (115). In a series of early books including *Motivos de son, Songoro cosongo,* and *El son entero,* Guillén accomplished a breakthrough in Cuban letters parallel to what Langston Hughes and Sterling Brown did by basing a literary art in the form of the blues. Guillén's intention was, as he put it, "to incorporate into Cuban literature—not simply as a musical motif but rather as an element of true poetry—what might be called the poem-*son*" (qtd. in Marquez 18). Turning from the tortured dialect of earlier popular Africanist verse, Guillén increasingly drew on the inventive potential of his polyglot culture. Spanish is spoken differently in the Americas, in part thanks to its forced marriage with the idioms of Yoruba and Dahomey. Guillén used a novel word, *jitanjáforas,* to describe the coinage of terms in everyday Afro-Spanish, words that suggest a mestizo linguistic history and that tunnel under the fortifications erected in the Spanish of the Conquistadors. The title of his book *Songoro cosongo* is itself a *jitanjáfora,* an Africanesque neologism creating a syncretic metaphor wedded to the meters of the *son.* In his introduction to his 1931 collection, *Motivos de son,* Guillén speaks of the injection of Africa into Cuba so deep that "many capillary currents cross and interweave in our well-irrigated social hydrography" (qtd. in Marquez 20). Because of this deep capillary network, "the two races that emerge on the surface of the island, though apparently distant, are linked subterraneously to each other, like those underwater bridges which secretly join two continents." It is just this deep capillary network that Cortez brings to the surface in "I See Chano Pozo," the same capillary network joining this chanting woman to the musicians surrounding her in her performances of the poem.

Guillén's use of *jitanjáforas* conjoins him to a lineage of modernist and postmodernist linguistic experimentation that, when discussed in most contemporary criticism, generally elides Cuba, the Caribbean, the Spanish language, and all things Yoruban. Such a critical oversight would likely not have been made by William Carlos Williams, for despite his many and overt prejudices he liked to draw attention to the Caribbean hydrography of his own familial and intellectual past. Guillén's turn to the quotidian idioms of Cuban speech links him again to the modernisms of Williams and of Hughes. Most important, for Guillén there is no inherent political opposition between the novel, perhaps partially opaque, construction of the *jitanjáforas* and the deceptive seeming-transparence of everyday language. What Guillén, Hughes, and Williams recognized was that "the people" experiment with language every day of their lives. This was the sort of "populist modernism" that Amiri Baraka was to make a rallying cry for the first generation of postmodernists, the generation of Jayne Cortez.

In his "*Son número 6*" Guillén writes:

*Yoruba soy,*
*cantando voy,*
*llorando estoy,*
*y cuando no soy yoruba,*
*soy congo, mandinga, carabalí.*
*Atiendan, amigos, mi son, que empieza así.* (61)

Guillén is the post-*modernismo sonero* who commands the reader's attention to the opening out of his *son*. His *son* commences midpoem, in medias res, calling out from the Middle Passage of song, that subterranean capillary network that conjoins continents and epochs. This is the call Cortez hears in the drumming of Chano Pozo: "Chano," she calls him, "connector of two worlds" (66). Guillén's drumbeat reads the roll of diasporic languages: "*soy congo, mandinga, carabalí.*" It is a roll Cortez continues on her return from "the cemetery of drums":

> Lucumi Abakwá Lucumi Abakwá
> Olé okay (67)

Earlier, Cortez asked a question that might well have been addressed to that mode of Anglo-American modernism that sealed itself off from all this, embargoed itself, all the while reserving unto itself the right to vacation in the spiritual Cuba of Wallace Stevens's florid mundo. In the poem "Do You Think," Cortez asked, "Do you think time speaks english?" (*Coagulations* 13). In the rooms that open beneath the foundations of modernity (rooms marked "Conquest," "Middle Passage," and "Slavery"), those rooms that connect continents in time, English is one of many idioms from which America's *jitanjáforas* might emerge. In "I See Chano Pozo" Cortez wonders aloud, "[W]hat made your technology of thumps so new?" (*Coagulations* 66). What Cortez calls to in her poetry is a modernity that constantly makes itself new by attending to the accents that speak its conditions of possibility. For decades the postbop, post–Free Jazz Art Ensemble of Chicago has had as its slogan, "Great Black Music: Ancient to the Future." The late Lester Bowie knew exactly the technologies of newness that link Nicolás Guillén to Langston Hughes and William Carlos Williams, that bring Chano Pozo together with Dizzy Gillespie, that Charlie Haden hears in Gonzalo Rubalcaba. It is the technology of thumps (school of hard knocks?) that Billy Higgins hears echoing from out the Congo as he propels a harmolodic Ornette Coleman. It is the congress of *jitanjáforas* that Roscoe Mitchell, Lester Bowie, Joseph Jarman, Famadou Don Moye, and Malachi Favors Magoustous heard bubbling from beneath the Chicago streets and shouted out to the world, what sets the Urban Bushwomen singing. It is what Jayne Cortez heard flowing from the fingertips of Chano Pozo one night in 1948 and refigured thirty-two years later as black American contemporaneity, a capillary action drawing up ancient centuries into our anaphoric future:

A very fine tree stump of drones
a very fine shuffle of shrines
a very fine turn of the head
a very fine tissue of skin
a very fine smack of the lips
a very fine pulse
a very fine *encuentro* (67)

II

"When you removed the gag that was keeping these black mouths shut, what were you hoping for?" (Sartre 115). This is a more than usually rhetorical question, set as it is at the opening of the essay "Black Orpheus," with which Jean-Paul Sartre introduced the 1948 anthology of Negritude poetry edited by Léopold Sédar Senghor. Sartre is memorializing a repeating moment in which, as Brent Edwards characterizes it, "colonial 'mirages' were beginning to talk back" (84). That Sartre addresses himself to a white audience is never in doubt. His rhetoric positions his readers inextricably, discomfitingly, in a subject position *as* white readers. "In a word," he explains, "I am talking now to whites, and I should like to explain to them what blacks already know" (117). In the peculiar history of racial discourses there can be few so peculiar as this. On the one hand Sartre's gesture is directed, decades before the advent of whiteness studies in the American academy, toward making their whiteness visible to white readers themselves. "For three thousand years," he writes, surely mistaken in his assumptions regarding the antiquity of whiteness as a racial category, "the white man has enjoyed the privilege of seeing without being seen" (115). Yet how oddly this prefatory matter reads today, an introduction to a book of poetry in which, Sartre asserts, "these blacks are addressing themselves to blacks about blacks" (117), an introduction in which a white philosopher addresses himself to the whiteness of his white readers. Certainly any reader, ideal, implied, or actual, advancing on a selection advertised as new black and Madagascan poetry would have much to ponder in the face of this insistently white introductory apparatus. But what of the black, or even Madagascan, reader? Just how is a black reader interpellated by Sartre's rhetorical question? Where does any reader find a resting place among Sartre's display of pronouns: "Here are black men standing, looking at us, and I hope that you—like me—will feel the shock of being seen" (115). Even if Sartre makes clear, in a word, that he is "talking now to whites," what a curiosity this presents to black readers. What *are* black readers supposed already to know, that Sartre now proposes to explain? And how does that already knowing extend itself across the decades of reading since?

Sartre writes out of a profound literary/historical vacuum, writes, indeed, as if black people had never before written to one another. More recently, Eliot Weinberger, who does not choose to present himself as a white person writing to other white people, accomplishes a similar act of erasure while introducing another black poet. On one side, no one should deny the act of editorial generosity with which Weinberger devoted his section of a 1993 issue of the journal *Sulfur* entirely to the works of contemporary poet Will Alexander. Disturbingly, however, Weinberger seems to retreat from that very generosity in his efforts to present Alexander as sui generis. "He is probably the only African American poet," according to Weinberger, "to take Aimé Césaire as his spiritual father" (227). Where Sartre, in the act of introducing the revolutionary poetics of Negritude, manages to wipe out all that preceded it, including its African American forebears, Weinberger, introducing a significant American successor to Negritude, manages with one phrase to obliterate all that had transpired between Césaire's time and our own. Both Sartre and Weinberger operate in such a way as to disconnect black poets from one another, a move that simultaneously disconnects the histories of Francophone and Anglophone poetries from blackness in the act of introducing black poetries. To interrupt such generous introductions as Sartre's and Weinberger's may well strike some as impolite, but within the poetry itself there is already a history of eruptions and interruptions. The historical motion toward a reassertion of white privilege within poetics invites its own disruptions. A critical interdiction appears within poetry, a black mark against the white pages wielded by Sartre and Weinberger, a hiccup in the white noise of poetics-as-usual. To Sartre's "what were you hoping for," a question that constitutes the reader as white, there is an opposed interdictory rhetoric in a question posed, "exile to exile," by Jayne Cortez: "Won't you dance for this mean banjo player?" (*Coagulations* 54).

The poet's choice of instrument is not merely fortuitous. The banjo has its ancient antecedents in African musics. On our shores it is the instrument that conjoins the blues to bluegrass, early jazz to radio hillbilly, the flailing improvisations of both blacks and whites. Within our writing it is the signifier of modernity's black and folk affiliations, witness Claude McKay's titular *Banjo* as well as the "banjo jazz" evoked by William Carlos Williams. Cortez's rhetorical question poses a transcontinental, transgenerational instrumental demand. The question is not "Will you dance?" Rather, it is the imprecatory "Won't you dance for this mean banjo player?" Sartre does not truly implore us to any action. Somehow responsibility in Sartre's eyes always comes back to blacks. He proposes that "[i]t is when Negritude renounces itself that it finds itself; it is when it accepts losing that it has won; the colored man—and he alone—can be asked to renounce the pride of his color. . . . [H]e is the one who looks to the end of particularism in order to find the dawn of the universal" (138). Note the oddity of this grammar. The colored man "can be asked to renounce the pride of his color," as if there were some colorless master asker already safely lodged on the other side of that ridge between the particular and the universal that Sartre sees Negritude perched on, as if the revolution had already come . . . for some. Cortez's question, in contrast, addresses itself to a universal second person, one who has the hiccups.

In 1937 Leon Damas published his poem "Hiccups" in the book *Pigments,* a volume subsequently banned throughout French West Africa, where its poems had been taken up in Baoulé translation by African draft resisters (Kennedy 43). *Pigments* appeared with an epigraph drawn from Claude McKay, underscoring the book's consciously diasporic aesthetic by honoring a fellow Caribbean poet who had been instrumental in the Harlem Renaissance. The book bore an introduction by Robert Desnos, pointing to emergent Negritude's affinities with modernist Europe's most radical branch of surrealist poetics. Negritude's pan-Antillean genealogy is also evident in its profound kinship with the Haitian *Ecole Indigeniste,* the intellectual and arts movement foregrounding *indigenisme,* greatly influential in Caribbean philosophy and painting as the revolution of surrealism found its ready and "always already" answer in Wilfredo Lam and others, and paralleling similar movements in the Spanish-speaking Caribbean. (Indeed, Alejo Carpentier's development in the next decade of what came to be known in English as "magic realism" is in large part credited to his experience of *indigenisme* during his visits to Haiti.) It is

"Hiccups" specifically, though, that Cortez's question calls us back to, a poem also revisited by Lorenzo Thomas in his collection *Chances Are Few*. When Cortez speaks of Damas as a banjo player, she alludes to a particularly scathing moment among Damas's impolite "Hiccups." Damas imagines a color-struck, assimilationist mother berating her insufficiently class-conscious son:

I see you haven't been to your vi-o-lin lesson
    a banjo
    did you say a banjo
    what do you mean
    a banjo
    you really mean
    a banjo
    no indeed young man
        you know there won't be any
        ban-or
        jo
        or
            gui-or
                tar
                    in our house
They are not for *colored* people
Leave them to the *black* folks (Damas 50)

The imagined mother, who wants her son to speak "the French that Frenchmen speak" (49), will abide neither tar nor guitar in her home. Her wandering son, still, replies with an impolitic rhetoric. Where the mother asks incredulously, "You really mean a banjo?"—Jayne Cortez can read a statement of fact: "You really mean a banjo"—meaning Damas as a mean banjo player, the one who calls the tune Cortez recalls us to; the different drummer who compels the New World idioms of Cortez's measures. Cortez seizes on the proprieties of the mother's speech ("there won't be any ban or jo"), turning them to importuning (Won't you dance for this mean banjo player?).

Damas's *Pigments* was published a year before Aimé Césaire undertook the writing of his *Return to My Native Land*, eight years prior to Senghor's first book, and more than a decade before Sartre's introduction to the Negritude poets. Damas's "Hiccups" carries a dedication to Vashti and Mercer Cook, a dedication reasserting the interlingual traffic suppressed in Sartre's account of Francophone blackness and thus reasserting an account of black modernity left out of account by Sartre and Weinberger. If Weinberger would have us skip entirely the generation of Cortez and view Will Alexander as Césaire's probable only-child, Cortez's praise poem for "The Red Pepper Poet" sings a genealogy Alexander has long acknowledged. "Cortez's development as a poet," notes Tony Bolden, "seems to coincide with her development of an internationalist world view and an interest in Surrealism, whose radical politics are quite compatible with the ideas of Black Arts theorists" (64), and much the same could be said of such post–Black Arts artists as Will Alexander, though it will not get said by Weinberger, intent as he seems on forgetting both Cortez and the Black Arts. The interlinguistic black modernity embraced by Cortez and Alexander constitutes that within "what blacks already know" that Sartre does not undertake to explain for whites. Mercer Cook was a professor of French, later to become a dean, at Howard University in Washington, DC, the city to which Damas was to relocate years later. Cook was an avid visitor to Paris in the 1930s, collecting a sheaf of the new Negritude poetry that he took back with him to DC to share with his students and friends. Those poems, then, were among the first fresh reports of Negritude circulated in the United States.

Mercer Cook met with many of the artists and theorists of Negritude, including Damas, Senghor, and Césaire, in the home of the Nardal sisters, whose Paris salon was as obligatory a stopover point for traveling black intellectuals as Gertrude Stein's was for whites. Out of discussions among these young writers came such significant publishing projects as *Presence Africaine, L'Etudiant Noir, Légitime Defense, Tropiques,* and the Senghor anthology introduced by Sartre. Paulette Nardal was herself to serve as editor of *La Revue du Monde Noir*. In her essay "The Awakening of Race Consciousness" Paulette Nardal, more than sixteen years before Sartre's "Black Orpheus," refuses the whitening of Western culture on offer in the colonial education apparatus. She points to the undeniable contributions of Antillean writers, including Alexandre Dumas and José Maria de Hérédia, to international romanticism. She also points to a perhaps surprising early American progenitor for diasporic black modernism, William Stanley Braithwaite. "It is under the influence of Braithwaite," she insists, "that modern authors, starting in 1912, without abandoning Negro rhythms and the emotional intensity due to their ancestral sufferings, took these themes as the starting point of their inspiration and gave them universal purport" (108). Where Sartre presented Negritude as "a simple surpassing of itself" on the path to the universal, Nardal presents Negritude as a black modernity surpassing Western culture, the Western culture that Nardal says made blacks "conscious of who we really are" (110) and in *that* surpassing demonstrating the universality that it already knows. Nardal's is criticism as interdiction, an interruption of white noise, characteristic, according to Brent Edwards, of a black expression that "effects a crisis" by "highlighting contradictions in the Western fascination with the primitive" (89).

Cortez's poem commences in the conditional, summoning global diasporic forces:

> If you see a cycle of heavy breezes
> blowing backward
> into massive loops of heat
> crossing two oceans after sunset (53)

These lines describe a vortex of migratory motions: the northward passage of a Senghor out of Africa; the eastward progress of a Césaire from the Antilles to Paris; the recirculation of poetics from Braithwaite to Brathwaite, from modern to postmodern, from Middle Passage to diasporic convection. It is the historical mode of circulation anatomized by Paulette Nardal at the beginning of the 1930s and recited post-Sartre in Senghor's "Negritude and Modernity." Here Senghor argues again, as had Alain Locke within the pages of his *New Negro* anthology at the height of the Harlem Renaissance, that black arts are at the very core of the modern. "We all know well enough, nowadays," Senghor begins—adducing a something that "we all know" that nonetheless eludes Sartre's exhibit to white readers of what black people already know—"how the arts of the Paris School—painters, then sculptors, met with Black Art at the beginning of the century and worked in assimilating its virtues, as the European musicians, in turn, enriched themselves with Black music through the American detour" (160). Sartre had been concerned with possible black assimilations of dominant white aesthetic ideologies but had taken little public note of the significance to diasporic rhetoric of the "American detour." Still, others attended differently. Senghor recalls the painter Soulage remarking to him after a reading of the poet's "Black African Aesthetics" that "it is the very aesthetics of the twentieth century" (160). In Senghor's reading, as in Nardal's, Locke's, Du Bois's, and C. L. R. James's, "the aesthetics of the Paris school expresses, in modern terms, Black African aesthetics" (160). Where Sartre promises "to show in what way we can gain access to this jet-black world" (117), Senghor suggests that we, and his pronoun seems ever so much more encompassing than Sartre's, are already in it.

In quite another context, Stuart Barnett has made the case that "[t]he search for the other does not need to posit an exteriority to the West—which is, in fact, always a positing of the West—because the other inhabits its innermost structures. . . . [T]he larger Modernity is precisely this search for another too easily forgotten, an other that the West has repressed and yet is utterly dependent upon" (36). This is surely not, as some might suggest, another moment of the West's narcissistic self-regard. It is in part a recognition of the facts that *white* and *Western* are not synonymous, that whiteness is dependent in its very structures as an identity on the positing of blackness, that any culture claimed by whites as Western is inextricably bound up with African antecedents and black contemporaneity. Under this construction Negritude is an exemplary instance of what Barnett has termed "the larger Modernity," and it is just that mode of modernity that Sartre's description of Negritude as an antiracist racism effectively effaces. That point has been made most effectively by one outraged early reader of "Black Orpheus," Frantz Fanon. In "The Lived Experience of the Black," published in the journal *Esprit* in 1951, Fanon lodges a complaint that Sartre's essay essentially filches from the black poets it introduces even their opportunity to mean: "There you have it, I am not the one who creates a meaning for myself, but the meaning was already there, pre-existing and waiting for me" (196). Fanon comes to feel robbed by the experience of reading "Black Orpheus." As he reads Sartre explaining to whites that which blacks are supposed already to know, Fanon finds himself up against an all too familiar usurpation: "As far as consciousness is concerned, the Black consciousness is given as an absolute density, as if filled with itself, a stage prior to any crack, or any abolition of the self by desire. Jean-Paul Sartre, in this work, has destroyed Black enthusiasm. To historical becoming, the unforeseeable should have been opposed" (197). It would seem that for Sartre, Fanon's reading was the unforeseeable.

Assigning to himself the task of introducing to an audience he constructed as ineluctably white the source of black knowing, Sartre appears not to have foreseen the possibilities of the black reader as knowing subject.

This simultaneous presumption and failure to assume is a phenomenon Fanon remarks as a recurrent feature of interracial discourse. Du Bois, in *The Souls of Black Folk,* avers there is always an unasked question hovering in the air between himself and the other. Fanon's later philosophical revision of Du Bois is his proposition: "Between the White and myself, there is an irrevocable relation of transcendence" (199). There is, always and everywhere, a relation of transcendence between any one and any other. A certain presumption is an epistemological requirement of any relationship in language. But Fanon's charge is that Sartre has forgotten the very thing he purports to explain, and this strikes one as a surprising if not surpassing act of bad faith; Sartre has forgotten what black people must know. He has forgotten, Fanon reminds us, "that the Negro suffers in his body differently than the White" (199). This is not at all the matter of an essential biologism, though it might at first seem such a claim, for the categories of Negro and White as Fanon comprehends them are not essentially biological. They are social. Sartre's erasure of the past of blacks writing to one another, coupled with his promise of a future in which *they* can be asked to renounce pride of color, creates a situation in which Fanon felt "it was impossible for [him] to exist [his] Negrohood" (199). It is a moment similar in structure to that in which contemporary whites, having had the epiphany of the social constructedness of race, announce that race no longer exists, while changing none of the social structures that in fact continue to construct us as white and black. Though there may be localized essentialist moments within the body of Fanon's work, I do not believe that this is among them. For Fanon Negritude is something that must be existed. The fact that he finds himself in a situation in which he must exist himself as black is given to him by the other, "whether real or imaginary" (201). His existing will be a mode of response to the world's expectations; it will necessarily be an art.

Even when Sartre believes that blacks are addressing themselves to one another, "unconcerned," as he puts it, "with *us*" (116, emphasis added), it is still somehow *about* "us." In one sense this is inevitable. It is not truly possible to read, which is always a most radical act of opening to the other, as if the other's text were not in some deepest of ways concerned with we who read it. Sartre's error, as Fanon finds it, "was not only to go to the source of the source, but also, in a certain way, to dry up that source" (196). If Sartre has explained to white people what black people know, what is left for black people to know?

This is so important because it so nearly replicates what too often happens when students at historically white universities and colleges study black people's poems. The poets are frequently reduced as they are elevated. Election to the status of the syllabus is sometimes accomplished to an accompaniment of enlistment as native informant. "When Whites feel they have become too mechanical," Fanon hears from a friend who has been teaching in the United States, "they turn towards the men of color and ask them for a little nourishment" (194). (At the risk of logical fallacy I might suggest that the academy's simultaneous fascinations with the Internet and with rap partake at least in part of this pattern.) After reading "Black Orpheus" Fanon believes that Sartre's excitement masks an aesthetic devaluation. "The Whites had discovered a poetry that had nothing poetic about it" (194). Sartre's rather remarkable accomplishment was to have read black surrealism, the super realism that both Senghor and Cortez claim as a deeper stratum of the real, to have read these most resistant and material of poetic signifiers as if they were not poetic at all, as though they had arrived before him as transparent reports of black life. The "Lived Experience of the Black," as Fanon and Cortez have existed it, refuses any such reductions. Cortez does not stop at praising the Red Pepper Poet, at asking us to dance to his banjo lays; she demands that we "dissect the meaning of the strategy of Damas" (55). We cannot reread Damas, or Cortez, as if the poem had vanished, leaving in *our* hands the sources of black people's meanings. Fanon defines an ethic: "I define myself as an absolute tension of opening" (199). Cortez, as she weaves her international, interlingual net of mutuality *about us,* interdicts Sartrean forgetting. In the end she demands nothing less of us:

> when everything drops into your mask
> in that position beyond all grief
> at that second
> this very instant
> Won't you dance for the Red Pepper Poet (56)

# *Works Cited*


Acosta, Leonardo. Liner Notes to *Irakere*. New York: Columbia Records, 1979. JC 35655.

Alcalay, Ammiel. *Memories of Our Future: Selected Essays, 1982–1999*. San Francisco: City Lights Books, 1999.

Anderson, T. J., III. "Body and Soul: Bob Kaufman's *Golden Sardine*." *African American Review* 34.2 (2000): 329–46.

Atkins, Russell. "Abstract of the Hypothetical Arbitrary Constant of Inhibition's Continuumization Becoming 'Consciousness' (Nervous System, Etc.)." *Free Lance* 11.1 (1967): 24–36.

——. "Eloge." *Free Lance* 14.2 (1970): 26–27.

——. "Henry Dumas: An Appreciation." *Black American Literature Forum* 22.2 (1988): 159–60.

——. *Here in The*. Cleveland, OH: Cleveland State University Poetry Center, 1976.

——. *Heretofore*. London: Paul Bremen, 1968.

——. "How Would I Come upon a Corpse?" *Free Lance* 3.1 (1955): 26.

——. "The Hypothetical Arbitrary Constant of Inhibition's Continuumization." *Free Lance* 8.2 (1964): 33–62.

——. "The Invalidity of Dominant-Group 'Education' Forms for 'Progress' for Non-Dominant Ethnic Groups as Americans." *Free Lance* 7.2 (1963): 19–32.

——. "Langston Hughes and the Avant-Garde." *Podium* 1.3 (1965): 14–15.

——. "Letter to *Input*." *Input* 1.4 (1964): 6–7.

——. Letter to the author. July 28, 2003.

——. *Maleficium*. Cleveland, OH: Free Lance Press, 1971.

——. "May Twenty-Second, Nineteen Sixty Seven." *Free Lance* 11.2 (1967): 20–23.

——. "Notes on Negro Poets." *Free Lance* 2.1 (1954): 16–18.

——. *Objects*. Eureka, CA: Hearse Press, 1961.

——. Of. *Free Lance* 7.1 (1963): 21–23.

——. Of. *Free Lance* 11.1 (1967): 49–54.

——. Of. *Free Lance* 20.1–2 (1980): 1–5.

——. *Phenomena*. Cleveland, OH: Free Lance Poetry and Prose Workshop/Wilberforce UP, 1961.

——. "A Phenomenalist Perspective for Poetics Based on C (Negative) and B (Positive) Probabilities for Maxima and Minima." *Free Lance* 18.1–2 (1977): 16–24.

——. *A Podium Presentation*. Brooklyn Heights, OH: Poetry Seminar Press, 1960.

——. "Pseudo-Problematical Critical Values for 'More' in Poetry as Opposed to Technique." *Free Lance* 16.1–2 (1973): 45–59.

——. "A Psychovisual Perspective for 'Musical' Composition." *Free Lance* 3.2 (1955): 2–17.

——. "Psychovisual Perspective for 'Musical' Composition." *Free Lance* 5.1 (1958): 7–47.

——. Rev. of *Musophilus,* by Samuel Daniel. *Free Lance* 10.1 (1966): 12–13.

——. "Russell Atkins." *Contemporary Authors Autobiography Series*. Ed. Joyce Nakamura. Vol. 16. Detroit: Gale Research, 1992. 1–19.

——. "Some Thoughts Defining 'Mainstream' in Relation to 'Education' and Destructive Power." *Free Lance* 8.1 (1964): 26–27.

——. "Special Russell Atkins Issue." *Free Lance* 14.2 (1970). Commentary by Casper L. Jordan and J. Stefanski.

——. *Spyrytual*. Cleveland, OH: 7 Flowers Press, 1966.

——. *2 by Russell Atkins*. Cleveland, OH: Free Lance Poets and Prose Workshop, 1963.

——. *Whichever*. Cleveland, OH: Free Lance Press, 1978.

Baldwin, James. "Interview with Julius Lester." *New York Times Book Review* May 27, 1984. 24.

Ball, Gordon, ed. *Allen Ginsberg Journals Mid-Fifties: 1954–1958*. New York: HarperCollins, 1995.

Baraka, Amiri. "The A, B, C's." *Yugen* 6 (1960): 39–40.

——. Amiri Baraka papers. Moorland-Spingarn Collection. Howard University. Washington, DC. 72 boxes.

———. Amiri Baraka papers, 1958–1966. Special Collections, University Research Library. University of California, Los Angeles.

———. *The Autobiography of LeRoi Jones/Amiri Baraka*. 2nd ed. Chicago: Lawrence Hill Books, 1997.

———. *Black Music*. New York: William Morrow, 1967.

———. *A Burning Mirror = Memoirs*. Ms. Baraka papers, Box 37. Howard University, Washington, DC.

———. *Conversations with Amiri Baraka*. Ed. Charlie Reilly. Jackson: UP of Mississippi, 1994.

———. *Eulogies*. New York: Marsilio Publishers, 1996.

———. *The Fiction of LeRoi Jones/Amiri Baraka*. Chicago: Lawrence Hill Books, 2000.

———. *Home: Social Essays*. NY: William Morrow, 1966.

———. Introduction. *The Moderns: An Anthology of New Writing in America*. Ed. Amiri Baraka. New York: Corinth Books, 1963. ix-xvi.

———. *It's Nation Time*. Detroit, MI: Motown Record Corp., 1972.

———. Letter to Ken Stuart. Aug. 19, 1976. Ts. Baraka papers, Box 3. "Correspondence 70–79, Macmillan File." Moorland-Spingarn Collection. Howard University, Washington, DC.

———. Letter to Rosey Pool. n.d. Ts. Rosey Pool papers. "Correspondence 1959–1967." File 84. Moorland-Spingarn Collection. Howard University. Washington, DC.

———. "*Northern Iowa:* Short Story and Poetry." *Arshile* 4 (1995): 39–43.

———. "A Note on the Twelve Poems." Baraka and Di Prima 51–52.

———. "Notes on Lou Donaldson and Andrew Hill." *Cricket* (1969): 46.

———. "Philistinism and the Negro Writer." *Anger and Beyond: The Negro Writer in the United States*. Ed. Herbert Hill. New York: Harper and Row, 1966. 51–61.

———. *Poetry with Jones*. Audiocassette. Pacifica Radio Archive, 1964. BB1910.02.

———. *Preface to a Twenty Volume Suicide Note . . . .* New York: Totem/Corinth Press, 1961.

———. *Raise Race Rays Raze: Essays since 1965*. New York: Random House, 1971.

———. "The Rejected Buppie." *Streetlights: Illuminating Tales of the Urban Black Experience*. Ed. DorisJean Austin and Martin Simmons. New York: Penguin, 1996. 20–23.

———. Rev. of *A Form of Women* and *Hymns to St. Geryon*. *Kulchur* 3 (1961): 81–85.

———. "Rhythm Travel." *Fertile Ground* 1 (1996): 243–44.
———. *Selected Plays and Prose of Amiri Baraka/LeRoi Jones*. New York: William Morrow, 1979.
———. *Six Persons*. Ts. Baraka papers, Box 38. Howard University, Washington, DC.
———. "Suppose Sorrow Was a Time Machine." *Yugen* 2 (1958): 9–11.
———. *Transbluesency: Selected Poems, 1961–1995*. Ed. Paul Vangelisti. New York: Marsilio Publishers, 1995.
———. "Uncle Udom's Cabin." *Kulchur* 11 (1963): 88–90.
Baraka, Amiri, and Amina Baraka. *The Music: Reflections on Jazz and Blues*. New York: William Morrow, 1987.
Baraka, Amiri, and Diane Di Prima, eds. *The Floating Bear: A Newsletter*. La Jolla, CA: Laurence McGilvery, 1973.
Barnett, Stuart. "Hegel before Derrida." *Hegel after Derrida*. Ed. Stuart Barnett. London: Routledge, 1998. 1–37.
Bernasconi, Robert, ed. *Race*. Oxford: Blackwell, 2001.
Bérubé, Michael. *Marginal Forces/Cultural Centers: Tolson, Pynchon, and the Politics of the Canon*. Ithaca, NY: Cornell UP, 1992.
Bolden, Tony. "All the Birds Sing Bass: The Revolutionary Blues of Jayne Cortez." *African American Review* 35.1 (2001): 61–71.
Bourne, St. Claire, dir. *In Motion: Amiri Baraka*. The Chamba Organization, 1983.
Brooks, Gwendolyn. *Blacks*. Chicago: Third World Press, 1991.
———. *Primer for Blacks*. Chicago: Third World Press, 1991.
Byrne, Peter. "Artjournalism." *SF Weekly* Sep. 13–19, 2000: 24–35.
Charters, Ann, ed. *The Portable Beat Reader*. New York: Penguin, 1992.
Chow, Rey. *Writing Diaspora: Tactics of Intervention in Contemporary Cultural Studies*. Bloomington: Indiana UP, 1993.
Christian, Barbara. "Whatever Happened to Bob Kaufman?" *Black World* 31.11 (1972): 21–29.
Congdon, Kirby. "A Reply." *Input* 1.4 (1964): 9.
Cortez, Jayne. *Coagulations: New and Selected Poems*. New York: Thunder's Mouth Press, 1984.
———. *Borders of Disorderly Time* (audio recording). New York: Bola Press, 2003. BLP2003.
———. Liner notes to *There It Is* (audio recording). New York: Bola Press, 1982. BP-8201.
Cortez, Jayne, and Sascha Feinstein. "Returning to Go Someplace Else: An Interview with Jayne Cortez." *Brilliant Corners* 3.1 (1998): 53–71.

Creeley, Robert. "Letter." *Yugen* 6 (1960): 30.
Cruz, Victor Hernández. *Maraca: New and Selected Poems, 1965–2000*. Minneapolis, MN: Coffee House Press, 2001.
cummings, e. e. *Complete Poems, 1913–1962*. New York: Harcourt Brace Jovanovich, 1972.
Damas, Leon. "Fifteen Poems from *Pigments*." Kennedy 45–61.
Damon, Maria. *The Dark End of the Street: Margins in American Vanguard Poetry*. Minneapolis: U of Minnesota P, 1993.
——. "Triangulated Desire and Tactical Silences in the Beat Hipscape: Bob Kaufman and Others." *College Literature* 27.1 (2000): 139–56.
——. "Victors of the Catastrophe: Beat Occlusions." *Beat Culture and the New America*. Ed. Lisa Phillips. New York: Whitney Museum of American Art, 1995. 141–49.
Davis, Miles. *In a Silent Way*. New York: Columbia Records, PC 9875.
De Gruttola, Rafael. "A Reminiscence." Torra 29–30.
Derrida, Jacques. *Aporias*. Trans. Thomas Dutoit. Stanford, CA: Stanford UP, 1993.
——. *Who's Afraid of Philosophy? Right to Philosophy I*. Stanford, CA: Stanford UP, 2002.
Dery, Mark. "Black to the Future: Interviews with Samuel R. Delany, Greg Tate, and Tricia Rose." *Flame Wars: The Discourse of Cyberculture*. Ed. Mark Dery. Durham, NC: Duke UP, 1994. 179–222.
Dorn, Ed. Letters to Amiri Baraka. Amiri Baraka papers, 1958–1966. Special Collections, University Research Library. University of California, Los Angeles. Ed Dorn file.
Edwards, Brent Hayes. "The Ethnics of Surrealism." *Transition* 8.2 (1999): 84–135.
Ellingham, Lewis, and Kevin Killian. "*Cock Drill:* Jack Spicer, Steve Jonas, The 'Boston Renaissance' and After." Torra 40–43.
Fanon, Frantz. "The Lived Experience of the Black." Trans. Valentine Moulard. Bernasconi 184–201.
Feinstein, Dianne. "Proclamation." Office of the Mayor, San Francisco. January 26, 1987.
Friedlander, Ben. E-mail to the author. March 8, 2004.
Gaddis, William. *Agapē Agape*. New York: Viking, 2002.
Gilroy, Paul. *The Black Atlantic: Modernity and Double Consciousness*. Cambridge, MA: Harvard UP, 1993.
Goldberg, David Theo. *Racist Culture: Philosophy and the Politics of Meaning*. Cambridge, MA: Blackwell, 1993.

Guillén, Nicolás. *El son entero: Cantos para soldados y sones para turistas*. Buenos Aires: Losada, 1968.

Hall, Stuart. "What Is This 'Black' in Black Popular Culture?" *Black Popular Culture: A Project by Michelle Wallace*. Ed. Gina Dent. Seattle: Bay Press, 1992. 21–33.

Harris, William J. *The Poetry and Poetics of Amiri Baraka: The Jazz Aesthetic*. Columbia: U of Missouri P, 1985.

Henderson, Stephen. "Black Poetry: The Continuing Challenge." ya Salaam and Brown 144–55.

——. "Modernity and Other Directions in Afro-American Literature: Reflections on the Past Two Decades." ya Salaam and Brown 136–43.

——. *Understanding the New Black Poetry: Black Speech and Black Music as Poetic References*. New York: William Morrow, 1972.

High, Ronald Henry. "Russell Atkins." *Dictionary of Literary Biography 41: Afro-American Poets since 1955*. Ed. Trudier Harris and Thadious Davis. Detroit: Gale Research, 1985. 24–32.

Hudson, Theodore R. *From LeRoi Jones to Amiri Baraka: The Literary Works*. Durham, NC: Duke UP, 1973.

Hughes, Langston. "The Twenties: Harlem and Its Negritude." *African Forum* 1 (1966): 18–19.

Hunt, Erica. "Notes for an Oppositional Poetics." *The Politics of Poetic Form: Poetry and Public Policy*. Ed. Charles Bernstein. New York: Roof Books, 1990. 197–212.

James, C. L. R. *The Black Jacobins: Toussaint L'Ouverture and the San Domingo Revolution*. New York: Vintage Books, 1963.

Jameson, Fredric. *Postmodernism, or, The Cultural Logic of Late Capitalism*. Durham, NC: Duke UP, 1991.

Johnson, Abby Arthur, and Ronald Maberry Johnson. *Propaganda and Aesthetics: The Literary Politics of African-American Magazines in the Twentieth Century*. Amherst: U of Massachusetts P, 1991.

Johnson, Joyce, and Jack Kerouac. *Door Wide Open: A Beat Love Affair in Letters, 1957–1958*. New York: Viking Penguin, 2000.

Jonas, Stephen. "About the Poem and about Measure for George Stanley." Amiri Baraka papers, 1958–1966. Special Collections, University Research Library. University of California, Los Angeles. Stephen Jonas file.

——. "A Poet's Word to a Blue Painter." Baraka papers, UCLA.

——. "distend." Baraka papers, UCLA.

———. *Exercises for Ear: Being a Primer for the Beginner in the American Idiom*. London: Ferry Press, 1968.

———. *Four Letters*. *:that:* 23 (1994).

———. "'I' BEFORE E-quality OR I THE FEW, YOU THE MINNIE-SINGERS." Baraka papers, UCLA.

———. Letters to LeRoi Jones. Baraka papers, UCLA.

———. Letters to Robert Kelly. Robert Kelly papers. Poetry and Rare Book Collection. State University of New York at Buffalo. B66F1, B66F3, B66F4, B66F5.

———. "Orgasm 0." Baraka papers, UCLA.

———. "Orgasm X." Baraka papers, UCLA.

———. "Orgasm XXXVI–Second Series." Baraka papers, UCLA.

———. "Orgasm XXVIIII: First Series." Baraka papers, UCLA.

———. "Orgasm 52." Baraka papers, UCLA.

———. *The Poetry of Stephen Jonas*. Ed. Joseph Torra. *Lift* 10 and 11 (1992).

———. *Selected Poems*. Ed. Rafael de Gruttola. Boston, MA: Stone Soup Poetry, 1973.

———. *Selected Poems*. Ed. Joseph Torra. Hoboken, NJ: Talisman, 1994.

———. "Subway Haiku." *The Floating Bear: A Newsletter: Numbers 1–37, 1961–1969*. Ed. Diane Di Prima and LeRoi Jones. LaJolla, CA: Laurence McGilvery, 1973.

———. "III." Robert Kelly papers. Poetry and Rare Book Collection. State University of New York at Buffalo. B272, F14.

———. *Transmutations*. London: Ferry Press, 1966.

———. "What Made Maud Hum." Baraka papers, UCLA.

Jordan, Casper LeRoy. Afterword. *Phenomena*. By Russell Atkins. 76–78.

Jordan, Casper LeRoy, and J. Stefanski, eds. *Free Lance: Special Russell Atkins Issue* 14.2 (1970).

Joyce, Joyce A. "The Black Canon: Reconstructing Black American Literary Criticism." *New Literary History* 18.2 (1987): 335–44.

———. "'Who the Cap Fit': Unconsciousness and Unconscionableness in the Criticism of Houston A. Baker, Jr., and Henry Louis Gates, Jr." *New Literary History* 18.2 (1987): 373–84.

Kaufman, Bob. *The Ancient Rain: Poems, 1956–1978*. New York: New Directions, 1981.

———. *Cranial Guitar: Selected Poems by Bob Kaufman*. Ed. Gerald Nicosia. Minneapolis, MN: Coffee House Press, 1996.

——. *Does the Secret Mind Whisper?* San Francisco: City Lights Books, 1960.

——. *Golden Sardine*. San Francisco: City Lights Books, 1967.

——. *Solitudes Crowded with Loneliness*. New York: New Directions, 1965.

Kelly, Robert. "Llanto for Steve Jonas." *Hearse* 13 (1970): n.p.

Kennedy, Ellen Conroy, ed. *The Negritude Poets: An Anthology of Translations from the French*. New York: Viking, 1975.

Kerouac, Jack. *Lonesome Traveler*. New York: Grove Press, 1960.

——. *Selected Letters, 1957–1969*. Ed. Ann Charters. New York: Viking Penguin, 1999.

Kisselhoff, Jeff. "In the Beginning There Was Risk Taking." *New York Times* Nov. 29, 1998. AR 33, 41.

Kutzinski, Vera. *Against the American Grain: Myth and History in William Carlos Williams, Jay Wright, and Nicolás Guillén*. Baltimore: Johns Hopkins UP, 1987.

Lacan, Jacques. *The Four Fundamental Concepts of Psycho-Analysis*. Trans. Alan Sheridan. Ed. Jacques-Alain Miller. New York: Norton, 1981.

Laforgue, Jules. *The Last Poems of Jules Laforgue*. Trans. Madeleine Betts. Elms Court, Great Britain: Arthur H. Stockwell, 1973.

Lorca, Federico García. *Poet in New York*. Trans. Ben Belitt. New York: Grove Press, 1955.

——. *The Selected Poems of Federico García Lorca*. Ed. Francisco García Lorca and Donald M. Allen. New York: New Directions, 1955.

*Los Angeles Times* May 1, 1960, 1.

Lyotard, Jean-François. *Peregrinations: Law, Form, Event*. New York: Columbia UP, 1988.

——. *The Postmodern Condition: A Report on Knowledge*. Trans. Geoff Bennington and Brian Massumi. Minneapolis: U of Minnesota P, 1984.

Mackey, Nathaniel. *Discrepant Engagement: Dissonance, Cross-Culturality, and Experimental Writing*. New York: Cambridge UP, 1993.

——. *School of Uhdra*. San Francisco: City Light Books, 1993.

Mann, Ron, dir. *Poetry in Motion*. New York: Sphinx Productions and Giorno Poetry Systems, 1982.

Marquez, Robert. Introduction. *¡Patria o Muerte! The Great Zoo and Other Poems by Nicolás Guillén*. Ed. and Trans. Robert Marquez. New York: Monthly Review Press, 1972. 13–29.

McClure, Michael. "It's Nation Time." Charters 556–57.
Metz, Christian. *The Imaginary Signifier: Psychoanalysis and the Cinema.* Trans. Celia Britton, Annwyl Williams, Ben Brewster, and Alfred Guzzetti. Bloomington: Indiana UP, 1982.
Miller, Adam David. "The Negro Writer in the United States." *University of California Graduate Student Journal* (1965): 3–12.
Moore, Marianne. Letter to Russell Atkins. July 14, 1951. Copy provided to the author by Russell Atkins.
Moten, Fred. *In the Break: The Aesthetics of the Black Radical Tradition.* Minneapolis: U of Minnesota P, 2003.
Nardal, Paulette. "The Awakening of Race Consciousness." Trans. T. Denean Sharpley-Whiting. Bernasconi 107–11.
Nash, Susan Smith. "Apocalypse Enactments in the Work of Rochelle Owens." http://www.thing.net/~grist/l&d/owens/lro-ssn.htm. March 1, 2004.
Nicosia, Gerald. Editor's Note. *Cranial Guitar.* By Bob Kaufman. Minneapolis, MN: Coffee House Press, 1996. 6.
O'Hara, Frank, and Bill Berkson. "F.Y.I. 6/26/61 (The Picnic Hour)." *Locus Solus* 3–4 (1962): 104–5.
Olson, Charles. *The Collected Poems of Charles Olson.* Ed. George F. Butterick. Berkeley: U of California P, 1987.
———. *Collected Prose.* Ed. Ben Friedlander. Berkeley: U of California P, 1997.
———. *A Nation of Nothing but Poetry: Supplementary Poems.* Ed. George F. Butterick. Santa Rosa, CA: Black Sparrow Press, 1989.
Outlaw, Lucius. "African, African American, Africana Philosophy." *Philosophical Forum* 24.1–3 (1992–93): 62–93.
Perelman, Bob. *The Marginalization of Poetry: Language Writing and Literary History.* Princeton, NJ: Princeton UP, 1996.
Philip, M. Nourbese. "In the Matter of Memory." ya Salaam and Brown 21–28.
Piedra, José. "Through Blues." *Do the Americas Have a Common Literature?* Ed. Gustavo Pérez Firmat. Durham, NC: Duke UP, 1990. 107–29.
Pound, Ezra. *The ABC of Reading.* New York: New Directions, 1960.
Ra, Sun. *Black Myth/Out in Space.* 1970. Motor Music GmbH. 1998. 557 656-2.
Radano, Ronald M. *New Musical Figurations: Anthony Braxton's Cultural Critique.* Chicago: U of Chicago P, 1992.

Rattray, David. "Lightning over the Treasury." Torra 36–39.
Redmond, Eugene. *Drumvoices: The Mission of Afro-American Poetry: A Critical History*. New York: Anchor/Doubleday, 1976.
Rexroth, Kenneth. "Panelizing Dissent." *Nation,* Sep. 7, 1964, 97–99.
Roberson, Ed. *Lucid Interval as Integral Music*. Pittsburgh, PA: Harmattan Press, 1984.
Ross, Fran. *Oreo*. 1974. Rpt. Boston: Northeastern UP, 2000.
Sartre, Jean-Paul. "Black Orpheus." Bernasconi 115–42.
Senghor, Léopold Sédar. "Negritude and Modernity or Negritude as a Humanism for the Twentieth Century." Trans. Valentine Moulard. Bernasconi 143–65.
Simon, Adelaide. "Salvos for Atkins." *Input* 1.4 (1964): 8–9.
Smith, Dinitia. "A Poetic Love Affair with New York." *New York Times* July 4, 2000. B1, B5.
Sollors, Werner. *Amiri Baraka/LeRoi Jones: The Quest for a "Populist Modernism."* New York: Columbia UP, 1978.
Thomas, Lorenzo. *Chances Are Few*. Berkeley, CA: Blue Wind Press, 1979.
Torra, Joseph. Introduction. *Stephen Jonas Selected Poems*. Ed. Joseph Torra. Hoboken, NJ: Talisman House, 1994. 1–12.
Torra, Joseph, ed. *The Poetry of Stephen Jonas*. Somerville, MA: Lift, 1992.
Turco, Lewis. "Amiri Baraka's Black Mountain." *Hollins Critic* 31.3 (1994): 1–10.
von Hallberg, Robert. "Poetry, Politics, and Intellectuals." *The Cambridge History of American Literature: Volume 8: Poetry and Criticism, 1940–1995*. Ed. Sacvan Bercovitch. Cambridge, UK: Cambridge UP, 1996.
Ward, Geoff. *The Writing of America: Literature and Cultural Identity from the Puritans to the Present*. Cambridge, UK: Polity Press, 2002.
Weinberger, Eliot. "Eliot Weinberger Section: Poems by Will Alexander." *Sulfur* 32 (1993): 227.
West, Cornel. *Beyond Eurocentrism and Multiculturalism I: Prophetic Thought in Postmodern Times*. Monroe, ME: Common Courage Press, 1993.
———. *Beyond Eurocentrism and Multiculturalism II: Prophetic Reflections: Notes on Race and Power in America*. Monroe, ME: Common Courage Press, 1993.

Wieners, John. *Selected Poems, 1958–1984*. Ed. Raymond Foye. Santa Barbara, CA: Black Sparrow Press, 1986.

Williams, Sherley Anne. "Anonymous in America." *boundary* 2 6 (1978): 435–41.

Wright, Jay. *Transfigurations: Collected Poems*. Baton Rouge: Louisiana State UP, 2000.

ya Salaam, Kalamu, and Kysha Brown, eds. *Fertile Ground: Memories and Visions*. New Orleans: Runagate Press, 1996.

# Index